The Circuitous Route

Six LGBTQ+ Stage/Screenplays & VAPID
A Novella

Grant Sutor Vuille

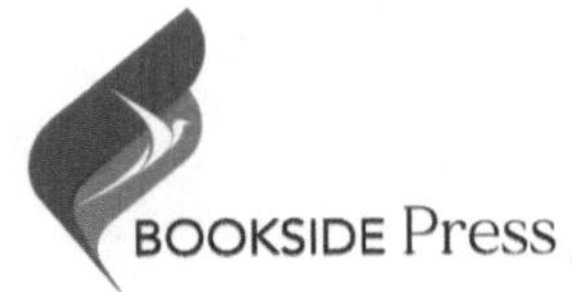

ISBN: 978-1-77883-048-8 (Paperback)

The original painting used for the cover was by my
friend & companion: Jeffrey Bryce Davidson

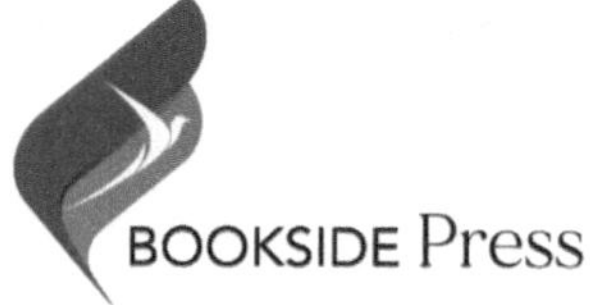

BookSide Press
877-741-8091
www.booksidepress.com
orders@booksidepress.com

Contents

Aquamarine. 1
Ascorbic Acid Freak 17
Doctor George's Magnificent Zeppelin 51
"Eternally Yours, Jayne Mansfield" 159
"Shamus Dragay" 173
"Twelve Tulips For Tinseltowne". 223
Vapid. 239

Aquamarine

A One Act Play

by Grant Sutor Vuille

Characters: ***Anthony*** *is a twenty-eight-year-old handsome young man who is sensitive and shy.*

Scott*, also twenty-eight, is strong, confident, and self-assured.*

Time: *The present.*

Place: *A small rowboat on Aquamarine Lake near the rocky Green Island.*

Setting: Tranquil Aquamarine Lake encompasses the entire stage. The rocky Green Island is up stage right, a dark sculpture with rocks, crags, trees and shrubs. The rowboat is left of center down stage with our two characters.

Scene: It is the beginning of summer. The night before our two characters had been to their first high school reunion. Anthony and Scott are fishing and drinking beer. They are slowly headed for the island which had been a childhood sanctuary of fun and fantasy. Scott's not wearing a shirt and Anthony is dressed casually. They are lost in thought as we begin. After a few moments Anthony feels a tug on his line.

Anthony: Hey, Scott, I think I've got something.

Scott: Well, come on, Anthony, pull him in.

Anthony: Oh, wow, it feels like a big one.

Scott: Don't tug so hard, just ease him in gently, play with him a little.

Anthony: Feels like he's fighting pretty hard. I think I'm going to need a little help, can you help me with him, Scott?

Scott: You don't need any help, Tony… come on now, bring him in, easy does it.

Anthony: Come on, Scott, I'm not kidding, it really feels like a big one, help me already!

Scott: *(Crouching behind him)* All right, that's it, steady now, come on now, pull that bad boy in… that's it.

Anthony: *(struggling)* Wow, he's really fighting, oh boy…

Scott: That's it, real him in… steady… here, let me do it.

Anthony: It's okay, I got him… I think.

Scott: That's it, don't let him go, now.

Anthony: *(The line pops up without a fish, then goes slack)* Oh, shit, I lost him. *(He reels in the unbaited hook)* Guess I never was much of a fisherman.

Scott: Well don't give up now, he's still out there, go for it.

Anthony: *(Examining the bait-less hook)* Yeah, but he's not hungry now.

Scott: Well, not to worry, we still have plenty of bait. Better luck next time, give the other fish a chance to be our supper.

Anthony: Sure, will you do the honors? *(He holds out his hook for him to bait)*

Scott: You're not scared of a few worms, are you?

Anthony: No, but you're so much better at it than me.

Scott: I beg your pardon?

Anthony: You know what I mean. I can't get the damn things to hold still long enough to wrap them around the hook… they squirm too much… ugh.

Scott: *(Disbelieving)* …uh huh…

Anthony: That's okay, Scott, forget it. *(He lays his pole down in the boat)* I need to let them all go home to their families.

Scott: Giving up so soon? We'll starve to death.

Anthony: Guess I'm not much of a fisherman. We've been out here for two hours and haven't caught a thing. All that partying at the reunion last night has worn me out. Besides, it's hotter than hell out here.

Scott: So take your shirt off macho and get a little sun… you need it.

Anthony: No, I'm alright, Scott.

Scott: What's wrong, you shy, take it off, relax and enjoy yourself.

Anthony: Not really, thanks, I don't want to burn.

Scott: How about another beer then.

Anthony: No, thank you. I'm wasted.

Scott: Aww, come on Anthony… *(He pauses, then opens the cooler and pulls out two crystal wine glasses and a bottle of champagne which he opens and pours)*… I've got just the thing… *(He hands Anthony his glass and raises his in a toast)* So here's to the Class of 'xx *(ten years after the present year)* May we live and prosper!

Anthony: Here, here! *(They drink and pause to reflect)*

Anthony: Here, here!

Scott: Hey, Anthony, what did you think about last night?

Anthony: I don't know… I found it a little depressing, but I had a good time. It was sad seeing how much we've changed.

Scott: Yeah… Mary Lou Wilcox… What happened to her? Talk about change… she was the fucking Prom Queen.

Anthony: She had cancer, Scott, but she's recovering and doing okay.

Scott: You're kidding me…

Anthony: No… she's okay now, though.

Scott: I didn't talk to her… should have, though.

Anthony: We only had a few classes together. She got married after graduation, had a couple of kids, then got divorced… and as if that wasn't enough pain and suffering, cancer got her.

Scott: That's really sad. It makes you think about what's ahead.

Anthony: I didn't ask her about that, Ellen Creason told me. I was afraid to ask. It made me ashamed. Like I didn't care… I don't know. Some things are too personal… Then I had a few drinks. I went back and spoke with her.

Scott: What did she say?

Anthony: After Ellen had filled me in and I had some booze in me I approached Mary Lou and began to chat. I got my nerve back and we started a conversation…

Scott: Full of courage now, Anthony?

Anthony: Well, just curious, trying to be respectful. You know. She was real sweet but had difficulty speaking… she had scars on her throat. She mentioned how she'd been sick but was okay. I was embarrassed to talk about it so I asked her about her kids. We talked about school events and such… she'd been very popular, had had a lot of boyfriends and attention back then. She'd been most likely to succeed and Prom Queen… just way above me and I saw she had trouble remembering me. I wasn't popular. I guess you were one of the few friends I had back then. But you probably remember all that stuff.

Scott: Yeah, buddy, we were very close friends… I remember. I remember lots about you back then… I think I called you queer a lot because of how shy and awkward you were around girls. Sorry I did that, Anthony.

Anthony: Yeah, but you were my friend so that was okay. But I did get that from other guys, you know... bullies... *(He hesitates)* Even girls, called me queer... so, I didn't date much... was scared to ask girls on dates.

Scott: That's pitiful, man.

Anthony: I told Mary Lou I admired her for all her achievements, and being popular and all. She gave me a look like I was a fool but then mentioned that she remembered I was good in art class. I could do portraits and stuff. She remembered I'd done pastel portraits of faculty members that staff hung in the library.

Scott: Yes, I do remember how well you could draw and paint. Cool.

Anthony: Also that I'd been good in drama class. She played a comic lead in a school play I wrote for a high school assembly. I remember being so nervous with excitement when I saw it performed onstage. I mentioned all that while chattering away foolishly.

Scott: Admit it, you were a regular drama queen.

Anthony: ... well, yeah, maybe that was it, she's thinking I'm queer... that's when she gave me a little eye roll and a side glance, like how stupid and queer I was or something. So she casually excused herself, returning to her other friends. I headed straight back to the bar. No wonder I'm wiped out today... and here we are still drinking!

Scott: Kids are cruel. I got in a few fights over that queer baiting shit... no one should get away with that. Remember me talking to you about other kids calling you queer?

Anthony: I think so. We were close you and I... you were my best friend. But I tried to forget about that stuff we did... you moved away for a while before coming back and I was heartbroken... and it hurts to think about it.

Scott: *(He pauses to reflect)* My parents took my family on a cruise to Jamaica and the Caribbean... but we were only eleven years old then... we were gone for months. My dad belonged to the yacht club... took us out of school for months.

Anthony: Yeah, but you sold your home across the street from us and moved back to another part of town. So I didn't see you for years until high school. Things changed between us. I felt a lot of remorse... and guilt.

Scott: Did you notice how everyone fell into the same old clicks? I couldn't believe how much the same everyone was last night. Same personalities in flabby disgusting older bodies.

Anthony: Until I saw you pop in last night, I hadn't really been enjoying myself. Now we're here on Aquamarine Lake together, just like being kids again headed for Green Island, our land of fun and adventure...

Scott: *(He pauses momentarily, recalling the past wistfully)*... Yeah, we had some good times together.

Anthony: My instincts kept telling me to leave in spite of the fact how glad I was to see you again. The reunion, I felt paranoid about being there, afraid I was going to be criticized. I wanted so much to loosen up and start having a good time. That's when I realized I hadn't changed either, I was just the same old kid again. I never had any school spirit, I missed all the sports, never went to but one or two games...just a nerdy kid with no close friends... I'd never fit in, and so I was ashamed of myself...

Scott: I don't think you need to feel ashamed, Anthony, you still look great to me... you are still very attractive. Shit, we're only twenty-eight, and not over-the-hill yet... cheer up, drink some more champagne! *(He fills both their glasses and they toast again and drink together)*

Anthony: Thanks, Scott, guess you saw things more like I did.

Scott: Yeah, it was a downer, that's why I was late getting there. If you hadn't been there the whole affair would have been a waste of time. *(He pours champagne continuously throughout their talk)*

Anthony: I remember being with you last night brought back a flood of memories. Same as right now, but maybe we shouldn't be rehashing it...

Scott: All right then, Tony, old buddy... cheers, drink up, let's finish her up! *(The champagne is toasted again and finished off. Their moods lighten and they loosen up)* Here's to the past, may it rest in peace.

Anthony: Cheers to that!

Scott: *(He tosses the champagne bottle, pulls out a small flask of whiskey, and takes a big sip, then offers it to Anthony)*

Anthony: Are you trying to get me drunk, Scott? Whiskey? Man, are you kidding? No thanks...

Scott: *(He reaches in the cooler and pulls out two more beers, tossing one for Anthony to catch.)* Here, you can chase it with this.

Anthony: Beer after Champagne... and Whiskey after that? You like me this way?

Scott: Yep. Come to think of it, so do you.

Anthony: *(Incredulous)* Bullshit.

Scott: Bullshit nothing, you had to have a few in you before you could dance on the ceiling last night... right?

Anthony: Every boring depressing minute of it. By the time you got there most everyone was half-lit... or drunk and no longer in pain.

Scott: *(Beginning a childhood game of theirs, he brings a hand to his ear as if using the telephone)* My point exactly, Mr. Peabody. *(He drinks his beer)*

Anthony: Point well taken, Mr. McCall. *(He drinks beer, also, as they laugh and mock using a telephone)*

Scott: That's more like it, hello, hello, are you there, Mr. Peabody? This is Mr. McCall!

Anthony: Yes, yes, Peabody here! Is that you, Mr. McCall?

Scott: Mr. McCall here, I say, McCall here! You there? What's new with you, Mr. Peabody? *(They laugh, take time for thought)*

Anthony: Come on, Scott, we don't want to get too plowed. We haven't seen each other or talked in over ten years.

Scott: Yeah, that's okay…it doesn't make sense our high school years… we were growing apart and childhood had been so sweet. Growing up is hard for everyone. I felt protective of you but we just weren't close like we were as kids. Sometimes I felt you were avoiding me.

Anthony: You were in band, you participated in sports, while I immersed myself in school work, art and drama, so we didn't have much in common anymore.

Scott: But we loved each other as kids. I felt hurt, too. Maybe guilty for having gone away or maybe because of what we left behind.

Anthony: We were just stupid innocent little kids.

Scott: Yeah, I think I tried hating you because maybe my feelings for you weren't so innocent.

Anthony: I'm sorry if I hurt you, but when you're really young emotions can be overwhelming.

Scott: *(He finishes the beer and takes another sip of whiskey)* Let's get off this subject, Tony…

Anthony: Okay. I like when you to call me Tony…we're kids again when you do.

Scott: Hey, the sun is out, we're on the lake, and we're having the time of our life… in this moment… right now.

Scott: No more being sorry the world's an accident waiting to happen. We are alive and well and I'm so damned happy to see you I could cry. No more gloom and doom… I want to see you smile, Tony! The past is over. Have a man's drink for Christ's sake, take a shot of whiskey! *(He hands him the flask)*

Anthony: *(Laughing, cheering up, he takes a sip and hands it back)* You're so pushy, you treat me like a sissy.

Scott: I want to make up for lost time. I want to make amends but I just don't know all the answers to things, so let's let go of anything that tore us apart long ago… let's be glad we're back together, Tony, old pal, you sweet piece of grab-ass.

Anthony: *(Laughing and again pretending to be on the telephone)* I'm just the same old pal you used to know, Mr. McCall. Same old pal doing the same old thing. So how be you be, Mr. McCall? … are you an old Bee, or a new Bee? Or are you a busy Bee? Be that as it may, I be sometimes a who be you Bee? … and never am I be going easy-on-the-sauce Bee… and you, Mr. McCall? What kind of who Bee do you be?

Scott: Same old thing as you be, Mr. Peabody, same old thing as you. I'm a horny Bee looking for a hot-ass Bee, where-some-ever you be, so will I be… and a very good, Bee, for damn sure. *(They laugh hysterically and nudge each other affectionately, then settle down quietly, feeling so much better)*

Anthony: Green Island, gee, Scott, I'm not sure I want to explore that place again. As interesting as it might be to see how it's changed, I don't think this is a time to bring back memories that ought to be left behind. Let's row back, go home and get some rest.

Scott: Stay positive, Anthony, we used to have a blast there. Remember the raft we built and launched it in this very lake. The island was our first destination. We explored that place many times.

Anthony: I need to go and visit my parents and spend time with them before I head back to St Louis. And I have to get back to work.

Scott: I got to be back in San Francisco on Tuesday, I have to work same as you, buddy.

Anthony: Your folks are in San Francisco, too, aren't they? Well, why don't we get back and go see my mom and dad. You remember them, they liked you a lot. Your family was special to me, too, when we lived here not far from Aquamarine Lake… we were always doing stuff with both our families. I think they would love to see you again.

Scott: Yeah, okay, we can stop in later. Right now, we've got time to ourselves so let's make the most of it. We might not see each other for another ten years.

Anthony: Some of those memories make me feel a little ashamed. You seem to see things different from my recollection. I sorta wish I'd stayed in St. Louis and skipped this reunion. I'll probably not return for the next one if they have it ten years from now.

Scott: *(He is hurt and gets serious for a moment)* I never felt ashamed of anything we did. I'm here to tell you how important being close to you back then was for me. I missed you a lot after we left town to go on that cruise. It's nobody's business how we felt toward one another. Who the hell cares what other people think, anyway. Well, enough already, I'll get you back in time to see your mommy and daddy…so, cheer up, Tony!

Anthony: Why do I get the feeling you don't hear me?

Scott: I'm listening. Lighten up, we're almost there, we can't quit now.

Anthony: You are determined to go ashore and risk exploring that rocky old Green Island fantasyland. It scares me, Scott, what are you up to?

(Scott has taken the oar and is paddling them towards the island. Anthony is uncomfortable but tries to relax as it seems he has no choice in the matter)

Scott: *(While concentrating on steering their little boat he speaks in measured tones, gentle in nature, softer in thought)* Spending a little time with you means a lot to me. I have things to talk to you about that I've been bottling up inside me for years. Personal things that I wanted to know if we felt the same way about. Unanswered questions most people ponder but never resolve.

Anthony: Why all the mystery, just spit it out and spare me the anguish.

Scott: *(A moment to ponder)* Did you happen to see Zelda Braddock at the reunion?

Anthony: Yeah, so what?

Scott: I spoke to her when you went off to the men's room. I asked her if her brother Bruce had ever been found... He had disappeared, maybe ran away... he should have graduated with us...

Anthony: *(Tightening up, alarmed)* Impossible, he was two years older than us. He couldn't have graduated with our class.

Scott: He was two years ahead of us but by the tenth grade we caught up with him because he'd flunked twice and then held back. He was a bully... obnoxious... always brawling with kids, picking fights and skipping class.

Anthony: I was terrified of him. He picked on me all the time. I avoided him as best I could.

Scott: I understand, believe me… He left me alone because I was on to him. It was rumored he was a hustler… Remember that huge gold ring with the diamonds he wore? Always had money and cash in his pockets…

Anthony: *(Fidgeting nervously)* So what did his sister say happened to him. Zelda must have known something… He disappeared you said… He never showed up?

Scott: No… just vanished into thin air… along with that gold ring. The talk of the town, poor Miss Brucie Braddock.

Anthony: That's a strange thing to call him, he wasn't queer, was he?

Scott: You're forgetting something, Anthony, don't be so naive… He had a sugar daddy, an old rich dude. Bruce had a dick the size of a cucumber. He was the admiration and terror of my gym class… especially in the shower… you had to hold your breath and think about Jesus Christ so you wouldn't get a boner and be humiliated to death.

Anthony: Ugh, I remember all that, I hated gym and stripping down and all the smelly jock straps, and the locker room… being in the showers, trying not to look at anyone or God forbid, getting caught checking someone out. Was there an investigation when Bruce disappeared?

Scott: No. There wasn't an investigation but the police held his sugar daddy for a night but let him go when he revealed how he'd basically been robbed and blackmailed. Bruce was just born bad, a thug and a thief, the town was glad when he disappeared. His sister, Zelda, or his parents never knew what happened to him. They figured he ran off and so they gave up on him.

Anthony: *(A moment, then remorseful, and sad)* …and a rapist, Scott… He was cruel, deliberately cruel…

Scott: To be sure, that, too. *(Gently urging him sympathetically)* … Why don't you tell me about it, Tony…

Anthony: I can't stand the thought of that guy. I need to forget, but I've never been able to... please, let's just turn around and go home. I want to be with my family.

Scott: We're here, Tony, our Green Island is at our feet... let's go ashore and have a new adventure together. Leave the past behind and savor our first precious moments in the new world.

Anthony: That's where it all happened. Bruce had followed us there but we didn't know he was on the island with us. He saw us together and knew what we were doing... it was our secret, that sacred bond we shared together... our love exposed and shamefully humiliated by uncaring eyes.

Scott: Tony, look around, that doesn't matter now. The devil has returned to hell and can't harm us anymore.

Anthony: Days later he approached me about what he'd seen us do. I blocked it out as best I could... carrying around years of shame and regret until years later and we were all back in high school... it was a stormy night when Bruce brought me out here on a little boat like this one... he said he was going to dig up that treasure box he said we'd buried. I said there wasn't any treasure and we'd made it all up but was nothing but junk if it existed at all. He told me if I didn't tell him where it was, he would expose us... that wasn't all he wanted. He wanted something else from me.

Scott: Bruce couldn't be trusted to slice tomatoes. We're here, our childhood paradise, land ho! All ashore that's going ashore! Come on, Tony, help me drag her up on the beach.

(They hop out and pull the boat onto the rocky Green Island upstage right set piece. Then Scott dashes around with excitement)

Anthony: Don't go running off without me!

Scott: It looks great, doesn't it. It's better than I remember! Looks like some trash around, like campsite kids still come out to explore here. *(Jumping around on the rocks and crags)* We used to play king of the mountain! Come on, stop dragging your ass, get up here. Let's explore the woods.

Anthony: *(checking around on the shore, Anthony moves around… hand for clues)* It was here, wasn't it? *(Rising to his feet, glancing up at Scott to get his attention)* The treasure we buried, it was here, right here.

Scott: Yeah, some old shells, comic books, and knickknacks, a few coins and bottle caps. Just junk… looks like it was dug up by someone, or we dug it up maybe. We were kids… elementary school kids… we used to brag about we had this secret treasure. Come on, let's explore.

Anthony: But it wasn't we who dug it up. It was Bruce. He dug and he dug… but he couldn't find it… so he got madder and madder. The sky was black and it was starting to rain and we were getting soaked. He grabbed me and shook me wanting to know where it was… I couldn't remember. I was scared to death. He beat me around and threw me to the ground. It was cold and wet. He pulled off my pants and penetrated me and I was in such pain I blacked out. When I came to, he'd vanished, he was gone.

Scott: His boat was gone but our raft was still here.

Anthony: The raft? Yes… the raft was here. Why was it here? I thought I'd been stranded.

Scott: I couldn't leave my buddy all alone out here without a way back.

Anthony: You mean you saw the whole thing? You were hiding somewhere? Why didn't you stop him?

Scott: I did. *(He reaches in his pocket and hands Anthony the gold ring with diamonds that had been Bruce's)* I think this belongs to you more than me.

Anthony: What? I can't remember, how did you end up with Bruce's gold ring?

Scott: It's hard to say. He was such a clumsy bastard. Maybe he ran away or maybe he fell into that treasure hole he'd dug for himself... He robbed his own grave maybe... that's the way I see it. Who knows?

(They share some quiet for a few moments. Scott moves to embrace Anthony in a long passionate embrace. They have their heads on each other's shoulder and hug and pat each other's back. They break apart taking deep breaths. Anthony comes alive and laughs with excitement. He runs to the boat)

Anthony: Scott, let's eat! I'm starving! *(He rummages in the cooler)* What have we got, junk food, snacks, sandwiches?

Scott: *(Racing back to the rocks)* Hell yes, all kinds, look in the sack next to the cooler! Come on, let's explore first, I want to search the island. We can eat like pigs later.

Anthony: The sun will go down soon. Let's eat our snacks on the way back. I don't want to row back after dark.

(Scott turns his back and drops his pants exposing his buttocks)

Scott: Hey, Tony, I hear there's a full moon out tonight. You don't have to be scared of the dark. *(He pulls his pants back up and jumps off the rocks and runs to Anthony)*

Anthony: You jerk, cut it out, I know what you're thinking! *(He is joyful and enthusiastic)*

Scott: *(Teasingly, shamelessly happy, and smiling broadly)* Anthony, there's no one out here, buddy, just you and me all alone.Let's strip and run naked all over the island, just like when we were kids!

Scott: We'll get hot and sweaty, make love getting all dirty and filthy, then go skinny dipping and wash away our shame!

Anthony: No! Absolutely, not… I mean yes, absolutely!

Scott: *(They embrace)* Yes, for old times' sake! *(Calmly, seductively)* Let me help you take off your shirt. We can't be savages with our shirts on, can we?

(Scott helps Anthony in removing his shirt, gently caressing his chest, they stroke one another softly. The lights have begun to fade and as they continue to disrobe, fade to black. The curtain falls. Music continues for a minute before BLACKOUT.)

AQUAMARINE

A One Act Play by *Grant Sutor Vuille*

THE END

Ascorbic Acid Freak

A Play in One Act
by Grant Sutor Vuille

CHARACTERS

Mark: *He is in his mid-thirties, has had a twenty-year career as an actor in semiprofessional show business, and is supposed to be dying of the incurable disease AIDS. The HIV virus had just been discovered.*

Stephan: *He is in his twenties and is Mark's live in companion, lover and friend. He is very good looking and somewhat immature.*

Julie Mofit: *She is an adorable young actress in her early to mid-twenties who adores Mark and wants him to return to the stage with her and raise funds to save the local Playhouse.*

Wanda: *She is the Manish sidekick to her actress friend, Julie. She is older and perhaps about thirty or so and is a gruff, in your face, overly protective lesbian.*

Doctor Purgess, M.D.: *He is Mark's personal physician and friend. He is determined to treat his patient, Mark with standard drugs and therapies of the times but is a bit quackish with conflicting ideas on how to treat this mysterious incurable illness that a cure has yet to be discovered.*

Zebulon: *Given the nickname, Zeb, he is in his twenties and is a very sexy and handsome younger man close to both Mark and Stephan.*

SETTING: *Smallville, U.S.A in 1988, at Mark's modest little home near a rural college community.*

SCENE ONE

(It is early Sunday morning and Stephan is up and around in his pajamas. He is making breakfast in a kitchenette in the corner of the living room)

(He is preparing Mark's special health drink in a blender with protein powder, egg, and milk. He also adds in Vitamin C tablets. After pouring this concoction into Mark's glass he fills his own glass halfway and tops in off with a few shots of vodka from a bottle)

(Mark is heard offstage shouting commands from their bedroom)

Mark: Be sure to put in at least ten thousand milligrams of Vitamin C, Stephan, I am not feeling quite myself today.

Stephan: Does that mean you're needing a little hand action in there?

Mark: *(Entering the living area from the bedroom, also in pajamas)* Ha ha! You attempting comedy? Nice try, don't use it in the act. I'm feeling a little congested. Don't forget the two raw eggs.

Stephan: I know the routine Melanie, save the eulogy for Scarlett, she can use some of that kind of action in the sequel when she's trying to win back Rhett Butler. But it is not 1939 anymore and Scarlett, Melanie, Rhett, and Ashley are "Gone With The Wind" and not coming back in bustling 1988, Smallville, U.S.A.

Mark: Yes, but a sequel is being planned, so I'm looking forward to that! *(Sadly, reflecting)* I wish Hattie McDaniel was here to protect us. Mammy would take good care of us. Stephan, it's been sucking forever and going on two years that I've been sick with this AIDS crap. Doctor Purgess, M.D. wants to do a special case study on me at the University Hospital.

Stephan: Well hooray for our dear Doctor Purgess, M.D. I think we can all breathe a little easier, now. Bully for him, the old fag.

Mark: Not to worry, I don't need him, just give me plenty of Vitamin C and I will be fine. Hospitals FREAK me out. You go in for a routine hemorrhoid exam and they cut off your balls instead.

Stephan: It's your friend Doctor Purgess, M.D. who freaks me out. Personally, I think it's the raw eggs in your breakfast drink that sticks you together... and a splash of vodka.

Mark: Raw eggs BIND you together, like in pancakes... not stick, I'm not stuck together am I, Stephan? And stop with the vodka, already, it's too early for that.

Stephan: Don't knock it till you try it... maybe a little spirits can help wipe out the HIV retrovirus, ever think of that?

Mark: People with AIDS will try anything... vitamins, yoga, voodoo... whatever it takes, whatever the cure, they'll try anything. Save that medicine show elixir for yourself. I don't need any mood elevation or enhancement.

Stephan: Could have fooled me, Mr. Poppers... a little sniff is all it takes, honey-bunch.

Mark: Give me my drink, lover boy, and go make the bed.

Stephan: I'm not your nurse maid. I made your drink so come get it. Hey, Mark, aren't you the guy I saw last night on televisions "Name That Cure"? *(He gives him his drink)*

Mark: Spare me your sarcasm, you skeptic pessimist. *(He drinks his breakfast)* Doctor Purgess, M.D. says he'll cure me if it kills him… or if it doesn't kill me first.

(As Mark crosses by him Stephan takes his vodka drink, picks up the morning paper and settles comfortably on the sofa)

Stephan: What's in the news today, any medical breakthroughs coming for my nerves? *(As Mark enters the bathroom with the door open the conversation continues)* You know, Mark, maybe you're not sick at all… maybe it's all in your head.

Mark: Yeah maybe… maybe it's all a plot to kill off homosexuals. But they test for HIV like last year when I got my positive reading. Then you got it and the test was negative… so maybe you are immune or something… *(He goes into the bathroom to freshen up, gargle, and wash his face, turning on the water in the sink)*

Stephan: It's all a plot, Mark, a scheme to make millions for the pharmaceutical industry.

Mark: I can't hear you, the water's running!

Stephan: *(Shouting)* I said the whole thing is a plot to kill gay people! The public is scared of us and the government is in a state of moral anarchy as the infected are ostracized and eliminated by the non-infected bureaucracy! Christians say it's God's punishment for queers!

Mark: Stop shouting, I'll be out in a second.

Stephan: Forget it, I'm just bull-shitting! Don't pay any attention. *(Mark comes out from the bathroom)*

Mark: What was that you said again, Stephan?

Stephan: Never mind, Mark, it's not worth repeating... sit down beside me and relax, buddy.

Mark: That's what I thought. *(He drinks)* Sure there's enough Vitamin C in this?

Stephan: *(Concentrating on his newspaper)* Of course there's enough.

Mark: There better be or your ass is all mine tonight.

Stephan: *(Pondering an article about unjust wars and military expansionist American values)* Why is it men kill each other in bloody wars but freak out over one man loving another man and expressing that love sexually. Freedom to love whoever we want regardless of gender, race, or sexual orientation seems to me to be the whole point of this freedom shit...since when is freedom isn't free a requirement for basic human rights? Why the conditional approach?

Mark: *(He plops onto the sofa)* You, airhead!

Stephan: If freedom isn't free then what is it? We can't be talking about freedom, can we?

Mark: An Olympic competition perhaps. Winners are set free and the losers become Christian republicans... slaves to Christ and guardians of Heaven's gate. Give me some of that paper... Give me the comics...

Stephan: *(They tussle over the newspaper)* Answer me first, Mark, then you'll get the funny papers. Well, which is it?

Mark: What? Which is what?

Stephan: Freedom... is it free if you have to pay for it?

Mark: There's a price on everything in life. Every second we exist we're paying our way by working, scheming, and sacrifice.

Stephan: What about human rights? Where's our freedom of choice if we're living in a free society that penalizes our choices... and discriminates against races, and religions, and gender and orientation? The United States Constitution is a myth.

Mark: We live by rules and laws based on promises made in that mythical constitution. Give me the comics, Stephan, you're hoarding them.

Stephan: I'm trying to focus on important political matters. LGBTQ citizens are treated like terrorists. We just want the basic human rights like the majority of society enjoys.

Mark: My basic human right is to what form of discipline I'm planning for you at bedtime.

Stephan: All God's creatures deserve a piece of the pie, don't they?

Mark: It's a fight to the death in order to survive. I'm fighting for my life every day, and so are we all.

Stephan: How can your will to live overcome an incurable disease? Can your will to fight HIV cure AIDS?

Mark: If my will to live is stronger than a virus' will to devour me then I shall be victorious.

Stephan: You certainly are sure of yourself. You don't think you need Doctor Purgess, M.D. hovering over you like the virgin, Mary.

Mark: No, but he's my friend and I like to humor him. As long as I can hang in there and cheat death, he will think he's the greatest doctor in all of God's green Earth.

(The phone on the end table by the sofa rings, they wrangle on who should take it, effectively lightening the moment)

Stephan: *(Picking up, he answers the call)* Hello? This is Stephan. Who's there, please?

Mark: *(Not wanting to engage he whispers harshly)* If it's for me, tell them I'm still in bed asleep.

Stephan: *(Sweetly)* Hey, Julie, what's happening, babe? … Ummm, Mark's still asleep. Should I wake him? *(Mark shakes his head no)* Oooh, Miss Mofit, on second thought why don't you tell me instead. I'll give him a message… uh, huh… yes… well, yeah… but I don't know, I can ask him… *(Mark waves and shakes his head no)*… sounds interesting, Julie, but you know how he is about going out these days. *(Mark shrugs, nods his head and rolls his eyes)* You want to come over? Noon-ish? Around lunchtime? … before one o'clock this afternoon? *(Sarcastically, glancing at Mark)* Okay, he ought to be up by then… you, know, when you're not feeling your best, you need all the rest you can get! *(Mark looks a little wary and unsure)* … Oh, I think he's well enough to have visitors… uh, huh… see you no later than one p.m. Thanks, honeybunch… *(Mark glares at Stephan)* Bye, bye, Miss Julie… *(He hangs up)*

Mark: So my favorite leading lady is paying us a call. I'm honored and touched. What's the occasion… what's she up to?

Stephan: The Smallville Playhouse wants to award you a lifetime membership.

Mark: I haven't performed there in over two years… what's the catch?

Stephan: It's the playhouses 25th anniversary. They want you and Julie to perform in a musical variety show to raise money.

Mark: They want me to jump through the hoop to save the theatre? Sounds like their usual tactic to fleece the town hall and build back their audience. Has-been variety acts is their go to fund raising grift.

Stephan: You're too cynical. The theatre needs you, Mark. They're cash poor and trying to revive the Playhouse. You did your best stage performances there, both you and Julie... you met me there as well. Remember, Shakespeare's "A Midsummer Night's Dream" and how the three of us met at their workshop? It was some years back but I remember it as if it was yesterday.

Mark: *(Wistfully recalling)* How could I forget... how happy I was back then after meeting you... and Julie, of course... I'm not sure I'd be up to it...

Stephan: You should be glad they still care... you know you still do, too. I think it would be good for you.

Mark: I'd rather receive a gift certificate to Hamburger Heaven than a lifetime membership for has-been starlets. If it wasn't for AIDS, we could have moved to New York City and been on Broadway.

Stephan: You have a bad attitude. You said you have a fighting spirit? An opportunity like this will boost your metabolism and get your juices flowing. Be a champion for life, Mark, or go sit in the corner and sulk. Mind, body, and spirit...the very key to life, Liberty, and happiness... and freedom... free to be well, healthy, and on your way to recovery.

Mark: *(Sadly apologetic, but hopeful)* Jesus Christ, Stephan...you make it seem like a miracle... nearly twenty years of amateur theatricals has led to a crucifixion by burn-out.Sorry, Sir Lawrence of Lamentia, our dreams burst and we've been laid to rest... a bummer for sure, my friend...

Mark: You could go to New York without me, Stephan, I'm holding you back...

Stephan: I can take care myself. I choose to be with you. I'm comfortable here and I do care what happens to you with all my heart.

Mark: The bright lights of Broadway are a long way from Smallville.

Stephan: Things aren't so bad here. You made a little money doing regional theatre and local television commercials. In a way you probably had more experience than you ever could've in that Broadway fish-bowl of broken dreams.

Mark: To be sure there are drawbacks and challenges everywhere. People are people, we're all vulnerable in the eyes of God. Audience members on Broadway cough, wheeze, and snort same as they do at the Smallville Playhouse.

Stephan: Some great artists aren't recognized until after they're dead. *(Embarrassed)* Oops, sorry, Mark... I didn't mean it I swear!

Mark: Truth is truth...that's okay, I'm realistic. My six volumes of scrapbooks might still impress someone somewhere... and I'm not planning on dying just yet...

Stephan: Auction them off, publish them, they might be worth something. You have old recordings and video, too.

Mark: The Smithsonian has warehouses full of archaic memorabilia that hasn't made it into the museum yet. I don't expect they'll be knocking at my door anytime soon. Why on Earth do we collect so much stuff in our lives?

Stephan: So thrift stores and the Salvation Army can support their communities.

Mark: I need to raise money for myself so I can pay the doctor bills. Maybe some of our old pictures of Julie and I performing are worth something. Wonder if they'd give me a cut of the profits. A few sympathy bucks my way might be helpful, much more than my wretched health insurance.

Stephan: Let's get them out of the closet and sort through them when Julie gets here.

Mark: Ah, a nostalgia festival... the lethal antidote to the cruelest form of revenge imaginable... showing off a has-been's press clippings.

Stephan: Cut it out, don't be depressing. Let's get out of the house and go for a ride. It's a beautiful Sunday morning. Come on, get dressed, we have all morning before company arrives.

Mark: Good idea, sexy, let's go for a spin. The past is a refuge for losers!

Stephan: *(Jumping up and pulling Mark up off the sofa)* We can get out the scrapbooks when we get back. *(He takes their glasses to the kitchenette sink, then goes to make himself a vodka drink)* You know, maybe the Smallville Historical Society would give you something for all those memorabilia. They've got funding for collecting stuff like that, don't they? It's proof of a life well lived, your life, Mark.

Mark: Yeah, good old Smallville Hysterical Society! *(Laughing pitifully at his own joke, hesitating, he becomes concerned)* Go easy on that drink. Wait till this evening, Stephan. Julie will be here in a few hours. You don't want to be tipsy when she gets here, do you?

Stephan: Just a little pick me up for the road... you, hysterical man-beast, you...

Mark: Then we're not driving. We can go for a walk instead.

Stephan: Aww... you drive us, then, stud-muffin.

Mark: Come to think of it, why don't we rest. Julie's coming over but so might Doctor Purgess, M.D. Let's relax now, finish the morning paper and just rest up. I feel a little weak.

Stephan: What are you talking about, you got a little fever so Doctor Purgess, M.D. is coming over to stick a thermometer up your butt? Get real, man, we're going for a drive.

Mark: This is like your second drink already. You can't drive.

Stephan: Yes, I can... I've barely got a buzz on.

Mark: No you don't, forget about it, no way man.

Stephan: *(Tossing Mark the car keys)* So, you're not helpless, you take the wheel.

Mark: *(Feeling his throat)* I think my glands are swollen.

Stephan: They're always swollen. You're okay, don't be a sissy, come on get ready. Hurry up, I'm suffocating in here!

Mark: I think I need to lie down. Sorry, Stephan. *(He goes to the bedroom)*

Stephan: Awww, come on, Mark, this isn't like you... you need the fresh air... and it's so nice out today.

Mark: Wake me up when Julie gets here... *(He enters the bedroom)*

Stephan: *(Going after him)* I don't understand you, man, one minute you're ready to conquer the world, and the next minute you're willing to give up without a fight!

Stephan: *(Mark turns around just inside the bedroom and tosses him the keys. Stephan catches them)* Thanks a lot, Mark, you're a real pal... *(The doorbell rings, followed by knocking)* See if I take you anywhere again. I'm tired of your shit. I'm getting the door.

Mark: Whoever it is, I'm sound— [asleep]

Stephan: *(Going to the front door)* —I know, I know, you're sound asleep and dead to the world... *(Mark shuts the bedroom door)*

(Stephan opens the front door and there stands a very attractive young man named Zebulon, a sexual heartthrob)

Zebulon: Hey, Stephan, dude... what's up good-looking? How are you and Mark doing?

Stephan: Hey, Zebulon... we're fine... Mark's still in bed...

Zebulon: So late? Get that hot ass up and make us some coffee!

Stephan: He's under the weather. I can make coffee or how about a real drink, Zebulon?

Zebulon: *(Noticing Stephan's car keys, he points)* Going out? Where? To church?

Stephan: No, the bar to get sloshed.

Zebulon: Bars are closed till brunch. Hope to go out later myself. So how is Mark?

Stephan: *(Gesturing for him to enter, leading the way to the kitchenette)* Okay...Feeling poorly... we were going out but he's still tired. Do you want me to make coffee or do you want a man's drink? *(He freshens his own drink with the vodka)*

Zebulon: The Lord would strike me dead with a lightning bolt from above!

Stephan: *(Making him a quick drink he offers it to him)* In that case, Zeb, drink up, fella, the master's asleep and the church mice have come out to play… cheers!

Zebulon: Sure why not, the Lord works in mysterious ways, down the hatch! *(He drinks)*

Stephan: God would've zapped us long ago for living a deviant lifestyle, and he hasn't, so here's to God, our protector and savior, *(They drink together)* praise, Jesus!

Zebulon: Amen to that! That's our boy upstairs!

Stephan: I'm glad you dropped by, we had wanted to go out, but Mark changed his mind. It's good to see you, we don't get out much these days. Zebulon, that's from the holy Bible, you're a Christian scholar, aren't you?

Zebulon: Maybe somewhat… it helps to believe in something. But just call me, Zeb… it's not so in your face as Christian fanaticism goes. I'm more comfortable just being a lowkey Jesus freak… no collars, no crosses around the neck, etcetera…

Stephan: *(Leading him to the sofa)* Come on, Zeb, have a seat. If we make enough noise, we'll awake Sleeping Beauty.

Zebulon: I don't want to disturb him while he's sleeping.

Stephan: *(Patting the sofa to encourage Zebulon to sit)* Sit down, Zeb, darling… sure you don't want me to call you Zeb-U-Lon? It's curls the tongue… kind of sexy… We won't disturb him, we'll be quiet as those church mice… *(Loudly for Mark's benefit)*

Zebulon: *(Getting uncomfortable, he sits next to Stephan)* No, really, let's not wake him, I worry when he's not feeling well. Honest, let's not disturb him.

Stephan: I know, I know, but the guy needs a little stimulation to keep the blood boiling. It's good for him, even the doctors tell him to keep active.

Zebulon: It must be tough taking care of him.

Stephan: *(A moment, a sigh)* ... Yes, it can be... *(Shaking it off, and the subject)* Man, it's so great to see you! You look great... and hot as a pistol... are you really wrapped up in spiritual things? I'm a bit afraid of far-right Christian's... Christ seems to be used as a weapon by them... sinners beware, you're bound for hell and all that.

Zebulon: My parents were faith healers in a traveling revivalist sideshow... I played the poor orphan crippled kid with crutches who magically could walk again after the power of Jesus was summoned.

Stephan: Weird, man, I don't remember you telling us that.

Zebulon: Yeah... I try not to think about those days.

Stephan: You're not ashamed of your past, are you?

Zebulon: No... I just don't mention it for personal reasons. People get all concerned or crazy... and so I keep it to myself.

Stephan: That's cool. So you and your mom and dad were entertainers or actors spreading the Gospel.

Zebulon: That's putting it nicely. But it's not Shakespeare... theatre perhaps... or Sunday school for suckers.

Stephan: For sure. Where are your parents now? Are they still out there saving people for Jesus?

Zebulon: Probably, but I don't know, I've not seen them for years. I ran off when I realized how fake it all was... and soon after they caught me with another boy.

Stephan: Oh...I see... so how does Jesus feel about you being gay?

Zebulon: Well, I still struggle with that question. You believe in Him, he saves you… as for forgiveness, I say what's there to forgive if you love someone? Love only counts if it's unconditional. So I think Jesus has to be okay with it.

Stephan: Now that's freedom personified… loving whomever you want without judgment or condition… bye, bye, Hell, and hello, Heaven on Earth…

Zebulon: So I'm careful to keep my Christian friends in the dark about my sexuality, but only because it generates so much hostility.

Stephan: And you skipped church today to come see Mark and me… naughty boy!

Zebulon: Jesus is with me wherever I go, so He's cool with it.

Stephan: That is cool. Are you a Presbyterian?

Zebulon: Yes and no, but I've been attending the Fifth Avenue Baptist church for years even though our reverend frowns upon the LGBTQ community… and so do a lot of the parishioners where I go to worship.

Stephan: Time to switch churches… maybe a Unitarian Universalist association would be a better choice. They're cool with our LGBTQ friends…

Zebulon: Too far to go… not here in Smallville, otherwise I would. I'm used to my Baptist brethren, I understand them, and there's a few closeted ones in the mix to make me comfortable there.

Stephan: Hell-fire! Let's start our own congregation of LGBTQ spiritualist souls. Come on, Zeb, let's blow this joint and go find some recruits! The Gay Spirits of Smallville out cruising for Jesus! *(Jumping up, they meander towards the door, drinks in hand)*

Zebulon: *(They begin to finish their drinks)* Hey, wait, what about Mark? We can't leave him behind. He might want to come.

Stephan: *(Putting his arms around Zebulon, he fails confidentiality)* Between you and me he can take care of himself when he makes up his mind to. We'll be back soon enough; he'll never notice we left.

Zebulon: You sure, Stephan, he's been so... I don't know... I worry about him...

Stephan: You're so sweet, he'd appreciate that, now let's get out of here... stop worrying, this disease is propaganda, a political tool to suppress our rights. I'll bet some people can have it for a long time and never get sick. *(He takes their empty glasses and puts them down on the end table)*

Zebulon: And a lot die, too. Aren't you afraid of catching it?

Stephan: Naw, I've been tested for HIV. We're safe, I don't worry like his doctor does when he's wanting to inject Mark with antibiotics and antiviral medications. If I were in Mark's shoes, I wouldn't fancy being a guinea pig for overzealous quacks. Let's take a drive down to the river and park.

Zebulon: Okay, but check to see if Mark's okay.

Stephan: He's out like a light, believe me. *(He tosses Zebulon the car keys)* You drive, I'm three sheets to the wind... *(Leading Zebulon out the front door)* Did anyone ever tell you what beautiful eyes you have?

(They shut the front door behind them. We hear the car doors open and shut. The car engine starts and the sound of it pulling out fades away. Mark enters from the bedroom in his pajamas, a thermometer in his mouth, and carrying a cold-water bag. He goes to the window and peers out to see if they've gone. He goes to the kitchenette and makes a fresh vodka drink.)

(He puts ice in his drink, and in the cold-water bag for his headache. He goes over and pulls a couple of scrapbooks off the bookshelf then plops down on the sofa with them, comfortably settling into place. He checks the thermometer, shakes it, then stirs his drink with it before putting it in his pajama pocket. He takes a drink and begins rifling through the scrapbooks, talking to himself with amusement)

Mark: *(Enjoying the solitude)* You son of a gun, what a brilliant career you've had... so many memories... *(He lifts out an old program)* My first starring role when I was sweet sixteen, maybe it is time for a comeback... *(He holds up an old photograph)* My first 8 x 10... Lovely, I was so adorably handsome, Julie will be impressed! I can't wait till she gets here... a triple threat onstage... we were a fantastic team! Move over Ginger and Fred, Miss Mofit and Mr. Mark have passed you by! ... Amazing, what incredible memories... She'll be so impressed when she gets here. Little Miss Julie Mofit, sat on my big juicy tofit, eating my... *(He stops to reflect remorsefully)* ... Must've slipped my mind, lovely girl, if only I could have given back the love you have given me...

(The stage fades to black as soft show tunes play)

SCENE TWO

(The lights come up, the show tune music fades as Mark sleeps comfortably on the sofa, scrapbooks strewn around him. The doorbell rings and there are knocks at the front door. Mark is startled as he wakes, remembering where he is, getting up as scrapbooks spill to the floor along with pictures and old programs)

Mark: Oh, my God, what time is it? *(Sleepy-eyed, forgetting his lover Stephan had left he cries out for him)* Stephan! Julie is here, I think! *(Adjusting himself in his pajama pants, he gets to his feet and goes to the door to open it, but checks out the window first to see who it is and then opens the door)* Julie, it's you, dear, come on in my love!

(Julie Mofit enters with her friend, Wanda. Julie radiates youth, beauty, charm, and glamour. Wanda on the other hand is gruff, mannishly overprotective, as Julie's somewhat defensive, lesbian companion)

Julie: Mark, it is so good to see you again! This is my friend, Wanda. I wanted you to meet her because she stage-manages all our shows now.

Mark: *(He shakes Wanda's hand, it hurts him)* Ouch! Jesus, nice to meet you, Wanda! *(Welcoming them)* So really glad to see both of you... sit down and make yourselves comfortable... drinks, anyone?

Julie: Not for me, thanks... Wanda?

Wanda: *(Gruffly demanding, she moves past Mark)* Where's the bar?

Mark: *(Taken aback)* By the kitchen sink, dear... help yourself, Wanda... uh... you probably know what you like...

Julie: Don't mind Wanda, she always takes charge. Where's Stephan?

Mark: Sowing wild oats, I suppose... off with a friend of ours... they should be getting back soon from wherever they have... uh... gotten off to...

Julie: That sounds ominous... you look well. Feeling stronger these days? We all miss you at the theatre.

Mark: Thanks, Julie, I've missed you and everyone as well.

Wanda: We want you back at the theatre... we need your help... I thought it would be good for you, a healthy experience to help you forget about being sick... your illness...

Mark: Oh, sure, you mean the plague... my infectious disease... AIDS.

Julie: Yes, it's difficult to talk about. I'm so sorry.

Mark: You needn't be... it's just a fact of life. I like to not worry too much about it...

Julie: Didn't Stephan tell you why we wanted to see you?

Mark: Sure did, the Smallville Playhouse is fundraising.

Julie: Yes, and you can help us! We'll have so much fun. We want you back onstage doing a variety act... we were so good together. We want to give you a lifetime membership award, Mark!

Mark: Yes, so kind and all... awards and honors... Not sure I can, but I appreciate your sympathy towards me...

Julie: We just want to show our appreciation for your years of contributions.

Wanda: *(Having been lurking close by, she butts in)* Don't be such a stiff. The fucking theatre needs the dough or we're all out of a job... Grow a pair, Bub, it won't kill you to hoof it up with Julie!

Julie: *(Embarrassed)* Wanda!

Mark: *(Putting his arm on Wanda's shoulder)* Not to worry, Julie, it wouldn't kill me. Wanda and I are going to be the best of friends!

Wanda: Damn straight. *(She lights a cigarette and takes a long drag before asking)* Mind if I smoke?

Mark: Go right ahead, my home is your ashtray. *(To Julie)* Your stage manager has a great sense of humor.

Julie: Wanda, you're being rude, the smoke bothers Mark.

Wanda: He said he didn't mind. *(She puffs and blows smoke his way)* He doesn't look sick to me.

Mark: Smoke until you self-ignite, Wanda, dear, I don't mind, just be sure you take yourself outside before you burn my house down!

Wanda: *(Chuckling threateningly)* Very funny, you made me laugh, pretty good considering it came from a has-been.

Mark: *(Being tolerant, a bit edgy and sarcastic)* Aptly put, has-been, that's me, out to pasture, hanging onto life by threads and stitches... I worked my tail off for years at your theatre. *(Pacing)* When I was the star of those productions the Playhouse made money and was never in the red. *(To Wanda)* You drag your butch lesbian ass-bitch into my home, try to set us all on fire, and then expect me to help save your theatre? Think again Lizzy Muffdiver, this thespian is not for sale!

Wanda: You got balls, banana blaster, I like that. *(Blowing smoke, she moves past him)* I think we're going to be chums.

Julie: *(Helpless, she consoles him)* We want you back, Mark, if you're able. You're looking strong, it would help us so much.

Wanda: We don't bite, Shakespeare, is it a deal? You don't want to lay around feeling sorry for yourself.

Mark: I'm not sorry for myself... I don't like being used.

Julie: The lifetime membership is only a lure to get you to come back to us. We all genuinely love you and need you.

Wanda: Be a good little fishy and bite the hook.

Mark: *(Touched)* Well I'll be damned. I can hardly believe it; the Play House wants me back?

Julie: *(Going to him)* Yes, Mark, we need you back, more than you know. *(Moving to embrace and kiss him)* We used to have such special times together, you must remember how much you meant to me. *(The kiss sets Wanda off like a firecracker)*

Wanda: *(Alarmed)* Julie, stop, are you nuts? *(Julie kisses Mark again)* Bitch, you belong to me, now! *(She tries to break them apart)*

Julie: *(Melting in Mark's embrace)* I've always loved you. You know it's true.

Mark: *(Lighting up inside)* You're not afraid to kiss me, are you Julie… I'm overwhelmed, I'm overcome with joy…

Wanda: *(Dashing into the bathroom)* You got any mouthwash in here? *(Grabbing it she returns to them)* Julie, stop, rinse your mouth out with this! You're not dealing with a full deck!

Julie: Kissing's okay, Wanda, you can't catch it that way.

Mark: She's right, kissing is okay, it's unprotected intercourse that's dangerous.

Wanda: Not the way you tongue twisters are doing it!

Julie: *(Breaking free of Mark)* Cut it out, Wanda, just stop with the hysterics.

Wanda: Rinse your mouth out with this now or we're through!

Julie: You bitch! You don't own me!

Wanda: *(Fiercely)* I've had it up to here with you, you stinking little tart! I call the shots in this relationship, not you! You do what I say or we're through! You take orders from me or I'm out of here!

Julie: I don't like you when you're bossy, and I'm getting sick to death of you! You're a control freak! Go wait in the car, I will be out in a minute!

Wanda: Yeah, I'll wait in the fucking car! *(Fleeing to the front door she turns back angrily, showing hurt and remorse)* You led me on, I thought you cared for me! And what I ever saw in you is gone… you're dead to me, Missy Polly Pussy-Pickle!!!

Julie: Calm down you cantankerous butch drama queen… smoke your Lucky Strikes and chill!

(Wanda turns and throws open the front door revealing Doctor Purgess, M.D. knocking on thin air. He is a kind older gentleman wearing his white lab coat, a stethoscope around his neck, and carrying his black doctor's bag. Wanda glares at him) Who the hell are you, Marcus Wellby?! Out of my way, stooge! *(She exits, pushing him aside, slamming the door behind her as the doctor now enters)*

Mark: *(An awkward moment, then calmly smiling)* Doctor Purgess, M.D, what a pleasant surprise! So good of you to drop by.

Julie: *(Greeting him politely, extending her hand)* You missed all the excitement, doctor. I'm Julie Mofit, from the Smallville Playhouse, perhaps you remember me. Mark and I performed there together not long ago.

Doctor Purgess, M.D.: *(Taking her hand and puzzling)* Can't say if I recall… wait a minute, let me see…

Mark: You remember, it was a few years ago. I got you and your wife tickets.

Doctor Purgess, M.D.: Yes, I think I might remember… *(To Julie)* You look familiar… did you work in the box office?

Julie: *(Annoyed)* Well… sometimes… Mark and I were onstage together. We were a team playing romantic leads… in many musicals… We were the darlings of the Smallville theatre set. Quite popular we were!

Doctor Purgess, M.D.: And you never looked more charming... excuse me, dear, I have to see Mark on an urgent matter. *(He turns and leads Mark a few steps away)*

Julie: Don't mind me, Doctor, I am just a common nobody...

Doctor Purgess, M.D.: Of course you are, Miss... errr, Jenny... and I promise to not tell anyone. *(To Mark)* She's quite a pip in the looks department... you're wearing a condom, I hope.

Mark: Always... wait minute... you mean Stephan and I are practicing safe-sex, don't you? Julie and I, you see... We are friends... We haven't seen each other for years, and— [we're not lovers]

Doctor Purgess, M.D.: —Listen to me, Mark, this is deadly serious! Stephan has tested HIV+...

Mark: What? Oh, God, no!

Doctor Purgess, M.D.: Have you and Stephan been having safe relations? Are you using condoms?

Mark: Of course, we have... We always have... Always... oh, no...

Doctor Purgess, M.D.: Yes? No? What are you telling me... be honest.

Mark: *(Opening up, Julie shows support, she moves with him as he speaks, perhaps touching him sympathetically as he relates his truth)* I'm often not feeling well so I'm not always up for... intimacy... sexual activities. I suppose I disappoint him a lot. I reject him and become distant. He tells me he's worried I don't love him anymore, but that's not actually true at all. I don't give him what he needs so he sometimes runs off. He needs friends. He gets bored with me, I sometimes think. This illness, it destroys everything about our lives!

Mark: It's relentless, fearful, and destructive. Maybe Stephan has found someone else… if he has, I cannot blame him. But I do have to be more responsible. I can only really blame myself. I was stubborn, selfish, my needs came first, and that's no way to live a life… no way to be grateful for our friends and families… or of being truthful to ourselves and to those we love…

Julie: Oh, Mark, I am so very sorry… please forgive me for not understanding.

Mark: Thanks, Julie, you mean everything to me. The memories we share, our love, our friendship, even our dreams… simply everything…

Doctor Purgess, M.D.: You must have Stephan come and see me right away. It will be strictly confidential; you don't have to say anything to him beforehand. I'll give him the test results, just see that he comes right away. Being HIV+ [positive] does not mean a death sentence. AZT is the current drug available. You must go on it immediately. *(He hands Mark a prescription)*

Mark: Thanks, Doctor…won't you make yourself comfortable…Julie…have a seat on the sofa. *(Looking at the prescription before putting it in his pocket)* AZT… an old drug used for something else… I don't know; it can make you sicker I heard.

Doctor Purgess, M.D.: Yes, Mark, it can lead to lethargy, being tired and anemic… but it's all we have right now. *(He and Julie settle on the sofa)*

Mark: You all care for a drink? Julie? Doctor Purgess, M.D?

Julie: No thank you… I have to run… Dance rehearsal at the theatre. You can come if you want. *(Offstage Wanda guns the engine and honks the horn)* Oh, Lord, Wanda's so pissed off right now. I've got to tell her I'm sorry for hurting her feelings. She's very sensitive…

Mark: Really? I hadn't noticed.

Doctor Purgess, M.D.: *(Laughing, scolding cheerfully)* Ahhh, no, no, no, Mark. You know I love spirits, but it's a wee too early… and if you're having problems with drugs and alcohol you must seek counseling immediately. This is no joking matter; your health and well-being are paramount.

Mark: Paramount Pictures? Cecil B DeMille and THE TEN COMMANDMENTS? Thou shalt not covet a man's boyfriend? … Sorry, doc, no can do, I need another good stiff one… *(Going for the vodka he mixes himself a tall drink with ice and a twist of lime)*

Doctor Purgess, M.D.: *(Sighing, shaking his head no)* Oh, Mark, my boy… you must take your health seriously. Although it has been proven that alcoholic beverages can help HIV+ patients do better than those who don't imbibe, it can only help in moderation! That's the secret… moderation.

Mark: Okay, Doctor, okay…I get it.

Julie: Doctor Purgess, Mark seems to be taking care of himself taking vitamins and eating right, perhaps he doesn't need these prescriptions.

Doctor Purgess, M.D.: You underestimate the power of HIV. It devours a person's white T-cells and their immune system.

Mark: Vitamin C has helped me in a lot of ways, Doc, if I take at least five thousand milligrams or more I can wipe out a sore throat or the beginnings of a cold overnight—

Mark: *(Enthusiastic)* —Common infections like zits, boils, and bladder infections, too! If an infection is being stubborn, I'll up the dose to ten or fifteen thousand milligrams, spreading the Vitamin C doses out over the course of the day and then for several days. It's a kind of miracle how effective it can be.

Doctor Purgess, M.D.: You are suffering from a delusional psychosis. I insist you make an appointment with a psychiatrist. Ascorbic Acid is not some kind of freaking catch all cure. It can't rejuvenate your immune system; I need to give you an injection of antibiotics.

Mark: I hate shots, please, Doc, let's forget about the shot.

Julie: *(Amused)* But darling, you're a big boy now, let Doctor Purgess, M.D. give you your shot. I'm sure he has a lollipop in that black doctor's bag for our brave little hero.

Mark: Shots and antibiotics... no thanks... they make me feel sick. *(Drinking some more)* I have an allergic reaction to them. I get dizzy and feel like I'm going to pass out.

Julie: You must be health conscious, Mark, please listen to Doctor Purgess, M.D. Come to the theatre with me just as soon as you can get ready. Save that drink for later this evening as a night cap.

Doctor Purgess, M.D.: You must stop drinking. You cannot drink and take your medicine, too. It reduces their effectiveness. Pills will sometimes upset your stomach and make you woozy, but you shouldn't have any problem with an injection.

Mark: Sure, Doc, I understand. *(To Julie)* And I promise to share my lollipop with you, my dearest theatrical diva!

(He toasts both Doctor Purgess, M.D. and Julie, raising his glass to them, shaking the tingling ice cubes, then finishing it off in one big gulp. He places his glass on the the end table, brushes his hands together triumphantly, and gives them a military salute)

Julie: *(Sweetly sarcastic)* Bravo, dearest Mark, my favorite leading man, well done! We will meet again upon your return to our former onstage glory! *(Offstage Wanda honks the car horn)* I must be going; I am late for rehearsal. Nice meeting you Doctor.

Mark: But can't you stick around, Julie? We haven't looked at any of my old scrapbooks.

Julie: Come to the theatre later. I have to run. If you can't, I will call about our schedule for our musical review fundraiser.

Mark: Okay. I'll try to make it... as soon as possible. Wish you would stay awhile. I miss you so much and all the good times especially.

Julie: Yes, me, too, Mark. I can run out and check with Wanda first, and skip dance rehearsal today. *(She is anxious to decide what to do and exchanges worried looks with Mark)*

Mark: *(Understanding her need to fulfill her obligations)* No, Julie, you run along... *(Wanda is revving up the engine again, she honks the horn loudly)* Later this week if I can psych myself up.

Julie: Promise? ... Call me, okay? I'm so worried about you... *(She kisses him and heads for the front door)*

Mark: Don't you worry, I'm fine, okay?

Julie: Okay, Mark, bye... *(She turns to go, looks back and blows him a kiss, then exits. The engine roars, Wanda and Julie are heard offstage)*

Wanda: *(Honking the horn)* Hurry up, sugar tits, we haven't got all day! Get in the car already!

Julie: Sorry to keep you waiting, Butchmeister! Cool off, shut up and hit the road! *(The car doors slam and they are heard driving away)*

Doctor Purgess, M.D.: *(Getting back to business)* Lovely girl, I detected sparks between you. Have you been taking the other medications I prescribed? The antibiotics to prevent opportunistic infections and pneumonia?

Mark: Once in a while if my throat gets sore or it's hard to breath and my lungs are congested. My glands swell and my throat will be raw. You see I get tired a lot and if I feel something coming on... I like to take a lot of extra Vitamin C.

Doctor Purgess, M.D.: *(Horrified he gets up off the sofa immediately)* Oh, my God, Mark, what are you trying to do to yourself? I must give you an injection immediately! *(He rifles through his black doctor's bag)* You're not taking those antibiotics the way their prescription demands. Read the labels, always read the labels on your medicines. *(He pulls out a hypodermic syringe and other items, clumsily in rapid fashion)*

Mark: Linus Pauling wrote a book on vitamin C. I eat healthy. I feel okay, what gives?

Doctor Purgess, M.D.: *(He pulls out an Ahhh-stick, his silver eye patch with the peep-hole, a slender flashlight, and goes up to Mark to depress his tongue and check his throat)* Open wide and stick out your tongue!

Mark: *(Mark can't speak well has he tolerates the tongue depressor)* ... Ahhh... Doctor you're overreacting... you don't understand... Ahhh... I want to treat AIDS with natural remedies...vitamins, and good nutrition...

Mark: … Gee, Doc, you're choking me to death! Vitamin C in large daily doses fights infections naturally. I don't need dubious drugs or constant medical attention.

Doctor Purgess, M.D.: *(Making him open wide he continues to depress Marks tongue and aim his flashlight into Mark's throat)* Have you lost your mind, my friend… open up, stick out your tongue again… Vitamin C has never been proven to be effective against anything. The HIV retrovirus must be making rapid progress within you. It's affecting your brain and your central nervous system. You are defiantly out of touch with reality. *(Mark gags some more)* Your throat is red and your glands are swollen and it's a good thing I came when I did! *(He removes the Ahhh-stick and goes to prepare the hypodermic syringe)*

Mark: *(Slightly worried, a bit fearful)* Gee, is that the shot? The needle looks more like a nail to me. Do I take it in the butt?

Doctor Purgess, M.D.: Yes, drop your pajama bottoms.

Mark: *(He obliges and bends over exposing his buttocks, he winces anticipating pain)* Okay, let's get it over with already. *(Doctor Purgess, M.D. administers the shockingly scary, huge, comical hypodermic syringe)* Ouch! Oh my God! Doc! *(He pulls up his pajama bottoms after it's over and rubs his forehead and starts breathing erratically)* Oh, Doctor, what a rush, just like snorting poppers… I feel woozy already… *(He staggers a little, catching his balance)*

Doctor Purgess, M.D.: *(Putting his medical materials back in the black doctor bag he turns to comfort Mark)* Don't worry about a thing.

Doctor Purgess, M.D.: You'll be fine, just get back in bed and rest awhile. I must be leaving, my wife Hilda and I have plans for this afternoon. I must take my leave.

Mark: *(Breathing harder)* I'm not kidding, Doctor Purgess, M.D. I feel like a rush, like when Stephan and I have sex and do poppers…it makes our hearts pound. Feel my heart pounding, Doc… I'm dizzy with sexual desire…

Doctor Purgess, M.D.: Stay away from poppers. Get in bed and lie down.

Mark: *(Breathing deeply, trying to recover)* Okay, okay, I will, thanks….

Doctor Purgess, M.D.: Bye, Mark, call me in the morning. *(He exits out the front door)*

Mark: Bye, Doctor Purgess, M.D. *(After a moment we hear the doctor's car start and pull away offstage. Mark staggers to the window and sees this before wobbling back to the sofa. He holds on to the back of it to support himself he mutters, slurring his speech as the combination drugs and alcohol take their toll)* What the hell did you give me, Doc?I feel like I'm blacking out. Water, I need water… ice water, I need a cool drink of water, I'm burning up! *(He goes to the kitchenette and the refrigerator shuffling around, getting ice cubes to rub in his face, splashing water from the sink in his mouth and on his face)* Oh, yeah, that's better. Much better… *(He makes it back to the sofa and clears it, stumbling around, knocking things over. He begins to sob and cry)* What have you done to me, I can't breathe, where is everybody, save me somebody… Julie, Doc, come back… Stephan, I'm so sorry… Stephan, you know I love you, you must care, please, please… Jesus… Christ…

(Mark finally blacks out and collapses onto the sofa. His head turns to the side and one arm drops to the floor. He sighs, exhaling slowly and remains motionless. During these last few moments Soft 1980's Music plays in the background. Fade to Black)

SCENE THREE

(The Music Continues in the Blackout and we hear the sounds of an approaching car which comes to a stop, the car doors opening, and the Music Fades as the intoxicated Stephan and Zebulon speak Offstage. Stage Lights come up slightly but remain dim. It is now early Monday morning after midnight)

Stephan: God damn it, why couldn't the motherfucker leave the porch light on.

Zebulon: Quiet, Stephan, it must be one of two in the morning... we'll wake him... He probably thinks we eloped or something...

Stephan: Zeb, you have a nice tight ass and I really liked being with you today, but you are too mother fucking sweet for your own good. Shhh, quiet now, handsome...

(Stephan awkwardly opens the front door slowly, flips on the porch light to reveal both men in the doorway, shirtless, being cuddly together, touching and flirtatious. Stephan reaches over and flips on a room light near the door, sees Mark on the sofa, then turns it back off)

Stephan: Shit, Mark is asleep on the sofa. Shhh, quite...

Zebulon: Uh, oh, I hope he doesn't think we've been messing around. Jesus Christ, he'll kill us.

Stephan: Relax, ass-hole, we're not going to tell him. He knows I like to go out once in a while, but there's no point in confessing.

Zebulon: Got you, we're not going to tell... but he will suspect we've been fucking around so I better go, see ya... *(He turns to leave but Stephan holds him back)*

Stephan: Don't go yet, let's sneak into the bedroom, I'm horny again.

Zebulon: You, crazy man, I'm not letting you leash another load in me without a rubber.

Stephan: You're being paranoid, I pulled out before I came inside you...Relax, Zeb, I'm not sick, you're safe with me.

Zebulon: Forget it, no way, I'm gone.

Stephan: Fuck you, Zeb, go on, get out of here.

Zebulon: *(Breaking away)* Bite me, Stephan. *(He heads for the car)*

Stephan: I did, and you loved it, didn't you? ... Hey, wait... I'll call you later... Bye, hot-stuff! *(We hear Zebulon getting in his car and driving away. Stephan enters into the dark dimly lighted home and goes carefully over to Mark on the sofa)* Mark, honeybunch, you awake man? *(Stephan takes a deep breath and sighs, becoming remorseful and apologetic)* I'm sorry I was gone all day. Wish you'd been with me. You still asleep? You okay, Mark? *(He touches him)* You okay, man? I'm sorry to disturb you... I just wanted you to know I'm back. And I am very... You know I love you, buddy... sorry I took off like that without you. *(He nudges Mark again more vigorously)* You hear me? Mark? Mark, sweetheart? *(He bends closer to Mark, suddenly becoming aware of Mark's condition, horrified)* Oh, no, Mark! My God what has happened! Mark! Mark! *(He begins sobbing)* No, no, it can't be true, you can't be dead! *(Grabbing the phone and calling 911 in desperation)*

Stephan: 911, 911, oh, God, pick up, pick up! Hurry! Yes, yes, I need an ambulance fast! My friend looks like he's dead! Come quickly!!!

Stephan: We're at 42392 Bratcher Lane! Hurry! *(He puts down the phone and tries CPR techniques on Mark. He performs mouth to mouth resuscitation between sobs and tears)*

Mark: *(Gasping for air, he comes back from near death, coughing and sputtering)* Oh, Jesus Christ, what happened!

Stephan: You're alive, your alive! It's a miracle, Mark, Oh my God! Oh my God, Mark! *(He grabs hold of Mark and they embrace on the sofa, kissing and hugging with tears and joy)* I thought I lost you, Mark, I thought I'd lost you…

(As the lights slowly dim and the soft 1980's music plays once against we can hear the ambulance siren approaching from the distance. Fade to Black and Curtain)

ASCORBIC ACID FREAK

A One Act Play by *Grant Sutor Vuille*

THE END

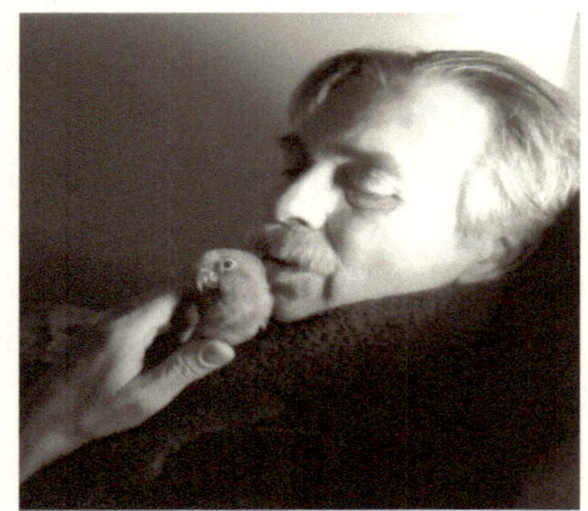

Jeffrey and Corabella

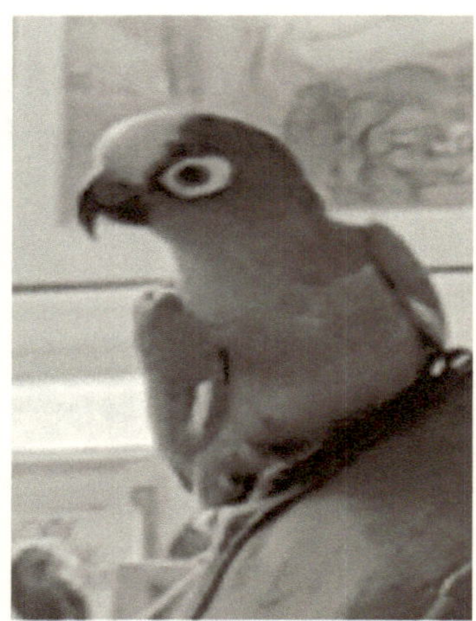

Corabella

Doctor George's Magnificent Zeppelin

A Musical Comedy Fantasy Stage & Screenplay
by Grant Sutor Vuille

SYNOPSIS / LOG LINE:

A Fantastical Musical Comedy Farce, DOCTOR GEORGE'S MAGNIFICENT ZEPPELIN takes us on a magical adventure to discover truth, justice, and the wonderful secret of living in a completely harmonious World of diverse morality-based relationships that end with the enlightening embrace of Unconditional Love

MAIN CHARACTERS

Doctor George	*An imaginative eccentric middle-aged philosopher, dedicated scientist & inventor who has grandiose plans to save the world from systemic character discrimination, widespread destruction & intolerant un-vanquished evil.*
Junie Moon	*A feisty romantic, young female actress, singer, & aspiring TV journalist with high intelligence & ambitions to succeed.*
Seymour	*A young crew member longing for love & adventure, but fearful, nervous & shy.*

Max	*A young witty, smart crew member & assistant to both Dr. George & Seymour, his closest friend and companion.*
Gloria Glamorude	*An outrageous nosey female journalist whose manners & ethics are often offensive & intolerant. She is always accompanied by her two subservient WHOP-TV nameless crew members.*
Cookie	*Junie Moon's misunderstood young female assistant, make-up artist, friend & confidant.*
Mr. Whopperberg	*Gruff WHOP-TV station's executive owner, mogul & producer.*
Captain Bandit	*A romantic, handsome & rugged adventurous pirate.*
Prince	*A dimwitted, but dedicated pirate & crew member & the Capt's first mate.*
Laddie	*A somewhat comic, dense & clueless pirate crew member.*
Corabella	*Capt. Bandit's green, blue, orange & yellow Conure Amazon Parrot, a witty, smart & highly intuitive, loving companion.*
Ethel Mermaid	*A divine, belting & singing showstopper & talented Mermaid.*
Queen Thirteen	*Antagonistic Fairie & egomaniacal evil dictator, tyrant & creator of a terroristic mega tourist trap name-saked Thirteenland.*
Gertrude	*Ethel's sidekick & talented Mermaid.*
Buffy	*Silly, talented singer & companion Mermaid.*
King Jaggar	*Usurped & jailed by his wife who has taken over as the ruler of the fantasy creature invested, Isle of Jaggar, a fairie's delight of a magical world.*
Jumper	*A large green fire-breathing Dragon & comic foil to the fairie Queen Thirteen.*

SUPPORTING PLAYERS — MISC. CHARACTERS / EXTRA'S

Winkie, Dinky & Twinkie *Jailed fairies, the King's companions, who only communicate in Xylophoneze, the official language of Fairies.*

Bernard C. Starmaker (B.C.) *An accomplished WHOP-TV top Studio Production Director.*

Cynthia *Child fan of Junie Moon.*

Mother *Cynthia's mom.*

Gloria's Two WHOP-TV Crew Members.

Actors, Singers & Dancers *Junie Moon's WHOP-TV Chorus*

Queen Thirteen's Fairie Souvenir's Factory-Slaves & Trinket-Makers

Junie Moon II *Junie Moon's beautiful yellow eyed fuzzy black rescue kitten.*

DOCTOR GEORGE'S MAGNIFICENT ZEPPELIN

A Musical Comedy Fantasy Screenplay
— by Grant Sutor Vuille

SCENE 1

(FADE IN)

EXT. DR. GEORGE'S ESTATE - DAY

(GLORIA GLAMORUDE, a pushy, middle-aged, THICKLY MADE-UP NEWS GLAMOR DOLL, HAIR COIFFURED in a blizzard of NOXIOUS TEASED BOUFANT CURLS, arrives with TWO (WHOP-TV) CREW MEMBERS. She is applying drippingly THICK RED LIPSTICK as they DRIVE up to the ZEPPELIN which is ANCHORED in the FIELD next to the GARAGE LABORATORY.)

(SEYMOUR and MAX, two young assistants and CREW MEMBERS, work with DOCTOR GEORGE on preparing the Zeppelin for their journey. DOCTOR GEORGE is a middle-aged lovable old scientist, sometimes bumbling, but always thoughtful and intelligent, if not always polite, determined and forthright.)

(GLORIA GLAMORUDE is the epitome of an obnoxious over-painted, over-glamorized, BAD NEWS VULTURE. She is hard-nosed and driven, never polite and always rude. Her TWO WHOP—TV CREW MEMBERS are subservient cowards who follow her around dutifully with portable VIDEO EQUIPMENT.)

(They APPROACH the ZEPPELIN and attempt to board it. MAX and SEYMOUR aid DOCTOR GEORGE in trying to control them, but they are inevitably pushed aside.)

(CUT TO)

EXT. THE ZEPPELIN'S LOWER DECK

(GLORIA and her CREW reach the DECK with a flustered DOCTOR GEORGE trying to interrupt her progress.)

Gloria: Doctor George? You are Doctor George, are you not?

Dr. George: Yes. Yes I am. Can I help you?

Gloria: *(to her crew)* Are we taping? Don't shut it off unless I give the word. *(to Doctor George)* Nice weather we're having, eh, Doctor?

Dr. George: Errr, yes, yes, it is. *(to his boys)* Seymour, Max. Keep working please.

Gloria: Nice day for a little trip into the outer stratosphere?

Dr. George: I should say so. Yes, it is as a matter-of-fact.

Gloria: Any vacation plans in the wind you'd care to communicate with our home viewers?

Dr. George: No, not at this time. Perhaps you could come back another day... when we're not here —

Gloria: Not so fast, Doctor George, you can't get rid of me that easily. I understand, Doctor, that you've been preparing this odd-looking contraption... this... this —

Dr. George: Zeppelin. It's a Zeppelin!

Gloria: Yes... so it is... but Magnificent? ... Perhaps... Most intriguing, and a very suspicious magnificent Zeppelin, I observably suspect, also!

Dr. George: You exhaust me, woman, be gone! Now, if you'd be so kind as to leave, my boys and I have a lot of work to complete. Thank you, Ms Roudimyer, my apologies for being so abrupt, and my sincerest sympathy to your bedraggled Crew and to your WHOP-TV Affiliates. So sorry to have met the lot-of-you... Good Bye!

Gloria: Not until I get what I came for, Doctor. I need a story. You can't brush me aside that easily. I happen to know from reputable political sources that you're on some sort of a top-secret mission. Something, I'm told, that has everything to do with a special device which the weapons experts in Washington are looking in to.

Dr. George: Please! I haven't the slightest idea what you are talking about. I beg you to take your leave. Max, Seymour, escort Ms. Ramaroodilla, or whatever her name is, off this vessel, NOW! *(To Gloria, who's fiddling with the CONTROLS)*

(CONT'D)—Madame, please! Don't touch anything! Boys! Get Madam Rude-Awakening off these premises, pronto!

Gloria: The name's GlamoRUDE!!! G - L - A - M - O - R - U - D - E. Rude! As in —

Seymour: —Rude bitch!

Dr. George: Seymour, watch your language!

Gloria: Quite right, young man, and because of my reputation, I always get my way, no matter what the obstacle. *(She backs him up against some ROPES and he nearly falls over but, getting tangled, manages to hold on to them.)*

(CONT'D) So don't get in my way, you rodent, unless you prefer to have your good name smeared across the airwaves of this nation.

Seymour: Right, lady.

Gloria: And don't you forget it. I've come for a story, and a story I shall have before I leave, unless you want me to make it up myself, which I often do.

(to Doctor George) So start talking, Doctor, before I expose you for the quack you obviously are.

(Doctor George storms down the GANGPLANK onto the GROUND.)

(CUT TO)

EXT. DR. GEORGE'S ESTATE

(Doctor George is frustrated and stands fuming.)

Dr. George: Quack? I dare say, my good lady… errr, Miss Glamorude, you are the only one around here whose feathers are flying! Now, I want you off my property this very minute, or I'll be forced to call the authorities.

Gloria: I'm the only authority around here. *(she charges after him)* If there is a story to be sniffed out, then that is where I'll be. No secret mission, no undercover government philandering, no corporate hanky-panky escapes my roving eye. I am not leaving until I expose you naked before the public conscience.

Max: Kinky lady.

(CUT TO)

EXT. DR. GEORGE'S ESTATE / GARAGE

(Doctor George heads for the garage. He summons Max and Seymour, who tag along helplessly after him.)

Dr. George: Madame, please, for the last time, you're making a grave mistake. I have nothing to hide as you can plainly see. Now, if you'll be so kind as to withdraw, I'll be happy to answer any future questions at a later date. You may call my secretary in the morning for an appointment.

Max: Secretary? Who's that, Doctor George? Me, or Seymour?

(Doctor George stands up against the GARAGE ENTRANCE, blocking the way.)

Gloria: Aha! Your secret devices are hidden inside. Stand aside. I command you.

Seymour: Command? Who are you, the First Lady of the United States of America?

Dr. George: You really have gone too far. The secrecy of my work is of grave importance.

Gloria: So. You admit your shenanigans. *(She barges forward and shoves a MICROPHONE in his face.)*

(CONT'D) Are you now, or have you ever been, a closet-bed-wetter? *(to her crew)* We've got him now, guys, I can see him beginning to sweat. He's about to confess. Is the tape running? Good. This is Gloria Glamorude for WHOP-TV. Our top story for today is the mysterious —

(CUT TO)

SCENE 2

INT. WHOP-TV STUDIO - DAY

(JUNIE MOON, a beautiful young performer and media personality is DANCING and SINGING in a ROCK VIDEO which is being TAPED by a TV CREW. LIGHTS, SMOKE and VARIOUS EFFECTS HIGHLIGHT the performance. Her COSTUME suggests a CAT. The dancers' costumes suggest DOGS. The song is titled "DOG BITES". At a CLIMACTIC MOMENT an EFFECT FIZZLES and BERNARD C. STARMAKER (B.C.) the accomplished top studio production director, STOPS the PROCEEDINGS. EVERYONE groans, then shuffles around, relaxing and chattering with one another.)

B.C.: *(Shouting in frustration)* Cut! What the hell happened, people?! Can we get it together, please?! What happened to the Flares? Huh? Can you hear me up there?! ... What Fizzled?!

Voice: *(O.C.)* Sorry. There was a short... it shorted out.

B.C.: Great, just great, we got to get it right or we'll be here all day! Can you fix it?!

Voice: *(O.C.)* Give me a minute.

(Junie Moon goes to B.C.)

Junie: *(Irritate and nearing exhaustion)* What happened this time, Bernard, I am losing my patience... what is the hold up?

B.C.: The flares were out of sync. You're doing great, honey, you and the cast take a break. *(shouting)* Be back in five, everyone!

Junie: Thanks Mr. Starmaker, hope this doesn't take too long....

(Junie's young assistant and makeup girl, COOKIE approaches.)

Cookie: You look great out there, but you're sweating like a pig. Let's hit the trailer, you need a touch-up.

(CUT TO)

SCENE 3

EXT. STUDIO LOT - DAY

(COOKIE and JUNIE head for Junie's dressing TRAILER.)

Junie: We were just about through with the number. This is the third take. I wish those techies would get it together.

Cookie: Me too. It's nearly lunchtime. I'm starved.

(A MOTHER and her young child DAUGHTER stop them just outside the TRAILER DOOR.)

Mother: My little girl just loves you, Miss Moon. She wants to ask you for your autograph.

(Junie leans down to speak to her.)

Junie: Well, aren't you a pretty little thing. What's your name sweetie?

Daughter: My name is Cynthia. I wanna be just like you when I grow up.

(CYNTHIA hands Junie a RECORD ALBUM COVER with Junie's PICTURE on it and a PEN. Junie takes them and writes.)

Junie: *(tenderly)* To Cynthia with love... Junie Moon. There you are Cynthia... that's a beautiful name. Take care now, and thank you.

Mother: Thanks so much Miss Moon. She's wanted to meet you for the longest time. Say thank you, honey.

Cynthia: Thank you, Mrs. Junie Moon... can I marry you?

Junie: Awww, You're so sweet... someday, Cynthia, darling, when you're all grown up...

Mother: You are most kind, Miss Moon, so welcoming to children and teenagers... Your parents must be very proud of your success.

Junie: *(hesitating, then sadly)* Oh, Well I... I don't have a mother or father... Excuse me, won't you. I only have a few minutes to freshen up. Bye now, have a nice day both of you. *(to Cynthia)* See you when you're all grown up. Bye, precious....

(CUT TO)

SCENE 4

INT. JUNIE'S TRAILER - DAY

(Cookie and Junie ENTER the TRAILER.)

Cookie: You're not upset, are you?

Junie: No, no… I'm much too busy to worry about the past… so many things on my mind…

Cookie: I just wondered. If I was an orphan, I'd be sensitive about not having any family.

(Junie sits at her VANITY as Cookie touches up her face and hair.)

Junie: WHOP-TV is my family. Growing up in a dozen foster homes is not something I care to think about, now. It's over and done with. Guess I was too much for them to handle… that's why I got passed around so often.

Cookie: How sad. *(reflecting, then cheerfully)* That little girl has a crush on you.

Junie: Hmmm… that's so sweet… so innocent… but my experience made me tough. I have had my work on stage and in films and I am grateful as can be, and happy… that's my life now and I love it.

Cookie: … You're special to me, too, I feel like that little girl sometimes…

(Someone KNOCKS at the door.)

Junie: Be ready in a minute.

Voice: *(O.S.)* It's me, Junie. I need to see you.

Junie: Come on in, Mr. Whopperberg!

(MR. WHOPPERBERG, the station's EXECUTIVE PRODUCER enters.)

(He's an imposing gruff middle-aged man. He flips on her TV upon the DRESSING TABLE which plays the station's NOON NEWS BROADCAST. GLORIA GLAMORUDE, appears SANS MAKE -UP & SHOCKING UP-DO is the ANCHOR. Subdued, she is pleasant and smiles a lot as she calmly reports without sensation while the SCENE PLAYS in the F.G.)

Gloria: *(B.G. Pleasantly bantering, whistful)* The news is just breathtakingly beautiful today!

The flowers and trees are doing so well after that lovely spring shower we had last night. And the birds were tweeting sweetly and squirrels were scampering about, looking for love and romance, lovely, just a lovely sight to behold. Butterflies fluttering around like little fairies bewitching little tiny princes and princesses, all behaving like angels in a fantasy land of joy...

(GLORIA's monologue is continuous in B.G. throughout the scene.)

Mr. Whopperberg: How's the music video going, girls?

Cookie: Fine, Mr. Whopperberg, sir.

Junie: Fair. How's my favorite mogul these days?

(On TV, CONT'D in B.G.)

(GLORIA GLAMORUDE, not at all her usual self, is rambling on. Her personal appearance and her NEWS AT NOON TV show is TRANSFORMED. Now without makeup, hair straight and naturally soft, she holds a FLOWER in her hand. Her news monologue progresses and her voice is pleasant and sweet, totally changed.)

Mr. Whopperberg: *(indicating TV)* Okay, except we have a serious problem on our hands.

Cookie: Oh my gosh, is that who I think it is?

Mr. Whopperberg: *(dismayed)* Our very own, Ms. Glamorude. Hard to believe, isn't it.

Cookie: Is she trying out a new look?

Gloria: *(ON TV she winds it up.)* ... and I just want everyone out there in TV land to know that I love each and every one of you. So from now on, just to show you how much I care, I'll report good news only. So, let's keep big smiles on our cheerful little faces. This is your afternoon news anchor woman, Gloria Glamorude, signing off until later this evening at seven o'clock. Don't forget to tune in for more good news across the nation and the world... Bye, bye...

Mr. Whopperberg: Worse. Take a look at this.

(He plugs a VIDEO TAPE into Junie's VCR. It CUTS into the TAIL END of GLORIA'S SIGN OFF.)

Junie: What's going on? I hardly recognized her. What happened to our hard-nosed anchor woman?

Mr. Whopperberg: Take a look at this interview she taped this morning at that wacky Doctor George's estate and you'll see.

(They watch TAPED MATERIAL on the TV SCREEN as GLORIA pushes her way into DOCTOR GEORGE'S GARAGE. As previously in SCENE 1, GLORIA's MAKE-UP is back to being thick as molasses, her hair teased-up and curls lacquered down ludicrously. Doctor George, Seymour and Max back away, nearly helpless.)

Gloria: *(ON TV to her crew)* Is the tape running?

(Crew nods in the affirmative)

Gloria: *(CONT'D)* Good, keep it rolling no matter what happens.

Gloria: This is Gloria Glamorude for WHOP-TV. Our top story for today is the mysterious —

Dr. George: *(ON TV)* Now, just hold on there, Miss Glamorude, you have no right to come barging in like this.

Gloria: *(barging forward, mic in hand)* Is there some clandestine goings on here you wish to hide from the American viewing public?

Dr. George: *(backing away)* Of course not, errr, but I, that is there are certain experiments of such a sensitive nature which I don't care to divulge at this time and —

Gloria: Experiments? As in top-secret undercover unofficial United States of America dirty tricks?

(On screen, Doctor George stumbles over SCIENTIFIC GIZMOS, aided clumsily by his uncoordinated assistants.)

Dr. George: Dirty tricks? I should say not.

Gloria: Wiretapping? Hush money?

Dr. George: Wiretapping? Absurd.

Gloria: Arms sales to enemy foreign nations?

Dr. George: Ridiculous. The idea!

Gloria: It is common knowledge that you and the President of our country were fraternity brothers while in college, were you not?

Dr. George: Uh, yes indeed, but, what does that have to do with—

Gloria: Did you or did you not participate in a shoplifting spree through the lingerie department at a K-Mart during fraternity hell-week-initiations, high on pot and intoxicated with booze!?

(On the TV screen, Gloria turns on the doctor's VANITY-EGO-REFLECTOR by accident. Its lights begin to FLASH. It catches her attention.)

Max: A K-Mart panty raid?

Seymour: *(To Max)* K-Mart is not a fraternity... Nice going, Doctor George.

Dr. George: Nonsense. A harmless prank. *(to Gloria)* Hey, don't touch that, it hasn't been tested.

(She stares deeply into the bright FLASHING mirror.)

Gloria: Some sort of spying device, no doubt. A two-way mirror to hide behind while recording secret negotiations I bet.

(Doctor George moves in attempt to stop her but fails.)

Dr. George: Don't stare into it, I'm telling you, it could be dangerous.

Gloria: *(mesmerized)* Tell me, Doctor, do you now, or have you ever, slept in the nude?

(GLORIA SCREAMS BLOOD-CURDLINGLY as her HAIR is BLOWN BACK and her THICK GLAMOR MAKEUP MELTS AWAY.)

(The TV SCREEN in Junie Moon's trailer GOES HAYWIRE, then BLANK. Mr. Whopperberg SHUTS IT OFF.)

Junie: *(gasping)* Jeepers. What was all that about?

Mr. Whopperberg: That's what I want you to find out.

Junie: Me? I don't understand?

Mr. Whopperberg: You've been bugging me to host the news for months. Now's your chance!

Junie: Yes, but I've got my music videos to cut and my agent keeps bugging me to do stage and film work this summer. I'm booked solid. I haven't got the time.

Cookie: *(enthusiastic)* You can do it, Junie. Just think how it'll look on your Actor-Singer-Dancer theatrical resume.

Junie: *(amused)* Actor-Singer-Dancer-TV Journalist? Please.

Mr. Whopperberg: I need you to replace Gloria tonight. If she goes back on the air with all that gladness and good news garbage, our network ratings will go right down the toilet.

(B.C. POUNDS on her TRAILER DOOR and THRUSTS IT OPEN.)

B.C.: Let's go, Junie Moon, we're all set. Let's wrap it up!

Cookie: Give us a minute. *(to Junie)* Your hair's out of place. Here, let's powder you down.

B.C.: Remember, Everyone, to give it all you've got… Got that? Okay, Places!!!

Junie: Be right there, B.C.

Junie: *(She sighs)* Bernard C. Starmaker… What a Task Master! He never lets up, Cookie, he just corals us all together and Bang, Bang, Bang!!! He pounds a performance out of us!

(B.C. EXITS through the trailer door.)

Mr. Whopperberg: What do you say, Junie, is it a deal?

Junie: *(Coyly)* I will have to think about it… I'll let you know.

Mr. Whopperberg: You've got me on pins and needles, Miss Moon! *(Grumbling)* I'll double your salary. Anything you want. You name it.

Junie: *(getting up)* You twisted my arm.

Mr. Whopperberg: *(extending his hand)* It's a deal then?

Junie: As soon as my new contract is signed... Then yes, it's a deal, Mr. Whopperberg!

Mr. Whopperberg: Very shrewd, Miss Junie Moon, I like it... Great! Now get down to the news room after the shoot and they'll set you up. I Want you to crack this Doctor George business and scoop the air waves tonight at seven. Don't disappoint me. I'm counting on you.

(Mr. Whopperberg EXITS the trailer and Junie turns quickly to Cookie.)

Junie: Cookie, I want you to go with me on this assignment. I may need your help with the equipment. Can you operate a video camera?

Cookie: I shot videos of my brother's wedding. Does that count? But you'll have the station's TV crew. You don't need me.

(They EXIT the Trailer)

(CUT TO)

SCENE 5

INT. WHOP-TV STUDIO - DAY

(JUNIE MOON & COOKIE ARRIVE INTO THE STUDIO SOUND STAGE. EVERYONE is getting IN PLACE.)

Junie: Yes, I do. Moral support, Cookie, and secrecy. Run ahead to the news room and get things started. I'll meet you there in ten minutes.

Cookie: Roger, over and out. Break-a-leg, Junie.

(Cookie rushes off.)

Junie: Thanks, Cookie.

(JUNIE MOON takes her place on the SET. The DANCERS ready themselves. The LIGHTS go UP and everyone waits in anticipation.)

B.C.: Everybody set? Ready with the playback? Let's roll it. Action!

(The MUSIC BEGINS for "DOG BITES" (A rock song by G.S. Vuille). LIGHTS FLASH and FLARES GO OFF ON CUE as JUNIE MOON and her DANCERS rock 'n roll.)

Junie: *(singing) Dog Bites! They don't bother me. Dog Bites! Oh, baby can't you see? /*

Our hungry love was always, always meant to be. Come on hold me baby, and rough me up for spite. /

Sling me, tear me, baby. My soul is yours tonight! Don't let me run away, I'm your prisoner for all time. /

Junie: *My soul is yours to walk on, and love me for all time! (Chorus joins Junie)*

(Chorus) Dog Bites! They don't bother me. /

Dog Bites! Oh, baby, can't you see? Our love was always frightening, as frightening as can be. /

Oh bite me babe forever and forever we'll be free! Dog Bites! Dog Bites!

(JUNIE MOON and the CHORUS OF SINGERS/ DANCERS strike a FINAL POSE.)

(DISSOLVE TO)

SCENE 6

EXT. JAGGER'S ISLE - NIGHT

(It is a FANTASTIC ISLAND FAIRIELAND with ROCKY SHORES, FORESTS, VOLCANOS, MERMAIDS, DRAGONS, FAIRIES and nefarious PIRATES. The pirates are swashbuckling, but lovable, fierce, and bumbling, despite their fierceness.)

(LADDIE and PRINCE are two such pirates and CREW MEMBERS of CAPT. BANDIT's PIRATE SHIP. They are involved in CHASING FAIRIES most earnestly, but with comic intensity.)

(The FAIRIES are sparkling little tiny creatures who whip about with ease through the air on wings. Their leader is KING JAGGER, a humble figure, anxious, kind in appearance, resourceful, yet unfortunately has lost his power on the island from having married a mortal, QUEEN THIRTEEN, a full-sized human being of irrational evil intentions.)

(Laddie carries a BUTTERFLY NET and Prince carries a BIRDCAGE full of twinkling FAIRIES. The Fairies speak only in XYLOPHONEZE.)

(LADDIE and PRINCE are chasing KING JAGGER through the FOREST, swatting at him with the BUTTERFLY NET. Jagger manages to escape several times and the two pirates continually bump into, or fall over, each other in their pursuit. They trip over LOGS, trafficking awkwardly through the UNDERBRUSH nearly taking accidental dives into LAVA PITS and become tangled in FOREST VINES.)

(Lurking in the DARK FOREST waiting patiently for his men to return, is CAPTAIN BANDIT and his beautiful female companion, Amazon Conure Parrot CORABELLA who is often perched on his shoulder. Bearded, handsome and tall, he exudes confidence as he waits by the ROCKY SHORE of a MERMAID'S LAGOON.)

(Laddie swings at King Jagger and falls into the LAGOON. A lovely MERMAID spits water in his face, pushing him underwater. Prince tries to help Laddie out of the lagoon with a long stick, but King Jagger FLIES about his face taunting him until he loses his balance and falls into the water.)

(The Mermaid gives King Jagger a ride to the other side, laughing all the way.)

(King Jagger is in stitches laughing on a TREE BRANCH when Captain Bandit plucks him off it by his pants as Corabella squawks and whistles approvingly. He takes the fairie King and places him in the BIRDCAGE with the other disgruntled fairies, WINKY, DINKY & TWINKIE.)

Captain Bandit: Gotcha now, me buck-o. You'll soon be roasting in the hell-fires of Queen Thirteen's Hot-House dungeon!

Corabella: *(A squawk and a whistle)* A Toast to the Roast, on King Jaggar's Isle's Coast!

(Laddie and Prince climb up on the ROCKS exhausted.)

Captain Bandit: *(CONT'D)* Nice work, boys. Queen Thirteen will be pleased.

Prince: Thanks, Captain Bandit, sir.

Laddie: Can we go back to our campfire and dry off? I'm freezing. That mermaid tried to drown me. I was scared!

Captain Bandit: Poor baby. Prince, take your sniveling shipmate back to camp. I'll meet you there after I pick up the ransom loot for our prissy glitter ridden prisoners.

Corabella: *(Whistling)* Sing a song of a Prince, and my Laddie will Wince! Don't freeze yourself Cold, as campfire-stories be Told! *(Squawking and tweeting happily.)*

(King Jagger protests and shakes at the BARS defiantly. The other three fairies, Winkie, Dinky, & Twinkie huddle together in fear.)

(Prince and Laddie begin to laugh at their fairie prisoners' fate. The Mermaid spits water on both of them and swims quickly away.)

(DISSOLVE TO)

SCENE 7

EXT/INT. STREET NEAR JUNIE'S DOWNTOWN APT BLDG / INT. CAR - DAY

(DRIVING Cookie and Junie ARRIVE with their VIDEO EQUIPMENT. In the CAR, Cookie tries to sort through it, pushing aside CABLES and portable LIGHTS. She holds up the CAMCORDER.)

Junie: Do you think you can handle that equipment?

Cookie: I don't see why we need all this extra stuff when we have this lovely little portable camcorder?

(Junie PARKS the car and they get out.)

Junie: Let's get up to my apartment and grab a sandwich. I need to change into something more comfortable, too.

(CUT TO)

SCENE 8

EXT. JUNIE'S APARTMENT BUILDING / ALLEY

(In the ALLEY next to her apartment BUILDING are some DOGS BARKING viciously near some GARBAGE CANS. Junie and Cookie scare them away.)

Junie: Hey. Scram. Get outa there! How many times do I have to tell you to stay outa my garbage?

Cookie: You heard the lady, scram! Take a hike!

(The DOGS run OFF and Junie straightens up a garbage can, TRASH and some BOXES.)

Junie: I wish they'd stay out of my neighborhood.

Cookie: What can you do? They're probably hungry.

Junie: Yeah. Strays, I guess, so sad seeing animals without homes.

(As she's bending down, there's a tiny trembling MEOW. She pushes aside a garbage can and there cowers a small fuzzy BLACK KITTEN with big YELLOW EYES. She looks up at Junie and MEOWS pitifully. Junie's expression reveals that her heart is breaking.)

Junie: *(CONT'D, tenderly)* Hello there. How did you get stuck in this mess? Come here little girl.

(She picks up the little kitten, cradling her tenderly, and shows her to Cookie.)

Cookie: Oh, my goodness, gracious, a tiny precious kitten person. Poor little thing. Those mean old dogs were after you, weren't they?

Junie: Uh huh... let's take her inside. She must be lost. *(to kitten)* Are you lost, little girl? Can't find your mommie? Let's go inside and see if we can find you something to eat. You must be very hungry.

(CUT TO)

SCENE 9

INT. JUNIE'S APARTMENT/HALLWAY - DAY

(Junie, Cookie and the kitten enter. They go into the KITCHEN and Junie places the kitten on the COUNTER next to the WINDOW.)

(CUT TO)

INT. KITCHEN

(The SUNLIGHT shines in, BACKLIGHTING the kitten's BLACK fuzzy FUR to a glowing REDDISH HUE. The kitten MEOWS in its tiny trembling way, little BELL-LIKE, and the girls become more attached with each moment.)

Cookie: I wonder who she belongs to?

Junie: I don't know. She probably just wandered off and got lost. Poor precious thing. Her mother's probably looking for her in some alley nearby. Or maybe someone abandoned her because they didn't feel they could afford to take care of her. A shame, really, when there are animal shelters in most places.

Cookie: Maybe we should take her to the animal shelter.

(Junie takes MILK from the REFRIGERATOR and pours some out into a SAUCER and puts it in front of the kitten.)

Junie: I suppose so. Look how hungry she is. She was starving to death. *(to kitten)* Should I take you to the animal shelter?

(The kitten looks up at Junie and meows.)

Cookie: People often adopt pets from Animal shelters.

Junie: But what would happen if no one adopts her, Cookie? *(CONT'D sympathetic interaction between the kitten, Junie & Cookie as their hearts break)*

No...I could not take her there. *(to kitten)* You like it here? *(kitten meows)* Well then, I guess that settles it... *(picking her up Junie bonds with the kitten in a most special way... unconditional love)* Just what is your name, little girl?

Cookie: She has big yellow eyes like the moon.

Junie: So she does. Two Moon's in the same household. I'll name her after me. *(to kitten)* How does the name Junie Moon II strike you? *(she meows approvingly... Junie's heart breaks, her eyes glisten.)* Yes? Then, Junie Moon II — It is! ... My sweet precious Junie Moon II, I'm already madly in love with you... *(She nuzzles her sweet new kitty.)*

Cookie: *(Sniffling through tears)* And I think both of you are breaking my heart, too...

(Junie puts four pieces of BREAD in the TOASTER and she and Cookie set out to make BEAN SPROUT and CUCUMBER SANDWICHES. They slice the cucumbers, setting aside the bean sprouts, Junie puts JUNIE MOON II down next to her saucer of milk so she can finish it. They sit at the KITCHEN TABLE and talk.)

Junie: *(to Junie Moon II)* When you've finished your milk, you can have the whole apartment to play in. This is your home now, precious...

Cookie: I guess this is how you stay so trim. I didn't notice any meat in your refrigerator. I'm partial to hot dogs and hamburgers myself.

Junie: We can stop at a fast-food joint on the way if you like, but I think you'll like these veggie sandwiches. We can eat them in the car on the way to Doctor George's estate.

Cookie: Okay. Will Junie Moon II be alright while we're gone?

Junie: Sure she will. *(to Junie Moon II)* Won't you precious?

(Junie Moon II is swatting at her REFLECTION in the toaster. The toast POPS UP and she JUMPS back, ROLLING over comically. The girls LAUGH. Junie Moon II then goes to the WINDOW to swat at the PRISMS hanging from a cheerful MOBILE with CHIMES which the SUN reflects COLORFUL SPARKLES of LIGHT bouncing around the room)

Cookie: I think she's made herself right at home. Are you excited about anchoring the news tonight?

Junie: I've got butterflies just thinking about it.

Cookie: It'll be a cinch. All you need is this one story and the news boys at the station will handle the rest.

(Junie gets the toast and they make the sandwiches.)

Junie: Just read that monitor without flinching.

Cookie: No sweat. Any idiot can do it, right?

Junie: Right. Be a doll and finish making these for me. I'll run and get changed so we can be on our way.

(Junie LEAVES the kitchen.)

Cookie: Be ready in a jiffy.

(Cookie loads cucumbers and beansprouts between the two slices of toast, after spreading some mayonnaise.)

COOKIE: *(CONT'D)* How are these cucumbers gonna keep from sliding out? Come on, guys, say put. *(to Junie Moon II)* You like cucumber sandwiches, Junie Moon II?

(Junie Moon II purrs and meows while playing in the WINDOW in the sunshine, OUTSIDE of which CORABELLA can be seen landing on a TREE BRANCH)

(DISSOLVE TO)

SCENE 10

INT. QUEEN THIRTEEN'S HOT-HOUSE DUNGEON & SOUVENIR FACTORY - DAY

(QUEEN THIRTEEN is an imposing FAIRIE SORCERESS of mortal dimensions. She lusts for power and control of others. She is dressed spectacularly in BLACK with dashes of RED, ORANGE, YELLOW, PURPLE and SILVER. She brandishes a MAGIC SCEPTER which emits LIGHTENING BOLTS of destructive power. She uses it upon entering to attain the FAIRIE FACTORY WORKERS' attention by ZAPPING a DEFECTIVE SOUVENIR on the ASSEMBLY LINE.)

(JUMPER the DRAGON reacts to this display by leaping nervously backwards. Jumper follows her around as she issues orders. He is friendly, yet tries hard to appear ferocious as he is in charge of the FAIRIE SLAVE LABOR FORCE of TRINKET MAKERS.)

(Jumper is tall, green, scaly with a long-spiked tail. He emits SMOKE when he speaks. He has a LARGE SNOUT, BULGING EYES, a LONG-FORKED TONGUE and SHARP TEETH. He has a comically effeminate expressive manner. He often LISPS, GAY-LIKE and STRIKES HAUGHTILY INDIGNANT POSES.)

(Queen Thirteen ZAPS a defective SOUVENIR.)

Queen Thirteen: Only quality merchandise is produced in my Hot-House Souvenir Trinket-Factory. Back to work you lazy fairie-flitterers! Jumper!!!

Jumper: Yes, your Queen Thirteenship, ma'am?

Queen Thirteen: Your fairie charges are falling behind in their productivity. Thirteenland opens its doors within a week, just in time for a flood of summer vacationers. We need twice as many tacky trinkets to stock overload our souvenir shops. How else can we succeed in my plan to bilk the tourists out of their cash reserves!

Jumper: You hear that, fairies? Snap to it. Put some sparkle into your work or I'll singe your wings and flame-broil your fannies.

(The FAIRIES twinkle and jingle with fear and speed up their ASSEMBLY LINES which produce remarkably MOROSE SOUVENIRS such as SHRUNKEN HEADS, PLASTIC VOMIT, MINIATURE GUILLOTINES, ELECTRIC CHAIRS, HANGMAN'S NOOSES, DRAGONS, LIZARDS, SNAKES, SPIDERS, TOADS, THIRTEENLAND T-SHIRTS, ETC. Queen Thirteen picks up a novelty SHRUNKEN HEAD.)

Queen Thirteen: What do you call this?

Jumper: *(helpfully)* That's a shrunken head... the deluxe edition.

Queen Thirteen: I know what it is, you foppish oversized Iguana. But they're not ugly enough! The patrons of Thirteenland demand ugly.

(Jumper takes it from her.)

Jumper: Maybe a little slime bath will help.

Queen Thirteen: My personal reputation is at stake. If Thirteenland doesn't deliver terror and masochistic horror, then my plans to control world tourism will be ruined.

Jumper: I don't see how it can miss. I'm scared to death myself of these rides you've designed.

(He indicates a working SCALE MODEL of THIRTEENLAND, a MANICAL THEME PARK filled with frightening hair razing THRILL RIDES, such as ROLLER COASTERS through VOLCANIC CRATERS, SPOOK HOUSES, PARACHUTE DROPS dangling perilously over CROCODILE PITS, TERROR-DACTYL SWINGS, etc. Jumper indicates his personal favourite ride, a gigantic DRAGON SLIDE into a LAVA PIT.)

Jumper: *(CONT'D)* This is my personal favorite. The Dragon-Slide into the Lava Pit-of-Hell Fire… it's a shame we have to fake it, but if we zizzled our customers, we'd lose the return business.

Queen Thirteen: The best advertising gimmick I thought up is the FREE admission. They must PAY to get OUT! … Now, what we need is some salaciously CHEAP publicity…

(CUT TO)

SCENE 11

EXT. DR. GEORGE'S ESTATE - DAY

(JUNIE and COOKIE pull up to the GARAGE LABORATORY as DOCTOR GEORGE supervises SEYMOUR and MAX, who are carrying the CRATE containing the VANITY-EGO-REFLECTOR DEVICE to the ZEPPELIN.)

(Cookie has just finished her cucumber and bean sprout sandwich, beansprouts still dangling from her lips and she sucks them in.)

Cookie: Not bad. I think I can handle it.

Junie: Can you handle the electronic gear?

(Cookie gathers up the electronic gear, lights and camcorder.)

Cookie: Can you help me with this stuff, Junie?

Junie: Just bring the camcorder. Leave that other junk in the car. We have plenty of light. Should be no problem.

Cookie: Fine. I'm no electrician. Need your makeup touched up?

Junie: There isn't time. Can you operate that camera?

Cookie: Sure. I told you. I did it once before at my—

Junie: Your brother's wedding. I know. Great. Just keep it aimed at the good Doctor. Here he comes.

Cookie: *(aiming the camera)* He doesn't look too pleased. Let's see some action.

(Doctor George is a bit peeved from the earlier experience with Gloria Glamorude.)

Dr. George: No, no, no, absolutely not. I forbid any more interference today. You newspeople are more trouble than I ever anticipated.

Junie: Just give us a few minutes of your time, Doctor George.

Dr. George: Another reporter was here this morning and nearly destroyed my experimental prototype.

Junie: I've seen the footage. What happened to Ms. Glamorude, Doctor?

Dr. George: That brazen woman ransacked my laboratory. It will be weeks before her perfume dissipates from the premises. I may be forced to fumigate.

Junie: The transformation, Doctor?

Dr. George: People will now be able to tolerate her.

Junie: Her broadcast career may be at an end.

Dr. George: A blessing in disguise. Perhaps she can host a garden show. Good-day, ladies, I must be off. Excuse me.

Junie: No, please, one more question—

Dr. George: —I haven't the time to spare. We lift-off momentarily—good day once again.

(He trots off to board the Zeppelin. Junie turns her attention to Cookie who stops shooting.)

Cookie: Good stuff, Junie. Mr. Whopperberg will be very pleased. That's that, I guess. We'd better head back to the studio.

Junie: Hold it, Cookie. Give me the camera.

Cookie: I thought we were through?

Junie: I'm tagging along on board that Zeppelin.

Cookie: That's not possible. You'll miss the seven o'clock news.

(Junie leads Cookie to her CAR and gives her the KEYS.)

Junie: Take my car and go back to the studio. Tell Mr. Whopperberg this story is too big to let go. Someone in the newsroom can sub for me if I don't make it back in time.

(Cookie gets in the driver's seat.)

Cookie: But there might be danger. *(contemplating the Zeppelin)* That thing's supposed to fly?!

Junie: I'll soon find out. Now go on, get outa here.

Cookie: You're the boss... be careful.

Junie: I will... don't worry.

(COOKIE starts the CAR and backs away. JUNIE turns away and then remembers her kitty, JUNIE MOON II. She turns and shouts to Cookie.)

Junie: *(CONT'D)* Cookie! If I don't make it back, check up on the kitty, Junie Moon II, for me! Make sure she's okay, and look after her while I'm gone!

Cookie: I will. Hurry back!

(Cookie drives away. Junie turns and heads for the Zeppelin.)

Junie: Here goes nothin'...

(CUT TO)

SCENE 12

EXT. THE ZEPPELIN'S LOWER DECK

(The ZEPPELIN is a large cucumber shaped BALLOON with NETS and dozens of ROPES which support the GONDOLA, which resembles a small SHIP or BOAT. There is an UPPER DECK, the CAPTAIN'S STEERING WHEEL, control LEVERS, FLASHING LIGHTS and SMOKE EMITTING PIPES.)

SEYMOUR and MAX, the Doctor's young dashing crew, prepare for departure. DOCTOR GEORGE, in his baggy colorful vested suit, complete with cane, top hat, scarf, pocket watch and spats, recalls the comforts of earlier decades.)

Junie: *(chasing after him)* Doctor George, please, my name is Junie Moon and I work for WHOP-TV. Can't you please tell me more about this mysterious journey you're about to make? The public has a right to know. Might I please have a statement of your intentions?

(Doctor George is pre-occupied with his business as she laps at his heels.)

Dr. George: I'm sorry Miss Moon, but if I was to reveal anything to you then this mission, and its sensitive experiments, would be entirely undermined. Seymour! Max! Is everything secure?

(SEYMOUR is dashing about checking the ENGINE PROPELLERS and then the ANCHOR.)

Seymour: Aye aye, Sir, she's ready to fly. Props engaged and ready to crank. Standing by to hoist anchor.

(MAX FIDDLES with DIALS and LEVERS as SMOKE EMITS and LIGHTS FLASH.)

Max: Propane heater units are fired and ready, Sir.

Dr. George: *(delighted)* Excellent. Prepare to hoist anchor.

Junie: Doctor George, I must insist you allow me to travel with you. Top--secret or not, the public has a right to know what government officials have engaged our leading scientists to discover.

Dr. George: Have you newspeople no scruples? In good time, all my hard work will be revealed. I cannot at this time jeopardize myself or my dedicated crew.

(Seymour and Max show off for Junie. She aims her VIDEO CAMERA at them as they strike poses and make muscles.)

Junie: Your crew members are quite entertaining. Might I have a word with them?

(He glares at them and they return to their work.)

Dr. George: Most emphatically not. To your posts, boys. The idea. Seymour, escort Miss Moon from this vessel, then prepare for the ascent.

(DOCTOR GEORGE goes to the PILOT'S BRIDGE on the UPPER DECK. SEYMOUR leads JUNIE MOON off the ZEPPELIN and down the GANGPLANK.)

(CUT TO)

EXT. DR. GEORGE'S ESTATE

Junie: So, you're Mr. Seymour?

Seymour: *(impressed)* Yes, ma'am. Gosh, you sure are pretty. We gonna be on TV?

Junie: Yes, if you can tell me something about this mission.

Seymour: *(looking over his shoulder)* Can't. I'm sworn to secrecy. We are headed for some island over in the... guess I shouldn't say. Junie Moon. I like that name and I've seen your music videos, too. You're a terrific singer. Why have you taken up TV reporting?

Junie: Just a sideline. You must be very brave.

Seymour: *(blushing)* Yes, ma'am... er... I guess so. On the Isle of Jagger, we hope to test out our—oops—it just slipped out... cat's out of the bag—

Junie: *(camera poised)* The Isle of Jagger, uh huh, you were saying?

Seymour: Uh... sorry, Junie Moon... I've said too much. Doctor George will skin me alive. Gotta go. Nice meeting you. Bye. Wish you could go, but it's too dangerous.

(He runs back ONBOARD.)

Junie: *(to herself)* I live for danger... maybe. Anyhow, some opportunities are too exciting to pass by.

(CUT TO)

EXT. THE ZEPPELIN'S LOWER DECK

(She sneaks back ONBOARD without anyone seeing her and hides in a LARGE PICKLE BARREL. Seymour pulls in the GANGPLANK.)

Dr. George: *(irritably)* Seymour! Haven't you hoisted that anchor yet? Max and I are ready for lift off.

Seymour: Sorry, Sir. I had to get the gangplank.

(He goes to HOIST the ANCHOR.)

Seymour: *(CONT'D)* I've got it now, Sir.

Max: *(amused)* You were flirting with that TV reporter.

Seymour: Mind your own business, Max.

Dr. George: Blast. I hope that nosey wench has gone.

Seymour: I chased her away, Sir. Anchor's away!

(The ZEPPELIN RISES OFF the GROUND, BRUSHING against TREE BRANCHES as it heads for the SKIES above.)

Dr. George: Excellent. *(finger to the wind)* The skies are clear and the wind's at our back. We'll be past the land and out over the sea in no time at all.

(The Zeppelin FLIES over HOUSES and FIELDS. Their HOME TOWN passes FAR BELOW them. CLOUDS ROLL by and BIRDS FLY past, some nesting briefly in the TANGLE of ROPES attached to the GONDOLA.)

(DISSOLVE TO)

SCENE 13

INT. QUEEN THIRTEEN'S THRONE-ROOM - NIGHT

(QUEEN THIRTEEN has her back to her BALCONY overlooking the horrifying THIRTEENLAND. She holds the BIRDCAGE which contains KING JAGGER and his entourage of FAIRIES, WINKIE, DINKIE AND TWINKIE, which CAPTAIN BANDIT and CORABELLA have just presented to her and JUMPER the DRAGON is standing by.)

Queen Thirteen: *(laughing maniacally)* Ha ha, so there you are my darling fairie husband. Dethroned at last. With you and your fairie subjects safely behind bars, my powers will be invincible. Thirteenland is soon to be a thriving success. *(to Bandit)* You have done your job well, Captain, I am pleased.

Captain Bandit: Yeah? About that ransom… Eh? I believe it was to be gold dabloons and jewels.

Queen Thirteen: You shall have your reward soon enough.

Captain Bandit: What's wrong with now?

Jumper: You shouldn't oughta question her highnesses authority—she wields a mean zapper stick.

Captain Bandit: By Davy Jones' locker, I ain't afraid of no one. Me mates and I did our work and we expect to be paid in full as bargained.

(Queen Thirteen ZAPS a CHANDELIER with her SEPTOR. SPARKS FLY and Jumper LEAPS back with fear, but Captain Bandit doesn't flinch.)

Jumper: See what I mean? She doesn't fool around.

Captain Bandit: Maybe not, but a bargain's still a bargain.

(King Jagger jingles in Xylophoneze.)

Queen Thirteen: Jumper!

Jumper: Yes, your Majesty?

Queen Thirteen: What is my soon-to-be executed ex-husband saying? I despise Xylophoneze.

Jumper: He says no one will show up to Thirteenland on opening day because when you cheat others, you only cheat yourself.

Queen Thirteen: Ha! The world is mad for violence and thrills. The more horrific and bloodthirsty, the more they lust for grim satisfaction.

(CUT TO)

INT/EXT. QUEEN THIRTEEN'S THRONE-ROOM/ BALCONY - NIGHT - TRACKING

(Queen Thirteen goes out on the BALCONY holding up the CAGE.)

Queen Thirteen: See for yourself, my doomed fairie King, Thirteenland sprawling before you in all its malevolent grandeur. Once the announcement is out that we are open for business, the psychotic masses will swarm our shores like maggots.

(INSERT MONTAGE of horrifying IMAGES as described by Queen Thirteen)

(CONT'D) Vacation paradise will be given a new meaning by the tourist industry, which we shall monopolize with glee. *(King Jagger jingles angrily)* What's that, my pet?

Jumper: Vacation pandemonium is a better term, but you'll need a good press agent to sell it.

Queen Thirteen: Insolent glitter duster! *(She tosses the cage to Jumper.)*

(CONT'D) To the dungeon with them. I'll decide their fate later.

Jumper: Yes, your Thirteenship. *(Jumper leaves the balcony, taking the birdcage.)*

Queen Thirteen: As for you, my swashbuckling cut-throat; you and your salty buccaneers will receive double the promised bounty.

Captain Bandit: That's more like it.

Queen Thirteen: When, that is, you find me a way to exploit my vacation creation.

(CUT TO)

EXT. WIDE ON THIRTEENLAND - NIGHT

(Queen Thirteen turns around on the BALCONY to look down and over her magical THIRTEENLAND a sparkling but menacing sight to behold.)

Queen Thirteen: *(CONT'D)* The world must believe that nightmares really do come true! *(She cackles maniacally.)*

(DISSOLVE TO)

SCENE 14

EXT. THE ZEPPELIN'S UPPER DECK - DAY

(THEY ARE ALOFT. The GENTLE BREEZE catches in the crew's hair. As more BIRDS FLY BY, a STORK LANDS on BOARD and startles MAX.)

Max: Where's your baby bundle? Look, Doctor George, a stork!

(The Stork remains momentarily.)

Dr. George: Ask him if we're headed in the right direction.

(Before taking off again, the STORK squawks his approval.)

Dr. George: *(CONT'D)* Take the wheel for me, Max, while I scan the horizon for landmarks. Seymour, man the controls for Max.

(Doctor George takes his TELESCOPE to look around. Seymour takes Max's position.)

Seymour: Yes, Sir. Thank you, Sir. Isn't the world beautiful from up above? So peaceful. I wouldn't mind being a bird if I weren't afraid of heights.

Dr. George: Fear is at the heart of all the trouble in the world. To discover truth, you must face the fear within you. Look down upon the Earth in all its splendor, Seymour, and know that all you perceive is but a reflection of you. The Divine Creator is Within All of Creation.

Seymour: Unfortunately, what I perceive makes me dizzy.

Max: We've been flying this Zeppelin for months, Seymour, you should be used to it by now.

Seymour: Max is right, Sir, I feel foolish. I try to face my fear of heights, but I must be doing something wrong.

Dr. George: Take a deep breath, look fear straight in the eye, suspend all disbelief in yourself and know that the energy of the universe is at your command. You will discover that anything you desire is possible, so long as you respect all creation in the surrounding envelope.

(Seymour takes a deep breath, runs to the side, but faints backwards with terror. He dizzily gets back to his feet, with help from Doctor George.)

Seymour: *(woozy)* Whew. I'm sure glad this Zeppelin's under my feet. As long as we have it to keep us aloft, I'm not afraid.

Dr. George: And, oh, what a Magnificent Zeppelin it is, too!

(MUSIC begins and he sings "Doctor George's Magnificent Zeppelin" - Music & Lyrics by G.S. Vuille.)

Dr. George: *(CONT'D, Singing in key of F) I'm Doctor George and this is my magnificent Zeppelin. We're sailing high, so high up into the sky. With Seymour and Max along an adventure is imminent, So come along with us and your spirit will fly. We will take her up and spin around, don't worry about a thing. With Seymour and Max right by our sides, we then can really sing! I'm Doctor George and this is my magnificent Zeppelin, so come along.*

Max & Seymour: *(join in singing) So come along.*

Dr. George: *(singing) So come along. We're flying high.*

Max & Seymour: *(singing) We're flying high.*

Dr. George: *(singing) So very high. So high, so high.*

Max & Seymour: *(singing) So high, so high.*

Dr. George: *(singing) So very high.*

Max & Seymour: *(singing) So very high.*

Dr. George, Max & Seymour: *(singing together) Up into the skies!*

(The song repeats from the beginning as they dance. Seymour and Max sing the second verse with Doctor George joining in at the end.)

(Junie Moon slyly emerges from her pickle barrel hideaway to videotape their happy cavorting.)

(In the dance, they swing on ropes, spin the wheel, balance precariously on the railings and jump into each other's arms.)

Dr. George, Max & Seymour: *(CONT'D, Singing together)* He's Doctor George and this is his magnificent Zeppelin! He's flying high, so high, right clear through the skies! With us along we're sure to encounter adventures! So have no fears and soar with us through the air. We will fly about doing loop de loops, throw away your cares. We're the greatest crew he's ever had and that is why we blare!

Dr. George, Max & Seymour: He's Doctor, George and this is his magnificent Zeppelin! So come along.

Dr. George: *(singing) So come along.*

Max & Seymour: *(singing) So come along. We're flying high.*

Dr. George: *(singing) We're flying high.*

Max & Seymour: *(singing) So very high, so high, so high!*

Dr. George: *(singing) So high, so high!*

Max & Seymour: *(singing) So very high.*

Dr. George: *(singing) So very high.*

Dr. George, Max & Seymour:	*(singing together) Up into the skies!*

(DISSOLVE TO)

SCENE 15

EXT. THE ZEPPELIN'S LOWER DECK - DAY

(SEYMOUR is SWABBING the DECK. JUNIE MOON peaks out from her hiding place in the PICKLE BARREL. He catches a glimpse of her out of the corner of his eye. She ducks out of sight inside, under the LID. This cat and mouse game goes on until finally he catches her, removing the lid, timidly exposing her.)

Seymour:	*(quietly)* What ho? A stowaway!
Junie:	Shhh... please, Mr. Seymour, don't tell Doctor George I sneaked on board.
Seymour:	Ms. Moon, Doctor George can be very severe with anyone caught spying.
Junie:	I know it was wrong of me, but I just couldn't resist an opportunity like this. Please don't tell him just yet.
Seymour:	But I must. It's my duty. If I don't inform him, he'll discharge me for harboring a spy.
Junie:	I'm no spy, Seymour. I'm a documentary news reporter from WHOP-TV.
Seymour:	*(haughtily)* Ha! —A likely story at best! Can you prove it?

(Junie holds up the VIDEO CAMERA and Seymour adjusts his hair.)

Junie:	My video camera, for one thing. Here's my WHOP-TV — ID badge, and ... *(reaching in her pocket)* ... my credit cards... *(Unfolding a long plastic series.)* What else do you need?

Seymour: Hmmm, I guess this proves you're not a foreign agent spying on us. At least you're from the good old U.S.A.

Junie: I take it this means you'll help me and not cast me over the side in a parachute?

Seymour: That'll be up to Doctor George.

Junie: Surely, he wouldn't consider such a barbaric act?

Seymour: One never knows about such things. When you're airborne, you have to obey the law of the skies.

Junie: Which are?

Seymour: Anything goes! *(Shocked, she throws her arms around him.)*

Junie: Oh, Seymour, I beg you, don't turn me in. I'll do anything you ask. *(shuddering as she glances over the side)* Besides, I'm afraid of flying… ugh… and heights. I fell off my grandfather's knee when I was an infant. Oooh, I think I'm gonna be sick.

Seymour: This certainly is a coincidence.

Junie: You gonna be sick, too?

Seymour: *(tenderly)* No, nothing like that, Junie, it's just that we have so much in common.

(While Seymour comforts Junie, Doctor George shouts commands from the bridge where he has been scanning the skies with his telescope.)

(CUT TO)

INT. THE ZEPPELIN'S UPPER DECK

(Max is at the wheel, piloting the Zeppelin.)

Dr. George: Clear skies ahead, by thunder. Max, let me take the wheel. Run and fetch me a treat. I'm dying for a tasty, crunchy, dill pickle.

Max: *(surprised)* You're dying, Sir? Should I call a doctor?

Dr. George: Blast it all, Max, you nit-wit! —I'm either a doctor, or my name can't possibly be Doctor George, now can it?!

Max: Sorry, Sir. To your point then however, I am a young man, therefore I cannot be considered an old fool, now can I, Doctor?

Dr. George: Point denied, my dear young Max… And furthermore, we do not have a telephone aboard this Zeppelin.

Max: Oh, guess I forgot. You prefer secrecy I suppose, but in these modern times communicating is generally easier than it was in the past… *(sheepishly)* What was it you wanted me to do again, Sir?

Dr. George: Good, now you understand, secrecy on our mission is a top priority lest evil forces prevail to sabotage our future plans…. What did I ask of you before you rudely interrupted? … *(puzzling)* Hmmm —Oh, my yes… Max, my dear, would you be so kind as to allow me to take over the wheel while you fetch us a couple of pickles from the pickle barrel?

(Max springs to action with a salute.)

Max: Certainly, your doctorship, sir. Two pickles coming up.

(He moves towards the controls.)

Max: *(CONT'D)* Just let me finish up the calculations and adjustments for the propane hot-air-generator.

Dr. George: Blast it all, Max, I can take care of that myself. Snap to it, young man, I need a pickle now!

Max: But, Sir, it'll blow if I...

Dr. George: —Ridiculous! Don't be insolent! I invented this Zeppelin, so I know exactly what I'm doing! Bring me a pickle and don't dilly-dally!

Max: Yes, Sir, right away, Sir.

(Max drops what he is doing and Doctor George takes over the adjustments, managing to bumble a bit.)

(CUT TO)

EXT. THE ZEPPELIN'S LOWER DECK

(Seymour turns his head as he hears Max approaching.)

Seymour: *(Urgently to Junie)* Quick. Into the pickle barrel!

(Junie climbs back into the PICKLE BARREL. Seymour whistles a tune, dusts with a RAG, adjusts ROPES carelessly and finally has an awkward moment with a MOP and BUCKET. All the while, Max struggles to open the pickle barrel. Junie is holding it shut from the KNOTTED END of the rope HANDLE underneath.)

Max: *(frustrated)* Seymour, could you give me a hand with this confounded pickle barrel? The lid's stuck.

Seymour: *(feigning macho)* Stand aside, Max, and let a real man show you how it's done.

Max: Are you insinuating I'm not a man?

Seymour: Maybe not, my friend, at least, not enough for this job. If ya wanna impress the ladies, ya gotta show 'em a little beef. Rise to the occasion, so-to-speak.

(Seymour attempts to lift the BARREL LID.)

Seymour: *(CONT'D)* She's tougher than I thought.

Max: She? — She who, Seymour?

Seymour: Did I say she? Just a figure of speech is all that is, Max—just like this Zeppelin. SHE'S — A great Zeppelin, ain't she?!

Max: If you say so…

Seymour: Of course, I say so. I wouldn't lie about a thing like that, would I?

Max: No, I guess not.

Seymour: Very well then, I must say. Let's try HER, again!

(He tugs at the ROPE LOOP HANDLE, managing to lift it off enough to see Junie tugging at the knotted end. She pulls it shut once more. Max has a puzzled look.)

Max: Honestly, Seymour… That's a mighty feisty pickle barrel. Let me try HER, again!!!

(Max grabs the rope handle. Seymour panics and pushes him aside.)

Seymour: Not so fast, Max, I can do it.

(Seymour rubs his hands in preparation and SPEAKS LOUDLY to the BARREL.)

Seymour: *(CONT'D)* Guess I need a little elbow grease. Gee, I wonder if there are any pickles in there after all? It'd sure be a shame if there weren't any, being as we've worked up quite an appetite trying to pull the lid off. Max, you don't suppose a spy could have eaten all the pickles in this barrel and is now using it as a secret hiding place?!

Max: Spies? I seriously doubt that, Seymour. I don't think Doctor George has any enemies.

(Junie Moon opens the lid a little and hands Seymour a PICKLE. He jumps between Max and the barrel to hide this exchange and accepts the pickle from her backhanded. He grins sheepishly at Max who has suspicious look on his face.)

Seymour: Here you are, Max ... a nice, big, fresh one.

Max: ... Thanks, Seymour, you're my very special friend. Got any meat balls to go with it? —Just asking...

(Max starts back to the BRIDGE as Seymour hangs on the RAILING, sighing with relief, before he JUMPS BACK recalling his fear of heights. He sits down on the DECK and fans himself dizzily.)

(CUT TO)

EXT. THE ZEPPELIN'S UPPER DECK

(Max is munching on the PICKLE when he meets Doctor George, who eyes him scoldingly for forgetting to bring him one. Max does an about-face and returns to the DECK for another pickle.)

(CUT TO)

EXT. THE ZEPPELIN'S LOWER DECK

(When Max gets to the BARREL and lifts the LID, Junie Moon automatically reaches out with a PICKLE. He takes it without thinking and starts back to the BRIDGE before he reacts with a jolt. Puzzled, he scratches his head.)

Max: Gosh, did I see what I just saw? Amazing. That was easier than I thought. Guess I'm quite a man after all. Run for cover, ladies, here I come! Getting jealous, Seymour, brute strength, my special quality...

(Max climbs back up the LADDER to the BRIDGE on the UPPER DECK.)

(CUT TO)

EXT. THE ZEPPELIN'S UPPER DECK

(MAX hands DOCTOR GEORGE his PICKLE.)

Max: Here ya go, Doc. Nice weather we're having, isn't it? Perfect for cruising babes by the seashore. Maybe a little side trip to the Bahamas would be in order.

(Doctor George nervously fumbles the CONTROLS.)

Dr. George: Yes indeed, thank you dear boy, er, uh, I need you back at the controls now, as I, er, seem to be having a little trouble.

(SMOKE and STEAM emit from the MECHANISM. The GUAGES SPIN out of control. Max's head is elsewhere as he has a curious look of worry on his face, but looks a bit vacant while pondering the puzzling questions of self-reflection.)

Max: Trouble? Oh, yes, Sir, I know what you mean, Sir, I've always had trouble with girls ... and that reminds me, and I don't know exactly how to tell you this, but I think there's something strange about that pickle barrel.

Dr. George: Strange? This pickle seems tasty enough to me.

Max: No, Sir, the barrel, I mean... it's friendly, in a feminine sort of way.

Dr. George: How nice for you—now about these pressure gauges. I've been resetting some of them and —

Max: *(Alarmed)* — Resetting!? Oh, no, Sir!

Dr. George: Why, yes, my dear Max, I thought we needed more pressure to increase altitude and I —

Max: — But, Sir!

(There is an EXPLOSION of SMOKE and STEAM and FLASHING LIGHTS. They jump back in fear, but then try to regain control of the ZEPPELIN as it begins to lose altitude.)

(CUT TO)

EXT. THE ZEPPELIN'S LOWER DECK

(JUNIE pops out of the PICKLE BARREL and begins to VIDEO RECORD the ACTION as SEYMOUR rushes up the ladder to aid them at the WHEEL on the BRIDGE. She follows.)

(CUT TO)

EXT. THE ZEPPELIN'S UPPER DECK

(As THEY SCRAMBLE AROUND, they begin talking all at once, OVERLAPPING DIALOGUE and PARTIALLY AD-LIBBING their WORDS to increase TENSION)

Max: ... You busted a valve. Get me a wrench, quick...

Seymour: ... The Zeppelin will crash if we can't fix it! Let me take the wheel, Max! Tighten the valve and reset the gauges before we lose the hot air and crash-land! ...

Max: ... Doctor George, give me a hand, it's stuck ...

Junie: ... That's it, that's what I like to see—Plenty of Action! Stand aside, Seymour, I need to get a tighter shot of the Doctor. Doctor George, does this accident mean the mission may have to be aborted? ...

Dr. George: ... What? Did somebody say something? Who's asking me questions? ...

Max: … Never mind, Sir, help me tighten this valve. Seymour, help us. Let Doctor George take the wheel!

Seymour: … Junie! Take the wheel. Doctor George! Turn the pressure gauges down to half! I'll go and help Max …

(JUNIE takes the WHEEL in one hand and shoots VIDEO with the other. Seymour helps Max and Doctor George adjusts the VALVES.)

Junie: … Doctor George, are your crew members fully insured?…

Seymour: *(Straining with the WRENCH)* … Oh, why didn't I eat my spinach when I was a kid?! …

Junie: … Can we expect any survivors? …

Dr. George: *(Anxiously befuddled)* … I must be losing my mind. I swear I hear voices! …

Max: … I think we've got it, Sir! We're regaining control!

(The Zeppelin Stops Losing Altitude And Levels Off And Overlapping Dialogue Can Cease, Easing Tensions.)

Seymour: She's coming around — Here, Junie, I'll take over!

(Seymour takes the wheel. The smoke and lights return to normal. They breathe a sigh of relief. Junie continues her interview.)

Junie: Doctor, can we now safely assume that the mission will continue as originally planned?

Dr. George: *(confidently)* Yes, I think we've recovered from our little mishap, eh, boys? And of course, we plan to… errr… My stars! Young, lady? However, did you manage to sneak on board?!

Max: Sir! In case you haven't noticed, there's a female stoaway present!

Dr. George: Quite so! How extraordinary!

(Seymour goes to her side to comfort her.)

Seymour: Please, Sir, it's all my fault. I encouraged her to come along with us. She wants to document the mission. I hid her in the pickle barrel.

Max: *(Unimpressed)* Now I get it. The mysterious pickle barrel gag.

Junie: I beg you, dear Doctor, please don't throw me over the side. If I'm able to sell my video to the WHOP-TV network, the profits can be used to finance your experiments, ... whatever they might be...

Dr. George: ... Do tell, young lady... Why I should I not hesitate to toss you overboard?

Junie: Because by documenting your journey it could reach people all over the world who would be inspired by your adventure and of your unique... hmmm... inventions? Am I getting warm? Perhaps your... experiences and experiments... —Think of all the school children whose dreams of success would inspire them to go on to college!

Max: Maybe I'll be able to go back to college and become what I was meant to be...

Seymour: ... Oh, yeah, Max? What's your dream of success?

Max: *(sarcastically)* ... Being a Rocket Scientist, Seymour... Zeppelins are passed their prime, I need a challenge.

Dr. George: *(Grumbling with concern)* Perhaps, Max, you don't realize that the Zeppelin is the noblest form of aircraft, the forerunner of all commercial airships. As for you, my dear, your offer is most generous and you may continue to travel with us to document our journey without fear of reprisal. I shan't be tossing you over the side—too uncivilized to be sure.

Max: *(lecherously)* Va-Va-Va-VOOM!!! Hey, babe, if you're free later this evening, I'll show you my Altimeter!

Seymour: Knock it off, Max, I saw her first.

(Seymour clutches her possessively, but she breaks free.)

Junie: Sorry to disappoint you boys, but I have other plans. My documentary comes first. Doctor George, exactly where are we headed?

Dr. George: To the ancient Isle of Jagger, land of the fairies, to test out my secret invention.

Junie: The device which transformed Gloria?

Dr. George: Yes, my Double-Refracting Vanity-Ego-Reflector—It allows anyone to see themselves exactly as they truly are. A most humbling experience to say the very least. Fairies, being completely innocent, will enable me to fine tune the instrument successfully.

Junie: Fairies? You mean like in the innocence of cats and dogs?

Dr. George: Precisely, all of God's creatures are innocent. Our pets are a good example of that as they love us unconsciously, provided we care for them responsibly with love and compassion.

Junie: I'm beginning to see why our government is so interested… especially among politicians.

Dr. George: Precisely, Miss Moon, they rank high on the list for Ego-Exposure. All manner of conflict is the direct result of their egotistical bumblings.

Junie: May I see it, this curious vanity mirror you've invented?

Dr. George: There will be plenty of time for that later. Seymour, Max, set the table for dinner. Our guest must be famished.

(DISSOLVE TO)

SCENE 16

EXT. CAPTAIN BANDIT'S PIRATE VESSEL - DAY

(The PIRATE SHIP has MASTS and SAILS despite being more modern-day with an ONBOARD ENGINE for high speeds. It has a somewhat battered appearance. It flies a SKULL and CROSSBONES FLAG and sports a small CANNON.)

(PRINCE and LADDIE are watching TV and straining to do the LOTUS POSITION for MEDITATION exercises. They are BREATHING DEEPLY and EXHALING slowly while CAPTAIN BANDIT complains, while CORABELLA is perched on his shoulder taking all in.)

Captain Bandit: That bloody Queen Thirteen and her blasted Thirteenland. She cheated us out of our ransom and I have a bad mind to sabotage the whole bloomin' mess and sail clear of these cursed waters.

Corabella: *(Squawking)* Bloody-Queenie, a cheating old Thirteenie! Saboteur Sally, a Blooming-Sis from Ransom Alley! *(She squawks and whistles)* Corabella, Raising Hell'a, for a Cracker I'll never Tell'a!

Laddie: *(nearly succeeding)* I think I'm getting the hang of this.

(Prince, all twisted up, comes undone.)

Prince: My legs are falling asleep.

Captain Bandit: What in blazes are you two blockheads up to? *(He notices that the TV program features Gloria Glamorude teaching a meditation class on her news program.)*

Gloria: *(ON TV)* ... keep breathing deeply... that's it... exhale slowly... be sure and sit erect... imagine a bright yellow light enveloping you in complete bliss... empty your minds of useless thoughts... relax... relax... become one with the light...

Captain Bandit: Snap out of it, you bums. On your feet, pronto, both of you!

Corabella: *(Squawking, doing a Birdie-Dance)* Hang like This, or Fall Asleep, you Blockheads are my Souls to Keep! *(A squawk and a whistle)*

Prince: *(struggling to rise)* But I was just getting the hang of it.

Captain Bandit: You'll both be swinging from the yard-arm if you don't cut out this foolishness.

Laddie: Sorry, Captain, we was just relaxing.

Gloria: *(ON TV)* That's all the time we have, darlings. If you see my friend Doctor George flying around in his magnificent Zeppelin with WHOP-TV's very own video personality, Junie Moon, blow them a kiss for me, hmmm? We hope she'll be home soon with some wonderful documentary footage.

Captain Bandit: *(Kicking the TV over, hollering at Gloria Glamorude.)* Shut your trap, Wench! No TV privileges for you Mates until we find a way to steal the bounty that's owed us.

Prince: What's a Zeppelin, Laddie?

Laddie: The thing what keeps your fly closed, ya Barnacle Brain!

Captain Bandit: Idiots! It's a blimp. A flying machine? A...? —

(Corabella looks up and sees Doctor George's magnificent Zeppelin approaching overhead in the distance.)

Corabella: *(Squawking warningly, she interrupts)* — Barnacle Brains is the Zeppelin's Game, she approaches Nigh, from the Pale-Blue-Sky! *(Whistling, dancing and squawking)*

Captain Bandit: *(Spoting it)* There's one now!

(He takes out his SPYGLASS and sees Junie Moon with her video camera.)

Captain Bandit: *(CONT'D)* Blow me down, if this sight's the break we've been looking for! Man the cannon, boys, we'll shoot her out of the skies!

(CUT TO)

SCENE 17

EXT. THE ZEPPELIN'S UPPER DECK - DAY

(DOCTOR GEORGE and MAX are at the WHEEL as SEYMOUR and JUNIE MOON share a romantic moment. He catches her alone near the STERN of the GONDOLA where she is shooting SCENERY with her CAMERA. The AERIAL VIEW of the SEA and ISLANDS BELOW through WISPY CLOUDS is peaceful and serene, setting the mood.)

Seymour: Miss Moon? ... Junie?

Junie: Yes, Seymour?

Seymour: I've been wanting to ask you something personal.

Junie: Yes?

Seymour: Would a guy like me, say, in your wildest imagination, ever be... ever be considered by you to be attractive?

Junie: You don't give up easily, do you?

Seymour: If I could get you out of my mind, it'd be easy. So, what's the answer to my question?

Junie: I don't know. Perhaps.

Seymour: Yeah?

(Junie smiles and glances sweetly at Seymour.)

Seymour: *(CONT'D shy and awkward)* Gee. I'm sorry I keep making such a fool of myself.

Junie: ... That's quite alright, I'm sure it comes natural.

Seymour: Then, you must understand how I feel...

Junie: I'm not falling for that line, Seymour, but I can tell you what I feel... and only that.

Seymour: Which is?

Junie: I haven't found what I'm looking for where men are concerned.

Seymour: Guess I'm not in the running.

Junie: Not at the moment, but, if I should change my mind, I'll let you know.

Seymour: Can you at least give me a hint on what it is you expect in a guy? Maybe I can change.

Junie: If I had to ask someone to change for me, then they couldn't possibly have the qualities I find attractive to begin with.

(The romantic mood is lost to the wind. Seymour decides to go about his work.)

Seymour: I can see I don't exactly turn you on. I'd better get back to work.

Junie: If I've hurt your feelings, I didn't mean to. It's just that I have guys coming on to me all the time. I think you're very nice, but I only just met you. I like to get to know a person first before developing relationship.

Seymour: I suppose you're right. Just the same, I think I'd do anything for you.

Junie: Thank you, Seymour.

(He goes back to his chores. Junie smiles and savors the beautiful scenery.)

(CUT TO)

SCENE 18

EXT. THE PIRATE SHIP - DAY

(CAPTAIN BANDIT'S PIRATE SHIP ADVANCES. They FIRE the CANNON at the ZEPPELIN. A CANNON-BALL TEARS a HOLE through the ZEPPELIN'S BALLOON.)

(CUT TO)

EXT. THE ZEPPELIN'S UPPER DECK - DAY

(DOCTOR GEORGE grabs his TELESCOPE to see from whence it came.)

Max: What shall we do, Doctor George? We're losing altitude fast!

Dr. George: We've been attacked by Pirates. Seymour! Climb up immediately and mend that tear!

Seymour: But I'm scared of heights.

Junie: Seymour, you must, or we'll crash into the sea!

Dr. George: You're the only one strong enough to climb the ropes. I need Max at the controls. Miss Moon, hand me that umbrella and take the wheel.

Junie: Yes, Sir.

(JUNIE hands him the HYPNOTIC UMBRELLA which has a SPIRAL DESIGN painted on it. and then she takes the WHEEL. DOCTOR GEORGE opens it and spins it around, aiming it at SEYMOUR, who becomes HYPNOTIZED.)

Dr. George: Seymour. Listen to my commands. You are in my power and will do as ordered. You are no longer afraid of heights. Begin the necessary repairs, now.

(SEYMOUR, in a trance, takes a NEEDLE, some STRING, and climbs the ROPES and begins making the REPAIRS. He SEWS THE TEAR CLOSED as they cheer him on.)

Junie: You can do it, Seymour. Be careful. This is great stuff for my documentary.

Dr. George: As long as I keep the umbrella spinning, you will have complete confidence in yourself.

Max: That a boy, Seymour. Hurry, we're losing altitude. We're going to hit the water. Brace yourselves.

(The ZEPPELIN GONDOLA HITS THE WATER. The vibrations from impact cause the balloon to bob, loosening ropes which tie it to the deck.)

(SEYMOUR loses his grip and practically falls, but dangles and sways dangerously, swinging from ROPE to ROPE precariously. On his last near fatal swing to the DECK he knocks the UMBRELLA out of Doctor George's hands.)

Dr. George: So much for the wonders of hypnosis!

(Seymour falls at Junie's feet. He holds on to her, trembling.)

Seymour: I can't believe I did it!

Max: If we'd hit any harder, we'd have sunk. Nice going, Seymour. Wow, you were amazing!

(He hugs him, then, embarrassed, pushes him away sheepishly)

Junie: You saved our lives, Seymour. You're very brave. I'm impressed.

(Getting up he takes the WHEEL)

Seymour: Does this mean we can go steady?

(She goes to the RAILING.)

Junie: You don't give up do you? We only just met and you want a commitment already. I have to admit, you're cute, but I'm not sure you're my type. You're too skittish. I need a guy who's not so nervous. Someone who will <u>sweep</u> me off my feet and run away with me!

(CAPTAIN BANDIT'S PIRATE SHIP SPEEDS by and he SWEEPS JUNIE MOON OFF THE ZEPPELIN. THEY SAIL QUICKLY AWAY with her and her CAMERA as she screams.)

Junie: *(CONT'D)* Help! Help! I'm being kidnapped by pirates. Seymour! Max! Doctor George! Come and rescue me. Help. Help!

Seymour: *(Hysterical)* Oh, horrors! Captain Bandit and his pirates have kidnapped my precious Junie Moon. What ever shall we do?

Dr. George: Why, we must rescue her, of course!

Max: Of course, Dr. George, but how we are going to manage to do that? Hypnosis?

Seymour: Yeah, Doctor, maybe you could hypnotize me again!

Dr. George: *(Shrewdly)* Possibly, we've got lots of tricks up our sleeves. We'll follow them closely, and, at the right moment, just in the nick of time, we'll snatch her up, then run like crazy in the opposite direction.

Seymour: Yeah, Doctor George, that's a terrific idea... but first, let's hypnotize each other.

Max: Hypnotized or not, well never catch up to them, their pirate ship is way faster than this Zeppelin.

It's impossible, we can't outrun vicious pirates, or do we have to hypnotize them first? They'll capture us and make us all walk the plank. Come on, Doctor George, you're a genius, think of something. There must be a safe way to rescue her?

Seymour: Yeah! Think fast, Doctor George! Hurry!

Max: It's impossible, we can't outrun vicious pirates, I'm not kidding when I say they'll capture us all and make us walk the plank! That's what pirates do, that's there thing! Is that what you guys want?

Seymour: You're such a pessimist, Max, Junie Moon is a damsel in distress, and I'm her future boyfriend and now I'm in distress... we must go after her!

Dr. George: We'll make an aerial attack in the Zeppelin, hoisting Miss Moon on board with a rope.

Max: Oh, fine, except we're grounded... er... stuck in the water, that is.

Seymour: You mean our Zeppelin won't fly?

Max: Not until I make some repairs, and by that time, the pirates will be long gone.

Seymour: Can't we sail after them in the water? The Zeppelin gondola floats just fine. You said so yourself.

Max: She'll drift at about two knots—forget it, and forget about Junie Moon, she can document her pirate adventure instead... and Seymour, don't forget, you've still got me to comfort you. *(He whips out a pickle)* Care for a pickle, Seymour?

Seymour: *(glibly)* Does it come with meatballs, Max?

Dr. George: Pull yourselves together, boys, let's not be downhearted, drowning ourselves in self-pity does not mend a broken heart, but focusing on the task at hand does. Get busy, Max and Seymour on those repairs while I scan the horizon with my telescope.

Max: Come on, Seymour, let's get to work.

Seymour: Yes, let's hurry, we've just got to save her.

(SMOKE SPURTS OUT where MAX is TINKERING.)

Max: The seal on the main valve has worn out and I've nothing to replace it with. Unless this leak is fixed, we'll have no hot air pressure and won't be able to fly.

Dr. George: Blast, that does sound serious. *(looking through his telescope)* Wait a minute, boys, I think I see something. Yes! It's the Mermaids of Mermaid's Isle! This is a spot of luck---Perhaps they can help us!

(CUT TO)

SCENE 19

EXT. MERMAID'S ISLE - DAY

(MERMAID'S ISLE is a ROCKY CRAG which JUTS OUT of the OCEAN. The WAVES SPLASH AROUND IT. ON IT SIT THREE MERMAIDS: ETHEL MERMAID, GERTRUDE and BUFFY MERMAID. They SING happily away in THREE PART HARMONY as they BECKON the ZEPPELIN CREW. They sport BEHIVE HAIRDOS, each a DIFFERENT COLOR. Their GREEN SCALED OUTFITS are STRAPLESS.)

They wear FLOWERS in their HAIR. There are PALM FRONDS and SEAWEED and SEASHELLS all about them.)

(ETHEL is a REDHEAD and the LEADER of the group. GERTRUDE is a BRUNETTE, & BUFFY a BLOND. The MERMAID'S SING — "THE MERMAIDS OF MERMAID'S ISLE" (A song by G.S. Vuille).

Ethel, Gertrude & Buffy: *(singing in key of C, 3 part harmony) We are the Mermaids of Mermaid Isle, and have we got a rousing tale for you. / Just a few minutes ago some pirates came along, and shot some crazy videos brand new. / I'm Ethel, I'm Buffy, I'm Gertrude Mermaid, and boys you won't believe, those pirates were the scariest that we have ever seen. / That poor girl that they kidnapped, a reporter we've been told, she screamed and screamed and screamed and screamed like the Siren's legends old. / And where do you suppose they were headed, those pirates and that poor girl? To the Isle of Jagger and Queen Thirteen who's anger will surely unfurl. Queen Thirteen has imprisoned, King Jagger and the fairies, and woe be to those who interfere, a wicked grudge that old Queen carries. /*

Ethel, Gertrude & Buffy: *She's a fairy herself but was cast out of fairyland long ago, for making a fuss by consorting with pirates and becoming the fairies' foe! / So, please, dear Doctor, don't go there, stay and chat with us a while. There's trouble there and we're lonely here be a sport come make us smile - ile - ile - ile! /...*

On Mermaid Isle, Mermaid Isle, Mermaid Isle!...

(The MERMAIDS begin a CONVERSATION with the ZEPPELIN CREW.)

Dr. George: *(applauding)* Splendid, ladies, splendid, and thank you for the advice, but my crew and I must go to Jaggers Isle to rescue Miss Moon.

Ethel: Those horrid pirates have taken her to Queen Thirteen to publicize Thirteenland. If she doesn't cooperate, she'll be fed to Jumper the Dragon.

Seymour: My darling Junie Moon is in dire peril! What ever shall we do?

Max: We need to fix this Zeppelin before we do anything.

Buffy: Would it help if we reprised our song?

Gertrude: *(Nudging Buffy)* Pipe down, we're on a break.

Dr. George: This Fairie Queen puzzles me. Fairies are supposed to be harmless creatures. What's she up to with those pirates?

Ethel: They helped her capture her husband King Jagger and all the Fairies. She's enslaved them in order to open an amusement park of horrors. It's a jealous move to destroy the reputations of all Fantasy Creatures. Jaggers Isle will no longer be the paradise it once was.

Dr. George: This is diabolical. How soon can we ascend, Max?

	(holding up gasket) This gasket is shot and I need a replacement. The hot-air pressure won't hold without it.
Buffy:	Gee, Ethel, that looks like one of your earrings.
Ethel:	Why, so it does.
Max:	Dear ladies, what good fortune. Might I borrow it for a while? It looks like a perfect match and is certain to do the trick.
Ethel:	*(taking it off)* Why certainly, but on one condition.
Dr. George:	Oh, what's that?
Ethel:	My girls and I wish to accompany you. We'd be at the mercy of those Pirates out here on Mermaid's Isle all alone.
Dr. George:	By all means, hop aboard, ladies!
Ethel:	Come along, girls, hold on to your tails!
Gertrude:	Thank you, Doctor George!
Buffy:	This ought to be fun… we'll flip and fly our way to Heaven!

(CUT TO)

EXT. THE ZEPPELIN'S LOWER DECK - DAY

(THEY SCURRY ONBOARD, HOPPING on their TAILS with a little help from SEYMOUR, DOCTOR GEORGE, and MAX)

Seymour:	*(Lusting for the Mermaids)* Oooh, la, la, you fantasy creatures are fantastic!
Max:	Show some respect for our guests, Seymour. Pay attention to your job! *(Jealous of the Mermaids)*

	... And show some respect for me, I need your help flying this Zeppelin! They don't know how to sail the skies.
Dr. George:	Pull yourself together, Seymour, and help Max get this Zeppelin aloft.

(ETHEL hands her EARRING to MAX, who is busy working on the VALVES.)

Ethel:	Here's the part you ordered, cutie-pie. Hope it fits.
Max:	*(Taking it)* Thanks ma'am, you're a life-saver... now make yourselves comfortable while we men man the controls... and keep away from Seymour, he bites!
Ethel:	No problem, Max, I think you have a twinkle for Seymour's tinkle... *(Taking in the Zepellin)* Say, girls, what do you think of this bird? Snazzy!
Gertrude:	Groovy, I mean, like wow!
Buffy:	For sure. I always wanted to fly like those seagulls who taunt us when we sing.
Dr. George:	Welcome aboard my magnificent Zeppelin, Ladies. I am at your service.
Gertrude:	Thank you, dear Doctor. If those Pirates had come back, I don't know what we'd have done. They have such untidy minds.
Buffy:	They shot videos of us from very unflattering angles and made us flip our tails in a saucy risqué manner. It was positively embarrassing.
Ethel:	I purposely sang off-key in order to scare them away.
Gertrude:	Savage chauvinists, that's what they are; although, the one they called Laddie was kinda cute.

Buffy: The one named Prince was a handsome dog of a guy. I'd like to wrap my tail around him.

Ethel: *(sighing)* Captain Bandit—those muscles, so ripply, and sin-ually sensual… Say, Doctor George, sweetie, how soon do we hit the beach at Jaggers Isle?

Dr. George: In no time at all… once we're aloft. May I remind you that those pirates are the scourge of the sea, and not to be trusted.

(Max and Seymour have been testing the VALVES. They pull LEVERS, releasing SMOKE.)

Max: Eureka, she's fixed!

Seymour: Nice going, Max. She's ready to fly, Sir.

Dr. George: Fantastic, let's have lift-off. Man, your stations, boys—I'll take the wheel. Hold on to your tails, ladies, we're off to rescue Junie Moon. With any luck, we'll have her and her documentary of our adventure back to the States in time for the eleven o'clock news.

(The ZEPPELIN SOARS into the SKY. The MERMAIDS hold on tight to the RAILING. The WIND ruffles their UPDOS. SEAGULLS taunt them and they laugh gleefully. SEYMOUR shoos the GULLS away with his MOP.)

Gertrude: This is thrilling. We seaborn gals are air-born!

Buffy: Oooh, I feel like a fish out of water.

Ethel: Don't you mean flying fish?

(They REPRISE a THIRD VERSE of "DOCTOR GEORGE'S MAGNIFICENT ZEPPELIN" in THREE PART HARMONY.)

Ethel, Gertrude & Buffy: *(singing) He's Doctor George and oooh! What a magnificent Zeppelin. We're flying high, so high, up into the skies. / The six of us will surely have thrilling encounters.*

Ethel, Gertrude & Buffy: *Let's flip our tails with glee at clouds passing by. / We will show those pirates a thing or two, Queen Thirteen beware, splashy stewardesses, that's what we are and that is why we care. / He's Doctor George and oooh! What a magnificent Zeppelin. So come along...*

(DOCTOR GEORGE, SEYMOUR & MAX join in the SINGING.)

Dr. George, Max & Seymour: *(singing) So come along.*

Mermaids: *(singing) So come along. We're flying high.*

Dr. George, Max & Seymour: *(singing) We're flying high.*

Mermaids: *(singing) So very high, so high, so high.*

Dr. George, Max & Seymour: *(singing) So high, so high.*

All: *(Singing together)* So very high, So very high, Up into the skies!

(DISSOLVE TO)

SCENE 20

EXT. THIRTEENLAND TICKET ENTRANCE - DAY

(TICKET BOOTHS shaped like DRAGON'S HEADS line the GATES. LIFE-SAVING'S PLAN SIGNS encourage future tourists to sacrifice all for a good time. JUNIE MOON is lashed between TWO POSTS on a PLATFORM. JUMPER has her CAMERA and he aims it at JUNIE while QUEEN THIRTEEN directs.)

Queen Thirteen: For the last time, Miss Moon, you will cooperate and make this commercial for Thirteenland if you wish to return home alive.

Junie: I refuse! This vile disgusting place is against everything I stand for.

Queen Thirteen: And what might that be?

Junie: Truth, Justice and the American Way!

Queen Thirteen: Honey, who are you? Super Woman? Where do you think I got the idea?

Junie: Harm one hair on my head and my producer, Mr. Whopperberg, will have you investigated on our "Current Affairs and Lifestyles of the "Lustfully Wealthy" show.

(Queen Thirteen holds up an IDIOT CARD with the phrase: "At Thirteenland, Your Worst Nightmares Will Come True - It's worth going broke for ... Make your vacation plans today!")

Queen Thirteen: Are you going to read this card or am I gonna have to brand it on your chest? *(Aside to Jumper)* ... That'd be a nice touch!

(Jumper claps his claw paws in agreement, hopping up & down enthusiastically.)

Junie: Go ahead. Torture me, if you dare. I'll never give into your demands. Kidnappers. Help! Help!

Queen Thirteen: Ugh! She reminds me of my baby sister after I abducted our parents and sold them to white slavers... Jumper! Remove this wretched girl and destroy her!

Jumper: *(Consoling Junie)* Don't worry, sweetie, it'll all be over in a split second. You won't feel a thing—I take big bites!

(DISSOLVE TO)

SCENE 21

EXT. THE ZEPPELIN'S UPPER DECK - DAY

(SEYMOUR takes the WHEEL from DOCTOR GEORGE, who looks through his TELESCOPE.)

Dr. George: Land ho!
Max: Land ho!

Seymour: *(securing ropes)* Land ho! Ladies, hang on tight!

Ethel: Link tails, girls, this landing might be rough on our scales.

Dr. George: Prepare to drop the anchor, Seymour. Release hot air pressure, Max. Set her down gently … easy does it!

(MAX opens VALVES, SMOKE escapes. DOCTOR GEORGE takes the WHEEL.)

Buffy: Oooh, this is scary. Can you see any pirates?

Gertrude: Not yet, maybe they're out to lunch.

Seymour: Don't worry ladies, I'll protect your tails!

Max: Seymour, you're embarrassing me! Don't tease the Mermaids!

Ethel: If they're out to lunch, girls, I won't mind that, just so long as we're not dessert!

(The ZEPPELIN skirts a VOLCANO, spewing FIRE, SMOKE, and STEAM.)

Dr. George: Brace yourselves. I'm setting her down on the beach.

(The ZEPPELIN glides down between GROVES of PALM TREES. SEYMOUR drops the ANCHOR.)

(CUT TO)

SCENE 22

EXT. JAGGERS ISLE BEACH - DAY

(The ZEPPELIN lands on the BEACH. The MERMAIDS squeal with excitement. The PIRATES casually lay around on the ROCKS, their CAMPSITE. They drink WINE from JUGS as they roast MARSH-MALLOWS over a small CAMPFIRE.

The four Fairies, TWINKIE, WINKIE, DINKIE and KING JAGGER await execution in their BIRD CAGE. They jingle angrily in XYLAPHONEZE, taunting PRINCE and LADDIE. CAPTAIN BANDIT leaps to his feet as he sees the ZEPPELIN, brandishing his SWORD. CORABELLA swawks a warning.)

Corabella: The Zeppelin's here, take cover my dears!

Captain Bandit: Hold it right there, you blustering blimpettes! I thought me boys and I blasted you out of the skies with our cannon?

Seymour: Gee, Sir, they look kinda fierce… Quick, Max, the Hypnotic Umbrella!

(MAX hands DOCTOR GEORGE the HYPNOTIC UMBRELLA.)

Max: Uh, Sir, how about giving them a dose of this?

Dr. George: Splendid idea. Good thinking, Max. Perhaps we can avoid a conflict and rescue Miss Moon peacefully.

Captain Bandit: *(laughing)* Expecting rain, Doctor George? Nice choice of weapons. I prefer my saber. Attack, men!

Corabella: Get to your feet, you lazy conquists, or well soon regret, our conquistador's fleet!

(PRINCE & LADDIE don't budge as they still sit around the FIRE munching on MARSHMALLOWS, oblivious.)

Captain Bandit: *(CONT'D)* Laddie! Prince! On your feet, men, the picnic's over.

(They slowly get to their feet, still eating and sucking their fingers.)

LADDIE: But, Captain Bandit, sir, you know, like really, we's two is entitled to a break now 'n then, right, Prince?

(Prince checks a WATCH hanging out of one his POCKETS— one of many dangling on the pirates of their stolen TREASURES and from the CHEST close by.)

Prince: You is right, Laddie. Besides, we still got a few minutes before Queen Thirteen sacrifices the TV lady to Jumper the Dragon.

Laddie: *(nudging Prince)* Too bad, she'd make a great cabin girl.

Prince: I dig orderin' her around, doin' me special favors—hey, maybe we oughta kidnap her back from the Queen for ourselves.

Laddie: What d'ya say Captain, hmmm, can we, huh, Sir?

Prince: She can cook our marshmallows for us?

Corabella: Leave the Moonie to Junie, or the Queenie will Screamy! *(Whistling)*

Captain Bandit: *(flustered)* Attack now, men, or I'll cut you to ribbons and bake you in a marshmallow pie!

Laddie: Okay, give me a minute to lick my sticky fingers.

Captain Bandit: Now, you slimy snakes!

Prince: *(to Laddie)* Touchy, ain't he. Hey, look, it's those cute mermaid dames. Hi ya, girls.

Ethel: *(to her girls)* Don't pay any attention to them. I'm not about to forgive their crude behavior when they kidnapped that poor girl.

Corabella: *(Whistling)* Dig the Chicks with the Tails, and the Girls with the Scales!

Captain Bandit: That's quite all right, darlin's—cause we're gonna have to kill you, anyway. Attack, guys!

Laddie: Sorry, girls, orders is orders!

Prince: *(To the mermaids)* Close your eyes, sisters, and ya won't feel a thing.

(They take out their SWORDS and approach the Zeppelin menacingly.)

Seymour: Do something, Doctor George!

Max: Hurry, Sir, before they finish us off!

(Doctor George opens the HYPNOTIC UMBRELLA.)

Dr. George: Right, boys. *(to the pirates)* Nice weather we're having for this time of year. Don't mind us, we're going for a little stroll along the beach. Come along everyone.

Captain Bandit: *(sarcastic)* Oooh, how swell that is… mind if my boys and I join you?

(Doctor George aims the umbrella at them and spins it. Laddie and Prince freeze, staring gawkily into it.)

Dr. George: *(poetically)* Savage pirates with marshmallow bellies / Your actions will soon become jellies / Pleasant thoughts replace daggers / On the Isle of Jagger.

(to his crew) … It always helps to rhyme.

(Laddie and Prince sit down in the SAND. They begin to play like kids, building SAND CASTLES.)

Captain Bandit: Get up you lazy thugs, it's a trick! Show them of what you're made, lads! Let's have some good, clean, bloody violence!

Corabella: Don't give up, Ca'pin, your Crew is just Na'pin!

Captain Bandit: Is it me or does nobody want to be bad anymore?! *(to Doctor George)* I hope you're happy now. Look what you've done to my buddies.

(He walks away exasperated.)

Laddie: You fishy lookin' gals sure are pretty. We can't take our eyes off you. Come play with us!

Buffy: I'm not about to be taken advantage of by someone so immature... call me when your voice changes. *(Seymour puts the UMBRELLA away.)*

Seymour: Don't let those Pirate Romeos intimidate you. Give me and Max the word, ladies, and we'll whop 'em good just for you!

Max: Speak for yourself, Seymour. The pirates can have them.

Corabella: *(Whistling)* Max, take a Clue, your Meatballs be Blue! *(Squawk)*

Gertrude: You pirates are full of what makes this Zeppelin fly.

Buffy: What's that, Gertrude?

Gertrude: Hot air! *(beginning to swoon)* Oooh, Buffy, I think I'm gonna be land-sick.

Ethel: Take a few deep breaths, girls, we amphibians aren't used to all this sand and shrubbery.

Seymour: Breathe easy, ladies, I'm here to protect you.

(The Fairies jingle with excitement. They sense that Queen Thirteen is on her way and gesture inland.)

Dr. George: Oh, my stars. Max, set the Fairies free before Queen Thirteen shows up!

(Prince jumps up and dashes to the CAGE to free them.)

Prince: Me do. Me do. I wanna free the fairies!

(Prince lets them OUT and they kiss him as they FLY happily about.)

Prince: *(CONT'D)* I like fairies! We pirates are the toughest. We'll do the protectin'. *(He dances with them.)* See how pretty they are? They're happy, now. I've made friends with them. Hi ya Winkie, Dinkie and Twinkie!

(King Jagger FLIES about jingling frantically in Xylaphoneze. He anxiously points to something distant.)

Max: Look, Doctor George, King Jagger has spotted something. He's trying to warn us.

(Captain Bandit pulls Laddie to his feet.)

Captain Bandit: Get up, you, lazy sack of double cross-bones, you're embarrassing me! Look what your pal, Prince has done. He's set the fairies free and we're supposed to be guarding them!

Laddie: I was just mindin' my own business.

Captain Bandit: Queen Thirteen's gonna feed us to her dragon instead of that snotty news reporter.

Laddie: I ain't scared of no dragon. Come on, Captain, help me build my sand castle. You can be the daddy. I always wanted a daddy.

(Captain Bandit pushes him away.)

Captain Bandit: No! By Davy-Jones-Locker. *(skulking away)* Where did I go wrong? What have I done to deserve this?

(Prince cavorts with the Fairies. They dance with him.)

Prince: Don't worry, Daddy, we still love you.

(Doctor George checks the horizon through his TELESCOPE.)

Dr. George: By thunder, it's Miss Moon in the clutches of the Queen's dragon. Steady everyone. Prepare for some unpleasantries.

(CUT TO)

SCENE 23

EXT. THIRTEENLAND ENTRANCE - DAY

(JUMPER, the DRAGON, drags on a large WOODEN PLATFORM it is a SACRIFICIAL ALTAR on WHEELS. JUNIE MOON is LASHED between the TWO POSTS on TOP of it. Jumper wears a SUN DIAL WRIST WATCH with the NUMBER THIRTEEN in place of the twelve. He drags the platform with a long ROPE into POSITION near the OCEAN SHORE. Junie Moon SCREAMS incessantly as if she were Fay Wray. WAVES SPLASH about her. Jumper is exhausted from dragging her and is sick of her noise. With hands on his hips. The ZEPPELIN arrives and SETS DOWN on the BEACH.)

Jumper: Look, young lady, I've had just about enough of your noise. You might as well save your screams for when dinner is served. *(He puts his claw paws over ears, lisping)* That voice! It's agonizing! Goodness, are you any relation to that terribly untalented Ethel Mermaid?

Ethel: I resent that remark.

(Jumper leaps back with surprise, not having noticed the Zeppelin until now.)

Jumper: *(surprised)* Sorry, I didn't see you there with your girls… lovely… *(licks his chops)* I always was partial to seafood… *(to Junie)* I may have to save you for dessert, sweetie, the main course just arrived on that blimp there. *(Jumper does double-takes as he regards the Zeppelin.)* Do my eyes deceive me? My, you ladies certainly travel in style!

Ethel: Yes we do. And, if you know what's good for you, you'll keep your big mouth shut and go on a diet. You're a little green around the gills.

(Jumper's claw paws touch his own cheeks.)

Jumper: *(indignant)* I didn't think it showed. *(He checks his sun dial wristwatch.)* Anyhow, when the clock strikes thirteen, it'll be dinner time—which'll be any minute, now—so if I was you, screaming lady, I'd begin by saying grace.

Junie: Save me, Doctor George. Don't let this disgusting dragon render my innocent virginal flesh to bare bones. Thirteen o'clock is but moments away!

(SEYMOUR tosses out the GANGPLANK in a great show of courage. He LEAPS upon it.)

Seymour: I'm here to avenge thee, Junie Moon! Never fear, Seymour's here, coming forth to save you!

(He trips over himself at the BOTTOM of the GANGPLANK, doing a forward roll into the SAND. He lands on his BACK SPREAD-EAGLED at Jumper's claw paw FEET.)

Max: Nice coming forth, Seymour, didn't wet your pants, did ya, eh, buddy?

(Jumper checks his SUNDIAL WRISTWATCH again.)

Jumper: *(pleasantly)* Could someone please ring the dinner bell? It's just now thirteen o'clock and I'm famished. *(He licks his chops as he turns to Junie.)* Oooh, yummy, such a tasty morsel... nothing I like better than saucy TV journalist over-easy! Scrumptiously femme fatale, don't you think?

(Jumper nudges Seymour with his foot paw. Seymour leaps to his feet.)

Seymour: Stand back, you, green scaly barbecue pit torch!

(He LEAPS upon the SACRIFICIAL ALTAR and UNLEASHES Junie Moon.)

Seymour: *(CONT'D)* Don't you lay a claw on my precious Miss Moon! *(to Junie)* Run for your life, darling. Hurry to the Zeppelin!

(She flees to the ZEPPELIN and into Doctor George's arms. Jumper angrily leaps upon the PORTABLE ALTAR, threatening Seymour.)

Jumper: Hey, cut that out. Talk about a quick bite. *(to Junie)* It's not polite to eat and run, ya know. *(aside)* ... and I didn't even get a chance to lick the spoon, so-to-speak.

(Junie CLINGS to Doctor George, who comforts her.)

Dr. George: There, there, Miss Moon, you're safe now.

Junie: Yes, thank you, Doctor, but I'm afraid I lost my video camera and won't be able to make my award-winning documentary of your adventure.

Dr. George That's quite all right. I doubt if anyone would believe it anyway.

(The MERMAIDS, the PIRATES and MAX cheer on SEYMOUR, who darts about, outwitting the clumsy JUMPER. With a bit of the LASH ROPE, they play tug-of-war. Seymour begins to tie him up where JUNIE had been, and crawls underneath him, leaps over his tail, back and forth, distracting him.)

Max: You can do it, Seymour. Sack that slimy lizard!

Jumper: Slimy? Watch your language.

Buffy: Seymour, you're the most!

Gertrude: He's such a handsome specimen of manhood. (to Junie) You his girlfriend?

Junie: No… Not exactly.

Gertrude: Good. Gives us girls a chance. Pull his tail for me, Seymour.

Ethel: Show us some muscle, ya big tease!

Jumper: *(accepting the compliment by mistake)* Why, thank you—I try to work out three times a week. Keeps me from getting flabby, especially under the arms. *(Jumper shakes his flab and then turns back to Seymour.) (CONT'D)* Will you please hold still long enough for me to torch you!?

(JUMPER pauses to IGNITE his BREATH with a MATCH as SEYMOUR continues to dart about.)

Jumper: *(CONT'D)* Guess my pilot light went out.

(Jumper's SNOUT SMOKES profusely. He BREATHES FIRE.)

Buffy: Eeek. He'll barbecue Seymour!

Ethel: Why don't you lazy Pirates do something?

Captain Bandit: *(applauding)* Nice work, Seymour. Snap that dragon!

Ethel: You call that helping him?

Captain Bandit: I gave him a hand, didn't I?

(HE TURNS around to his CREW who are again are back to PLAYING in their SANDCASTLES.)

Captain Bandit: *(CONT'D)* Excuse Daddy, boys, but I'm off to dig for treasure.

Laddie: Bring me back a shovel, Daddy, my fingernails is gettin' dirty.

Captain Bandit: *(scolding)* Tsk, tsk, tsk, what will Queen Thirteen … er … Mommy … What will Mommy say? Shame, shame—I'll go see if Mommy knows where I left the shovel. Bye, bye, you little dickens' you.

Corabella: *(Whistling)* Snap the Dragon and Give Them a Hand, The Crew Needs a Shovel for Castles in Sand, Go Treasure The Queen or She Won't be so Happy, Get busy Me Maties, and do make it Snappy! *(Squawk & Whistle)*

(CAPTAIN BANDIT and CORABELLA EXIT to FIND QUEEN THIRTEEN.)

Prince: If ya need any help with that Dragon, Seymour, just holler. Me 'n Laddie'll pitch in some muscle.

Ethel: The only muscle you've got is the one in your head!

Buffy: You tell him, Ethel. *(to Prince)* I'll exercise those head muscles, handsome.

(BUFFY pulls a dead FISH out of her BODICE, shuffles OFF the ZEPPELIN, over to PRINCE and bops him on the HEAD with it.)

Gertrude:: While you're at it, hon, why don't you help Seymour out before he gets fried?

(BUFFY shuffles her way to JUMPER and smacks him on his FIRE BREATHING SNOUT. She hurries back ONBOARD. Jumper reels from the WHACK she gave him.)

Jumper: Foul, foul! Or should I say, trout? Trout! Ouch, that smarts. No fair fishing from the sidelines. I think she put out my fire. *(to Buffy)* Come on, baby, light my fire.

Gertrude: Light it yourself, we're not the fire department.

(JUMPER, having been distracted, is easily TIED to the POSTS by SEYMOUR. The FAIRIES jingle and dance for joy. They FLY about Jumper, teasing him.)

Seymour: How does it feel to be lashed to the spit like a barbecued chicken?

Jumper: Finger lickin' good? Hey! This ain't fair. I was only gonna take a teensy-weensy bite outa her. She wouldn't have felt a thing. This is no way to treat a dragon.

Seymour: And why not? I fought you fair and square.

Jumper: You've humiliated me. The Queen will strip off my lovely green scales, one by one and I'll be Naked!

Dr. George: If only I spoke Xylaphoneze. Why the fuss?

Ethel: Only Fantasy Creatures understand Xylophoneze.

Gertrude: And we qualify!

Buffy: King Jaggar says we should split before his Queenie-Wife gets here. Because she's bad, she's always really really Mad!

Ethel: Her destructive powers will always make us Sad.

Gertrude: Let's scram before we're Had!

(JUMPER struggles against his BONDS.)

Jumper:	They're not kidding. I'm with you, girls. Set me free, please, or she'll scale me alive.
Buffy:	This talk of scales is giving me the shivers.
Seymour:	No way, butane-breath, you can't be trusted after trying to flame-broil Junie Moon.
Jumper:	Simmer down, you tepid teapot show-off. Set me free and let me come with you and you'll never have to eat fried foods again. We'll be so slim and trim, no one will recognize us. No eating out—think of the money you'll save. I cook, I clean, I even do windows!

(JUNIE rushes to UNTIE him. In a moment, he is FREE.)

Junie:	What a bonus! With my busy schedule on TV, I never have time for domestic duties. I have a guest room you'll love with a great view. I take breakfast at five in the morning, so I can get to the studio early for my make-up call. That's why I like my coffee strong.

(She ESCORTS him up the GANGPLANK.)

Max:	You've been out-classed, Seymour—unless, of course, you do windows, too.
Dr. George:	*(shaking Jumper's paw claw)* Welcome aboard, Jumper. Fire up the Zeppelin, Max! To your station, Seymour! I suggest we take King Jagger's advice and escape while we may.
Jumper:	*(humbly)* Thank you, dear Doctor. Chomping the heck out of the Queen's victims was exhausting. Such a guilt complex you wouldn't believe, and working non-stop thirteen hours a day.
Ethel:	Exhausting yes... extinguishing is more like it!
Seymour:	Thirteen hours a day?

Jumper: And without a break. Unreal. *(checking his watch)* You see, now that Jagger's Isle is called Thirteenland, there's thirteen hours a day… oh, my, it's just thirteen o'clock now—see?

(He shows EVERYONE his Thirteen-Hour SUN DIAL-WRISTWATCH.)

Jumper: *(CONT'D)* A designer edition. Just imagine if you'd never come along —

Junie: *(startled)* — I'd be dessert!

(CUT TO)

EXT. THE BLACK CLOUD / ABOVE THE BEACH

(QUEEN THIRTEEN and CAPTAIN BANDIT — ENTER — FLYING IN on her AIR-BORN BLACK-CLOUD FLYING-MACHINE. IT HOVERS in the AIR, has CONTROLS which she uses for MANEUVERING and is capable of FIRING RAIN, HAIL and LIGHTENING BOLTS. As THEY APPROACH, these DEVICES are FIRED upon LADDIE and PRINCE, who DASH to the ZEPPELIN in fear. CAPTAIN BANDIT has JUNIE's CAMERA and SHOOTS VIDEO of the ACTION from ABOVE.)

Captain Bandit: So, it's mutiny, eh boys?!

(PRINCE is smarting from being SINGED by a BOLT of LIGHTNING.)

Prince: Help! Save us, Doctor George.

(LADDIE is SHOWERED with RAIN and HAIL, which leaves BRUISES on him.)

Laddie: Ouch, ouch. Help! Let us come with you. We promise to be good.

(CUT TO)

EXT. THE ZEPPELIN'S LOWER DECK

(THEY BOARD the ZEPPELIN and DOCTOR GEORGE tries to calm them down. The MERMAIDS soothe them, also.)

Dr. George: Hurry on board, boys, perhaps we can out maneuver them. Blast, I'll have to cancel my experiments with the Fairies and my invention.

Max: Forget it, Sir. She's got us cornered. Our Zeppelin's no match for her Black Cloud. One shot with those lightning bolts would send us plunging into the sea.

Seymour: We best stand our ground, Sir, and see what she wants.

Ethel: *(to her girls)* Strike while the iron's hot, girls, when they're the most vulnerable.

Gertrude: *(to Prince)* Save me, you scourge of the sea.

Buffy: *(to Laddie)* I just love a burly man with tacky tattoos all over his hunky muscled body.

(The BLACK CLOUD APPROACHES. QUEEN THIRTEEN SHOOTS WADS of HAIL at THEM. JUNIE holds tightly to SEYMOUR. MAX hides BEHIND the WHEEL, & DOCTOR GEORGE stands by firm, fearlessly and stalwart.)

Max: What are we going to do, now?

Dr. George: Remain calm, everyone. I'll think of something.

(CUT TO)

EXT. THE BLACK CLOUD

Queen Thirteen: *(Vainly to Captain Bandit)* Shoot me from my left side. It makes me look meaner. *(to the Zeppelin gang)* Who allowed those fairies to escape their cage? Why hasn't that prissy TV personality been reduced to bare bones by my dragon for refusing to publicize Thirteenland?

(CUT TO)

EXT. THE ZEPPELIN'S LOWER DECK

(Jumper looks up at the BLACK CLOUD as it DESCENDS and addresses Queen Thirteen.)

Jumper: In answer to your second query, it was brought to my attention that I needed to drop a few pounds. I elected to begin a faddish flesh-free-diet of fruits and nuts.

(CUT TO)

EXT. JAGGERS ISLE BEACH

(The BLACK CLOUD LANDS on the BEACH. Queen Thirteen and Captain Bandit get off. She charges over to the ZEPPELIN, waving her magic SCEPTER zapper.)

Queen Thirteen: Silence! Traitorous reptile. I'll zap your vegetarian jaws shut permanently for betraying me.

Buffy: Golly, she's ugly!

(King Jagger jingles something to Doctor George.)

Gertrude: Buffy, be still. Where are your manners? *(to Doctor George)* King Jagger says his mortal wife is merely misguided.

Dr. George: Mortal, eh? Hmmm... most interesting, that gives me an idea.

Laddie: *(to Buffy, in his arms)* If we're gonna die, can we get hitched first?

Prince: *(to Laddie)* The single life leaves more time for looting and pillaging. *(to Gertrude, in his arms)* Would you consider going steady?

Gertrude: Anything you want. Just get Buffy and me the heck out of here.

Queen Thirteen: Silence, trespassers. I'll zap anyone who tries to escape. You are my prisoners for life, doomed to slave in my Hot-House.

Junie: Fudge. Captain Bandit has my video camera.

Queen Thirteen: Silence, vacuous video vixen!

Ethel: Exactly what goes on in this… this Hot-House?

Queen Thirteen: Silence, you fillet of femme fatale, or I'll fillet your sole! You will discover that momentarily. Jumper! Escort these Zeppelin Zanies to my dungeon and remind me later to strip your scales for disobedience.

Jumper: Yes, your glorious Queenie Thirteenship, but if you'd care to reconsider my punishment, I promise to be good—er—Bad, and to never ever let it happen again.

Queen Thirteen: Traitor! Promises are made to be broken here in Thirteenland—once known as the tired and trivial Isle of Jagger, my soon-to-be_ex_ecuted ex-husband… *(to King Jagger)* You may begin counting the minutes, dear… Yes, yes indeed! And that is that…

(King Jagger jingles fearfully to Doctor George as QUEEN THIRTEEN pontificates, moving and pausing, flowing to emphasize her declarations.)

Queen Thirteen: *(CONT'D)* King Jagger, who's services are fortunately no longer required. Vacationers, lured to these very shores by sordid commercials featuring prancing fairies, won't be allowed to leave until they've spent their life's savings on worthless trinkets purchased in Thirteenland's mandatory gift-shops.

Queen Thirteen: If they refuse to cough up the cash, they'll be enslaved with all of you, trespassers in the Hot-House Trinket Factory, making tasteless souvenirs, thirteen hours a day for the rest of their lives!

Max: *(whispering to Doctor George)* Sir, excuse me, but, wouldn't this be an opportune moment for the ol' Hypnotic Umbrella trick?

(Max offers him the UMBRELLA, but he refuses it. He takes him aside.)

Dr. George: Thank you, Max, but I think we need something a bit more persuasive—my experiment may not have to go untested after all, but I need King Jagger and his Fairies cooperation. They must gaze into the mirror first.

Max: Why? It worked on Gloria Glamorude.

Dr. George: She was lucky it didn't kill her. I must set the intensity levels to that of innocence. If someone like Queen Thirteen stares into it, the unit might explode and kill us all. *(to Ethel)* Ethel, I need you to ask the King for his cooperation…

(Doctor George whispers to Ethel and in turn she does the same to King Jagger in Xylaphoneze.)

Dr. George: *(CONT'D)* Seymour, assist Max in carrying that crate with the invention over to her Majesty.

Seymour: Yes, Sir.

(They carry the CRATE with the VANITY-EGO-REFLECTOR down the GANGPLANK and set it down in front of Queen Thirteen.)

Queen Thirteen: What effrontery is this? What have you been whispering about? Answer me!

Dr. George: A gift for you, your Majesty. Something for the boudoir to ease the tension after a long day of misdeeds.

Queen Thirteen: Interesting, and it's not even my birthday. Let me see it.

Dr. George: Open the crate, fellows, and remove the Double Refracting Vanity-Ego-Reflector for her Majesty's approval.

Queen Thirteen: Approval? I warn you, I'm never in a mood for jokes. When I laugh, I only laugh maniacally at the contemplation of my doomed victims. *(They undo the crate, revealing the MIRROR with its many BRIGHT LIGHTS. The Mermaids are awestruck.)*

Gertrude: Oooh, Buffy, look! The perfect accessory for any mermaid on the go.

Buffy: Perfect, I'm homesick—let's go. She starts to leave, but Gertrude stops her.

Ethel: When we do our act at sea, that'd be perfect for our dressing room.

(King Jagger FLIES down to the MIRROR with the other Fairies close behind him. He taunts his wife, jingling haughtily and pointing at her gift.)

Queen Thirteen: What's that shrimp of a husband saying to me?

Ethel: He says you should let them look into the mirror first because it'll crack if it's gazed into by someone who's ego is already the size of the universe.

Queen Thirteen: I must be improving. Anything else on his glittery little mind?

Ethel: He says no one will come to Thirteenland because he and all the fairies would rather die than slave in your souvenir factory Hot-House.

Queen Thirteen: Ingrate! Stare into the mirror if you want to. It'll be your final request granted before I zap all of you into oblivion.

(The Fairies stare into it. The LIGHTS FLASH and SWIRL. A FLASH of SMOKE goes off on top of it and the Fairies flee back to the ZEPPELIN. Everyone is STARTLED.)

Jumper: Eeek! That was a close one. *(to the Queen)* Ya know, Queenie dear, I'm a Fantasy Creature, myself, and I think what your, um, husband, King Jagger meant to say was that you look really fabulous in black.

(Queen Thirteen aims her SCEPTER at Jumper and a BOLT of LIGHTNING ZAPS the railing next to him. He SCREAMS and runs behind Junie and holds onto her, trembling.)

Queen Thirteen: Traitorous Triceratops, take that!

Jumper: Can't you take a compliment? *(to Junie)* Save me, sweetie! Take me to your apartment, now. I'll start with the kitchen floor—strip it completely. I bet it's filthy and could use a thick coat of Bee's Wax.

Dr. George: My dear Majesty, I'm sure your subjects meant no harm in addressing you. As for my crew, Miss Moon, here, and certainly I, we are a hardy bunch used to the stress of mortal existence. I'm sure we'll serve you well in your Hot-House slave labor factory.

(Seymour, Max and Junie are noticeably shocked.)

Seymour: You talkin' about us, Sir?

Max: Doctor George, sir... what are you saying?

Junie: Really, Doctor, you must be mistaken. Surely you can't think to include me. I'm quite satisfied with my position at WHOP-TV.

Queen Thirteen: *(laughing maniacally)* Doctor George, you amaze me. Mortals are always such fools. That's why I'm certain they'll flock like sheep to Thirteenland, eager to meet their inevitable doom. *(laughing again)* And now, before I send you off to my dungeon, let me have a look at this fabulous gift you've designed with me in mind.

Dr. George: Max, Seymour, what are you waiting for? Present her Majesty with the lovely gift, designed especially for a thriving tyrant's egotistical needs.

(They begin to turn it toward her, but she ZAPS the GROUND in front of them.)

Queen Thirteen: Halt! Not so fast. What do you call this special gift, again?

Dr. George: Why, this is the incredible Vanity-Ego-Reflector. The perfect indispensable boudoir accessory that is ideal for guys and gals on the go. Just one peek and you'll see yourself in a whole new dimension. One quick glance and the —

Queen Thirteen: Silence! Enough with the sales pitch. If this is indeed a gift and not some fancy fail-safe device, then let us allow Miss Moon to test it out for me first.

(Junie fearfully turns to Doctor George. Jumper cradles her protectively. Doctor George nods his approval.)

Junie: Jeepers, Doctor George, dare I glance into the Vanity-Ego-Reflector?! I've seen what it can do. My ego is my living and I don't want to lose it... it gives me character, an edge when I'm doing my thing on TV.

Jumper: *(fearfully)* Don't do it, Junie Moon.

Dr. George: *(comforting)* There's nothing to fear so long as you don't mind seeing yourself as you really are. I got quite a kick out of it myself when I first gazed into its glassy depths.

(Junie walks down the GANGPLANK and goes to the MIRROR. Seymour and Max ANGLE it toward her. Its LIGHTS begin to SWIRL and SPIN hypnotically. Jumper cannot control himself.)

Junie: It's calling me....

(JUMPER leaps to the BEACH and pushes her aside. He STARES DEEPLY into the MIRROR, reacting strongly to it.)

Jumper: Don't do it I tell you. *(gasping as he stares)* Oooh, my goodness gracious, what lovely green scales, I must say... and such a noble snout. And just look at that tail. Have you ever in your life seen such a tail as this.

(He begins to have a DEEPER REACTION. The LIGHTS create DISTORTIONS which allow him to see his PAST.)

Jumper: *(CONT'D)* Oooh. Oh, my... Yes... yes... yes. I suppose I did chomp a few too many innocent fairies... but, I was just following orders. That's no excuse, is it? I am responsible, aren't I! Oh, please, forgive me. They didn't even taste that great.

Jumper: Forgive me, please, and I'll never, never, never do it again, I promise. Oh, tell me that you love me and that it doesn't matter anymore as long as I can change. Oooh, yes, I love you, too, you sweet, smokey, scaley green bombshell, you. Oooh, oh, oh.

(Jumper faints BACKWARDS, his paws LIMP and extended in the air. He SNORES. Junie kneels down at his side.)

Junie: Jumper? Jumper, are you okay? *(He revives and she helps him up.)*

Jumper: Never felt better in my life. *(to Junie)* Hey, tootsie, what's happening? Sorry I almost finished you off earlier, but I was just following orders like a good little soldier. *(to Doctor George)* Hey, Doc, this mirror set-up is great. Ya sure you wanna let Queenie here have it?

Queen Thirteen: Silence, ingrate.

(She shoves Jumper aside as she makes for the mirror.)

Queen Thirteen: *(CONT'D)* Out of my way, you treacherous fairie sizzler. Bring me that mirror. Lay it on me.

Junie: Of all the egotistical nerve. You said it was my turn.

(Captain Bandit is VIDEOTAPING the Mermaids with JUNIE's CAMERA. Queen Thirteen addresses him.)

Queen Thirteen: Aim that video camera at me and not those tuna-enticing-tramps.

Ethel: How rude. Girls, are we gonna stand for that kind of treatment?

(Buffy and Gertrude shrug. Queen Thirteen addresses everyone in song. "THIRTEENLAND EGO BUSTERS" — Music and Lyrics by G.S. Vuille).

Queen Thirteen: *(singing 1st two verses in F) It seems to me I have the right to say and do whatever I might. / So don't give me a hard old time, I'll zap you silly for it's a crime. / No one here is greater than I, for I'm the best and I know why!* (2nd verse) *Thirteenland is nightmares come true, a land where fairies in fairie suits turn blue. / As they slave away in my Hot-House I'll think up evil deeds to loosen up every good intention they have thought up just to get away!*

(The Mermaids sing the Chorus, in Three Part Harmony and the Pirates sing Bass — 'Bum, bum, bum, blow me down,' etc.)

Ethel, Gertrude & Buffy: *(singing) How rude, how rude, that's such an egotistical thing she plans to do. / Those poor sweet fairies don't stand a chance, her rudeness is supreme, / To shatter all those fairies hopes and dreams!*

Junie: *(singing 3rd and 4th verses to the Queen) Your ego knows no bounds it's true, but just the same, I've got one, too. / Because I am a video queen, a star of stage and sometimes screen, / don't think you can shove me aside. I'll spar with you and chance my hide* (4th verse) *To zapping with your magic scepter becoming at once oblivion's specter. / For ego is as ego does, so don't blame me you crummy scuz. / I'm video's finest broadcast from towers, all over this land for hours and hours!*

(The Mermaids repeat the Chorus. The Pirates and Zeppelin Crew sing Bass 'Bum, bum, bum, blow me down,' etc. During the chorus, the Zeppelin Crew and the Pirates dance, cavorting happily with Doctor George conducting. Queen Thirteen sings the 5th verse, intimidating Junie Moon with her movement.)

Queen Thirteen: Young lady I don't care if you think egos as yours can squelch me, too. / What's more I plan to make you prisoner, just like those glittering fairie flitterers. / King Jagger thought to reign all over, until I locked him up forever.

(Queen Thirteen continues onto the 6th verse, continuing her intimidation.)

Queen Thirteen: *(CONT'D) Those fairies, you and everyone else, will succumb to me for I'm so jealous, / of anyone who dares be greater, I'll toss you in volcanic craters. / Whose red-hot flames will make you scream, avenging my Thirteenland dream!*

(The Mermaids sing the Chorus one final time. Queen Thirteen obviously disapproves of their Dancing and Carrying on. The SONG ENDS and Seymour and Max turn the MIRROR toward her, with Prince and Laddie's help.)

Dr. George: Present her Majesty with the mirror, boys. We hope it will satisfy you.

Junie: *(disappointed)* I guess we know who counts around here. *(to the Queen)* Don't let those unsightly bags under your eyes wreck your day.

(Queen Thirteen LUNGES at the MIRROR, nearly knocking it from their grasp. The LIGHTS on it SWIRL and SPIRAL HYPNOTICALLY, as before. As they FLASH in her face, she's given a GUT-WRENCHING LOOK at her TRUE SELF. She GASPS, her EYES BULGE wide, as a MULTITUDE of IMAGES, which she describes, RAPIDLY FIRE before her, SURROUNDING her, ENVELOPING her in her past misfortune. She SCREAMS.)

Queen Thirteen: Ahhheeek! Oh, merciful universe. Can my fairie friends ever forgive me? How could I have nearly destroyed King Jagger and his fantasy isle?

Queen Thirteen: As their Queen, I made them suffer, knowing deep down I was a mortal undeserving of my fairie reign… they had adopted me as a young runaway… King Jagger married me out of sympathy, hoping to bridge the gap between fantasy and reality, but I was a fairie in name only. I didn't belong. The rejection I felt shattered me. My mortal past haunted me to extremes of paranoia. My true mortal family from the States had rejected me first because my baby sister was cuter and more loved. I kidnapped her and put her in a far-away orphanage. Then I stowed away on a fishing vessel which sank at sea not far from here. Mermaids rescued me and deposited me on this very beach … the rest is history. I became insanely jealous of my fairie saviors. My wings were fake, I was too large and couldn't fly, and a total glittering failure! Naturally, the only logical thing to do was to take over the Island and enslave everyone with the help of the pirates—they'll do anything for a little treasure… but even they can't stand me!

(She sobs, overcome with grief.) Oh, you poor, poor, wicked creature you… so fragile… so unloved…

(Queen Thirteen faints. Junie and Jumper rush to aid her. They help her up.)

Junie: Queen Thirteen! Queen Thirteen! Please, wake up. Please.

Jumper: Poor, Queenie, I had no idea how much you've suffered. If it's any consolation, I always thought you were a… er… interesting person.

Queen Thirteen: *(reviving)* Oh, my... what a relief... I feel lighter than air!

(Junie points to a small MOLE on her own cheek.)

Junie: Did that little girl who was your baby sister—did she have a little mole on her cheek like this one?

(Queen Thirteen RECOGNIZES her as her long-lost BABY SISTER. They EMBRACE in TEARS.)

Queen Thirteen: Merciful moonbeams! You're my long-lost baby sister. Oh, happy day, to be reunited at long last. Now I can give up my plans to destroy world tourism and free the Fairies of Jagger's Isle!

Junie: Gosh, if only I had been able to document this wonderful event for WHOP-TV!

(Captain Bandit, still videotaping, goes to her.)

Captain Bandit: Don't worry, doll, I got the whole revelation on tape for posterity. You and me and the good Doctor are gonna be rich when we sell it to the network. *(She rushes into his arms.)*

Junie: Oh, Captain Bandit, you saved my documentary. I'm yours forever to love and obey! Take me away in your pirate ship for our honeymoon.

Captain Bandit: We'll sail the seven seas and make plans to raid the TV industry, pirating videos!

Seymour: *(aghast)* My precious Junie Moon! What mischief is this? You belong to me. I saved you from the dragon.

Jumper: He's gotta point there... and, what about my position as housekeeper?

Max: Well, if that don't beat all—jilted, on top of everything else... take it easy, Seymour, there are other fish in the sea.

Ethel: He's right about that.

Max: Hey, Doc, if nobody else wants to take a look, can we put this contraption away?

Dr. George: Sure, boys, great job. Put that crate on board, and let's head for home.

(They PACK up the MIRROR and carry it ON-BOARD the ZEPPELIN.)

Seymour: *(grudgingly)* Women don't need Vanity-Ego-Reflectors when it comes to busting egos. Mine couldn't get more deflated if you sucked it out with a vacuum cleaner hose. Women!

Max: *(comfortingly)* Cheer up, Seymour, at least we have each other— and, Doctor George—and I love you like a... friendly companion... eh, brother?

(They set the crate down and give each other a hug.)

Seymour: Thanks, guy, you're a pal. I know you'll help me forget those long lonely nights ahead.

Dr. George: Now that things are looking up, does anyone need a lift home? My magnificent Zeppelin is yours to command.

Ethel: You can drop the girls and I off at Mermaid Isle.

Prince: Us too, come on Laddie.

Laddie: Don't forget us, girls, the captain doesn't need us now that he has a girlfriend.

(They get onboard the Zeppelin and join the Mermaids.)

Junie: Goodbye, Doctor George, I'll be staying here with my fiancee and my long-lost sister Blanche.

Queen Thirteen: How marvelous, you remembered my mortal name. This is not goodbye, Junie —

Queen Thirteen: *(She kisses her.)* — I've got to return to the States and patch things up with our parents... *(waving at King Jagger and the Fairies)*... sorry, hubby, to have put you through so much... take care of yourselves and this magical island. Bye! *(to Doctor George)* Don't leave without me, Doctor!

(The FAIRIES jingle happily and ZOOM about, DUSTING everything in sight with FAIRIE DUST and merriment. Queen Thirteen, a.k.a. now BLANCHE gets ONBOARD as JUMPER climbs ABOARD her BLACK CLOUD and HOVERS & ZOOMS around ABOVE THEM trying it out.)

Jumper: Guess you won't be needing this anymore, Queenie—Excuse me, Blanche! Thanks, Doc, for saving Fairieland... goodbye everyone...I'll remember you in my flames—er—dreams!

(Jumper waves goodbye and ZOOMS away in the BLACK CLOUD, crashing into PALM TREES, soaring across SMOKING VOLCANOS and RAINING, HAILING and SHOOTING LIGHTENING BOLTS all the way. EVERYONE cheers and the FAIRIES jingle approvingly.)

Captain Bandit: But then don't forget, Doc, you got a cut in the documentary video stakes. See you back in the good ol' United States in a few days. Right, doll?

Junie: I, I, Captain! *(They smooch)* Goodbye, Doctor, Seymour, Max and everyone... I'm sorry if I was a nuisance... forgive me, Seymour... you're very special to me... *(She blows him a kiss.)*

Seymour: Goodbye, Junie... I'll always love you... Max and I are going back to college and study to be rocket scientists.

Max: Now you're talking, Seymour! I'll race you to the university laboratory!

Dr. George: Goodbye everyone! I'm so glad things worked out and everybody is happy. Boys, to your stations. Let's have lift-off.

Ethel: Doctor George, you're the greatest doctor on the most magnificent Zeppelin in the world.

Dr. George: Yes indeed! Up, up and away!

(The ZEPPELIN FLIES into the SKIES. EVERYONE waves as it sails away.)

(DISSOLVE TO)

SCENE 24

INT. JUNIE'S APARTMENT / KITCHEN - DAY

(With the ADVENTURE is over, COOKIE and JUNIE are in a blue mood because JUNIE MOON II has disappeared.)

Junie: I just can't believe she's gone.

Cookie: I'm so sorry she got out. I'd been over to feed her and I opened the kitchen window just a crack to air the place out. I was straightening up when I noticed she was gone. I'm so sorry, Junie. I feel terrible.

Junie: It's not your fault. It was an accident. We can look for her after we get back from the studio.

(CORABELLA is seen LANDING on Junie's cracked open WINDOWSILL, she listens to their plight.)

Cookie: With both of us searching, we're bound to find her. I looked by myself throughout the neighborhood yesterday and again this morning, but didn't have any luck.

Junie: Come on, let's get to that rehearsal. I don't want to hold everyone up. Whopperberg never saw the documentary we tried to shoot while I was away, because Captain Bandit accidentally dropped my camera in the ocean. I shouldn't have trusted him.

Cookie: I bet you're glad not to be anchoring the news, what with Gloria's new popularity, and after all, your boyfriend was a loose cannon.

Junie: Ha! Good one, Cookie, loose cannon describes him perfectly. After my romantic fling with that crazy pirate, which only lasted a few short hours, our romance fizzled. We hit shore and that was it. He was off to the pubs to chase loose women. I've had it with men, they don't want us, they want fun and adventure, not a serious relationship... I need a vacation.

Corabella: *(Corabella shakes her head and squawks disapprovingly.)* Captain Bandit the Fink, Dumped our Junie, that Stinks!

Junie: *(grabbing her purse)* Let's get going, Cookie, WHOP-TV is calling for their lonesome star...

Cookie: I hear you loud and clear, girl, stick with me and I'll help you get through this.

(They head for the DOOR and EXIT)

(DISSOLVE TO)

SCENE 25

EXT. JUNIE MOON'S CAR - DAY - TRAVELING

(They are DRIVING to the STUDIO. Both of them are still blue, but hopeful that things will work out.)

Cookie: I hope you're planning on cheering up soon.

Junie: I'm sorry, Cookie. So much has happened lately, that I'm completely exhausted.

Cookie: Mr. Whopperberg would have loved the footage you shot of your adventures. Gloria had been planning a special segment featuring it for her new "Good News for An Enlightened Age Show". I'm so sorry, Junie... *(hugging her)*

Junie: *(laughing)* Amazing what one good hard look in a mirror can do—if it's the right one. Doctor George will have to get his Guru's license.

(Moments later they pass by the CITY PARK, where a HUGE CROWD has gathered. Doctor George's Magnificent ZEPPELIN begins its DESCENDING maneuvers.)

(DISSOLVE TO)

SCENE 26

EXT. CITY PARK / CAR LOT - DAY

(Junie PARKS the CAR and they get out.)

Cookie: There they are now.

Junie: *(happily)* He's brought my sister back with him from Jagger's Isle!

(They RUN over INTO the PARK and JOIN the CHEERING CROWD.)

(CUT TO)

EXT. CITY PARK

(GLORIA GLAMORUDE is covering the EVENT. She is dressed like a FLOWER CHILD as are her many FOLLOWERS & FANS surrounding her.)

Gloria: *(beaming)* They're coming in for a landing ladies and gentlemen. Our very own Doctor George and his magnificent Zeppelin!

(As the ZEPPELIN comes in for a LANDING, just skirting the TOPS of the TREES, SEYMOUR tosses out the ANCHOR, which gets caught in a TREE and he gets tangled in it and FALLS overboard onto a TREE BRANCH.)

(CUT TO)

EXT. CITY PARK / TREE BRANCH

(As SEYMOUR LOOSENS and UNTANGLES himself, while DANGLING from the BRANCH, CORABELLA swoops in to a higher branch beside him and SQUAWKS, indicating to Seymour to look.)

Seymour: Corabella?! What's that you say? *(Seeing Junie Moon II.)* … Hey, there, little kitty. You stuck up here like me?

(She MEOWS sweetly and GOES to him. He PICKS HER UP lovingly, cuddling her.)

Corabella: *(Whistling)* A match made times Seven, for a guy seeking Heaven! *(Squawk)*

(CUT TO)

EXT. CITY PARK

(DOCTOR GEORGE waves to the CROWD. MAX has taken the ANCHOR from SEYMOUR and dropped it to the ground. The ZEPPELIN lands safely. The crowd continues cheering as Max, Doctor George and Blanche come down the gangplank.)

(SEYMOUR drops out of the TREE carrying JUNIE MOON and runs up to greet JUNIE MOON, who is with COOKIE.)

Seymour: *(modestly)* Looks like I've found a friend at last.

Cookie: Look, Junie, it's your kitty!

Junie: Junie Moon II! Oh, Seymour, thank you for rescuing her.

Seymour: I finally did something right. Hey, I'm improving. Does this mean I stand a chance?

(He hands her JUNIE MOON II. She PURRS with glee. Junie Moon KISSES Seymour and he puts his arms around her.)

Junie: Oh, Seymour, how could I have been so foolish. You saved my life on Jagger's Isle and you've rescued my kitty. How can I ever repay you?

Seymour: Would you be my girl?

(Blanche, Max and Doctor George come over to them.)

Blanche: Don't let that boy slip away from you this time.

Junie: I love you, Seymour. *(They kiss.)*

Blanche: That's more like it, little sister, now we can all begin our new and joyful reunion!

Max: *(Sadly, remorseful)* Gosh, Seymour, where does that leave us? If you have Junie Moon to love, then who's going to care for me?

(CORABELLA swoops down from the TREE where JUNIE MOON II was found moments before and lands on Max's shoulder, startling him.)

Max: *(CONT'D)* Corabella! How on Earth did you find us?!

Corabella: *(Whistling & squawking happily.)* I longed to be Free, so Capt. Bandit's Junie, could be spooned without Cracks, from this bird wanting Max! *(Squawk)*

Max: Thanks, Corabella, I knew you should belong to me!

(GLORIA puts the MICROPHONE to Doctor George.)

Gloria: Would you say we have a happy ending, Doctor?

Dr. George: I can't think of a better one, can you?

(Everyone cheers.)

Gloria: Let's hear it for Doctor George's Magnificent Zeppelin! Hip hip, hooray!

Everyone: Hip hip, hooray! Hip hip, hooray!

(MUSIC begins a CHORAL version of "Doctor George's Magnificent Zeppelin." BALLOONS are RELEASED and the ENSEMBLE REVELS with DELIGHT.)

SUPERIMPOSED over FINAL CREDITS:

"In Loving Memory, JUNIE MOON, b.1987 - d.1989 & CORABELLA, b.2011-d.2021"

(FADE OUT)

A Musical Comedy Fantasy Screenplay
by *Grant Sutor Vuille*

THE END

"Doctor George's Magnificent Zeppelin"

Music & Lyrics by Grant Sutor Vuille © 2011

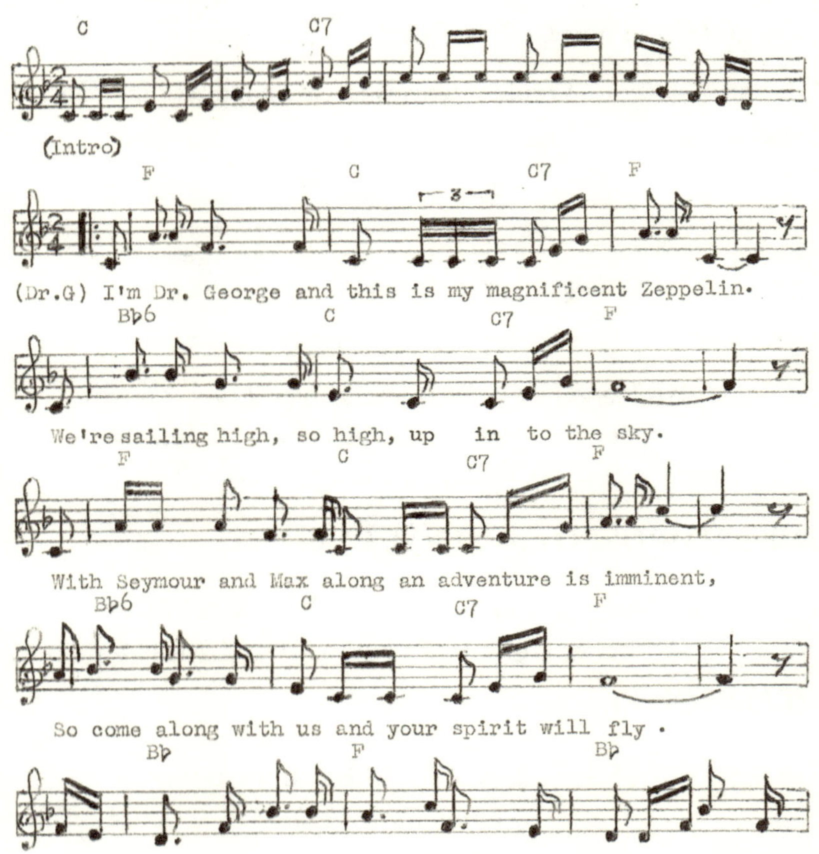

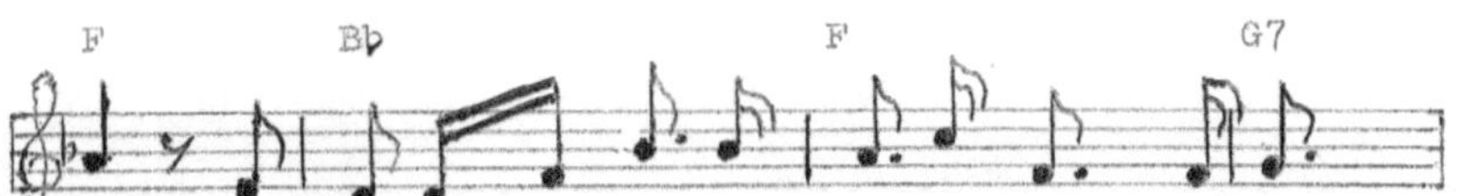

thing. With Seymour and Max right by our sides, we then

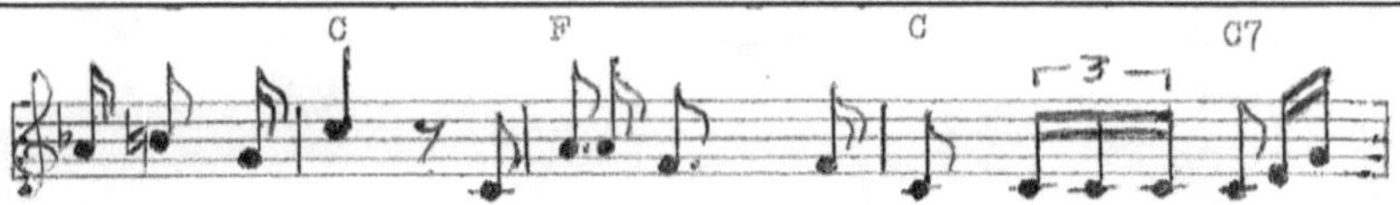

can really sing. I'm Dr. George, and this is my magnificent

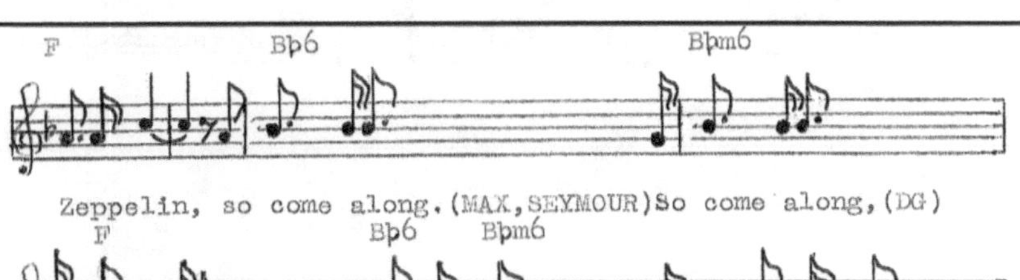

Zeppelin, so come along. (MAX, SEYMOUR) So come along, (DG)

So come along. We're flying high. (M, S) We're flying high.

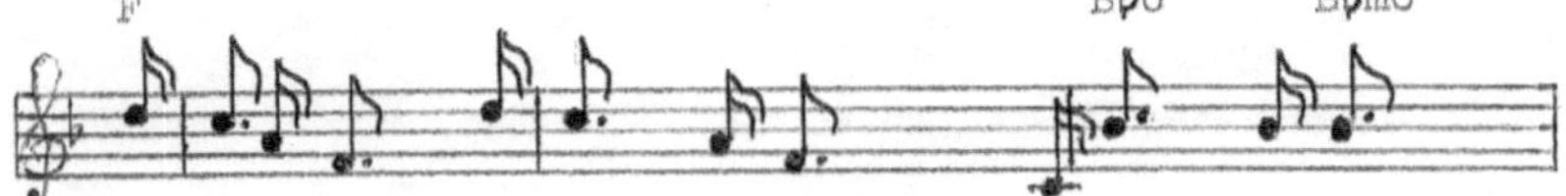

(G) So very high. So high, so high. (M, S) So high, so high.

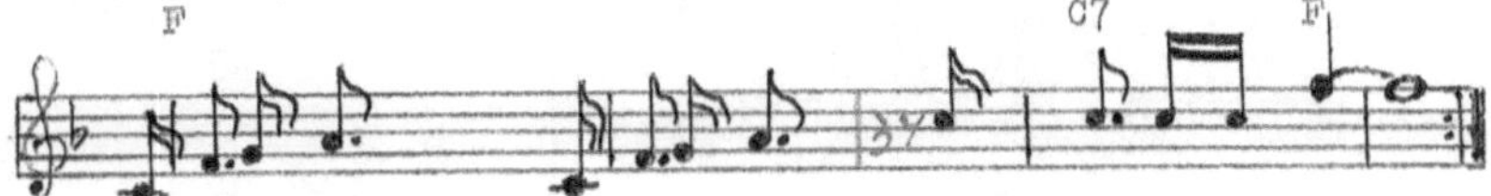

(G) So very high. (M, S) So very high. (G) Up in to the skies!

"The Mermaids of Mermaid's Isle"

Music & Lyrics by Grant Sutor Vuille © 2011

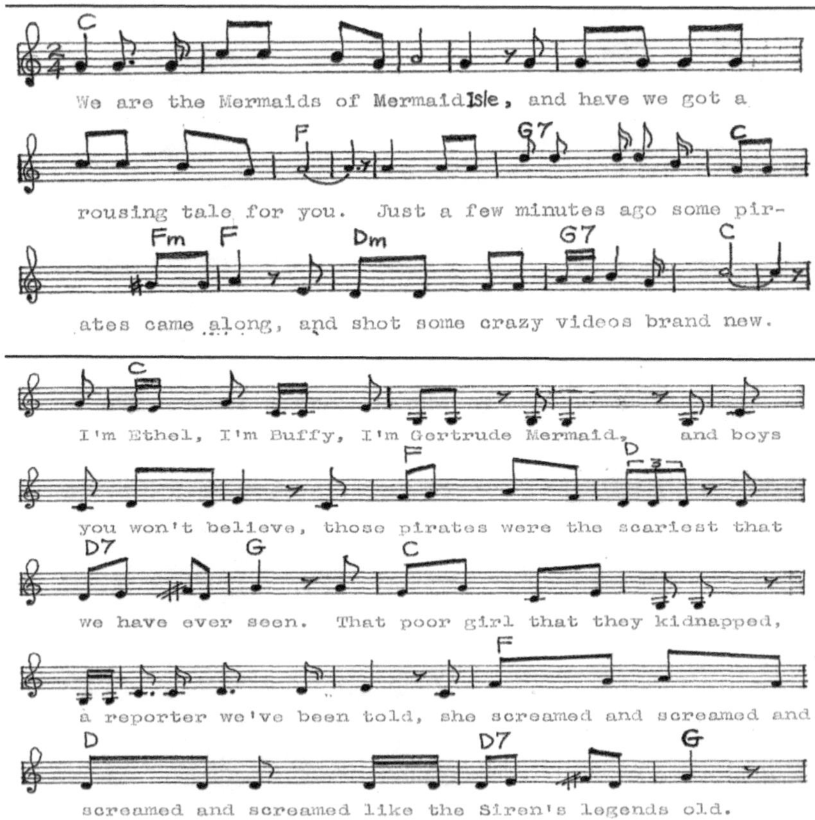

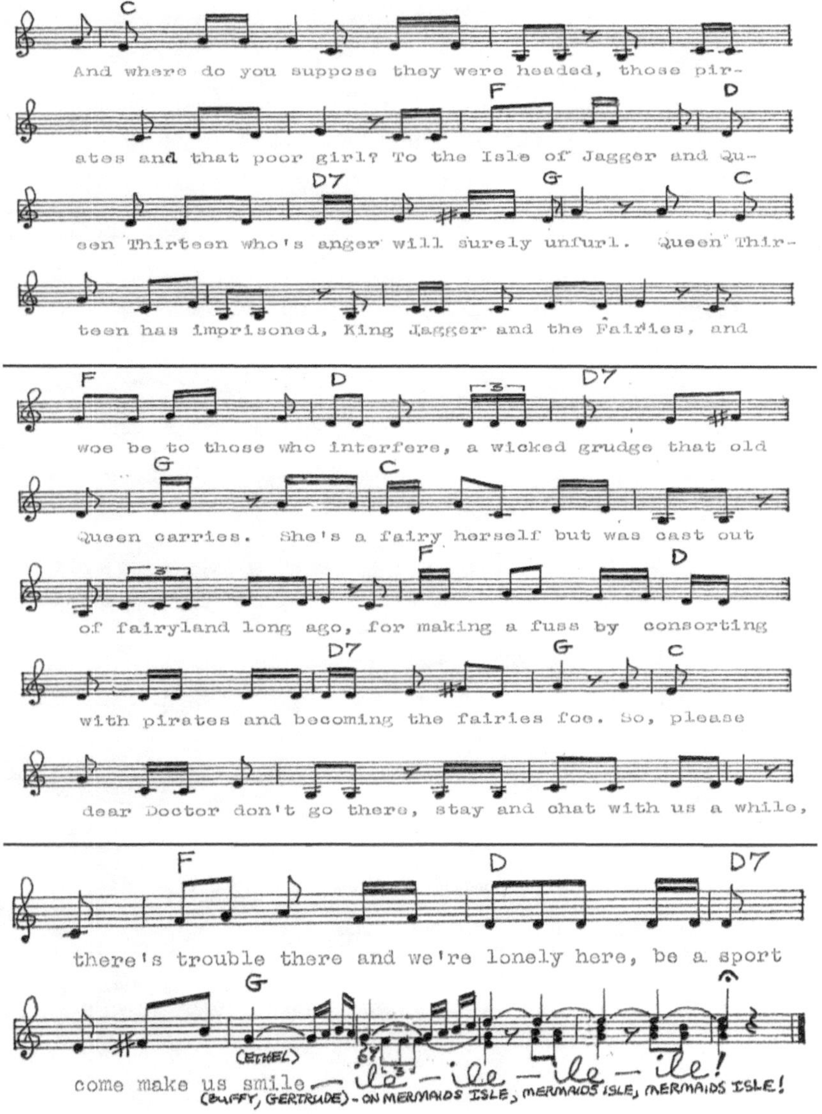
C
And where do you suppose they were headed, those pir-
F D
ates and that poor girl? To the Isle of Jagger and Qu-
D7 G C
een Thirteen who's anger will surely unfurl. Queen Thir-
teen has imprisoned, King Jagger and the Fairies, and
F D D7
woe be to those who interfere, a wicked grudge that old
G C
Queen carries. She's a fairy herself but was cast out
F D
of fairyland long ago, for making a fuss by consorting
D7 G C
with pirates and becoming the fairies foe. So, please
dear Doctor don't go there, stay and chat with us a while,
F D D7
there's trouble there and we're lonely here, be a sport
G
(ETHEL)
come make us smile — ile — ile — ile — ile!
(BUFFY, GERTRUDE) - ON MERMAIDS ISLE, MERMAIDS ISLE, MERMAIDS ISLE!

"Thirteenland Ego Busters"

Music & Lyrics by Grant Sutor Vuille © 2011

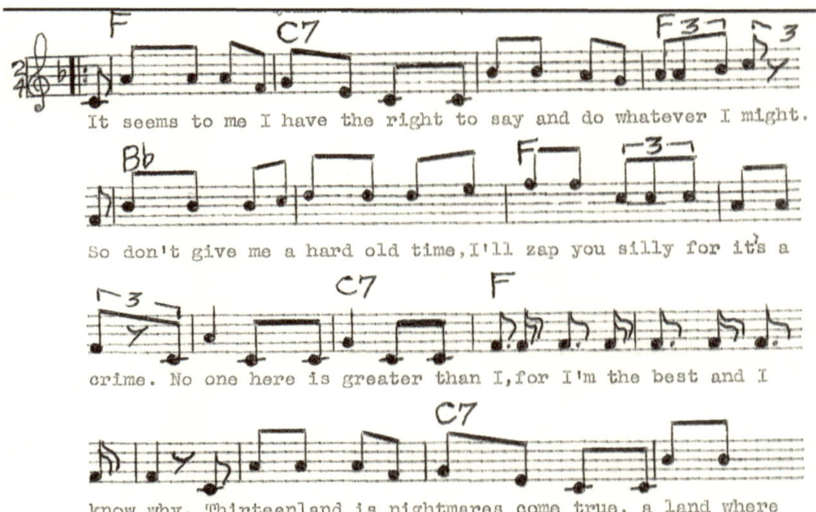

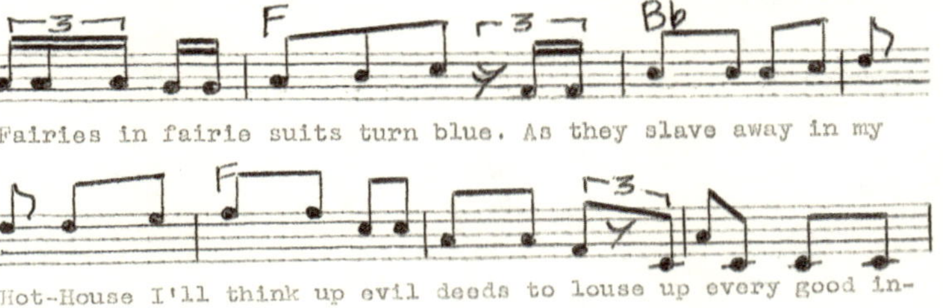

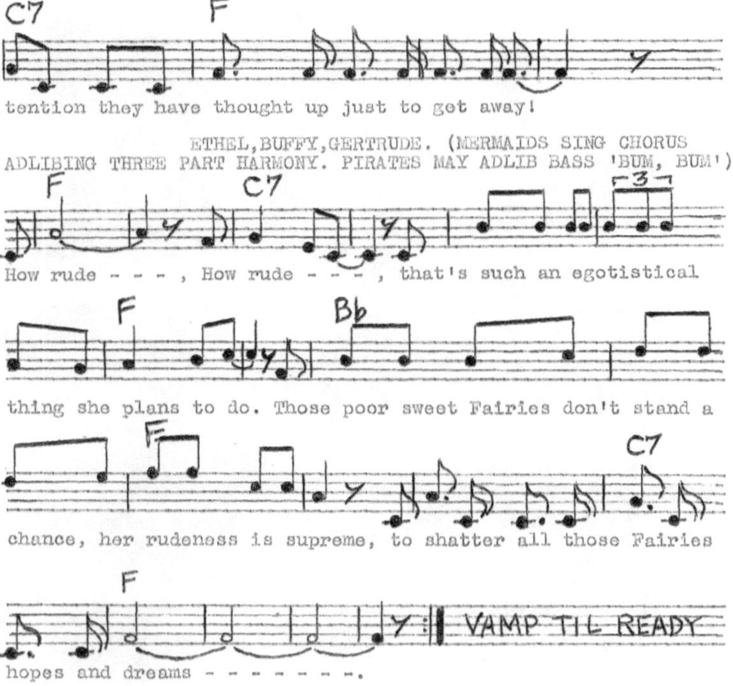
C7
F
tention they have thought up just to get away!
ETHEL, BUFFY, GERTRUDE. (MERMAIDS SING CHORUS ADLIBING THREE PART HARMONY. PIRATES MAY ADLIB BASS 'BUM, BUM')
F
C7
3
How rude - - - , How rude - - - , that's such an egotistical
F
Bb
thing she plans to do. Those poor sweet Fairies don't stand a
F
C7
chance, her rudeness is supreme, to shatter all those Fairies
F
VAMP TIL READY
hopes and dreams - - - - - - - -.

DOME GSVuille 2-9

THE MUSIC BEGINS FOR "DOG BITES" - **Song** by GSVuille.
LIGHTS FLASH AND FLARES GO OFF ON CUE AS JUNIE MOON
AND HER DANCERS ROCK 'N ROLL.

JUNIE MOON
(singing in Key of C)

```
 'C  C              '    (Bbmb)   '
 (CM) '       ' G    Bb  /'BbG  ' G  '/
(1)Dog Bites!  They don't bother me.
 'C  C    '       C     C     E   D'     (//:)
 (C)  '        G   ' G /'        '  (G7)  ' G
(3)Dog Bites!  Oh, baby can't you see.  Our
  C(E)    C          (mb)       C(M)   C           '  '/
  '  G   '     G  'BbG    '/' G      '       G  Bb(mb)
(5)Hungry love was always, always meant to be.
  C(M) C  D'   E  C(M)        C       C  D' E    C(M)
  '       (G7)      '   ' G   /'         (G7)      '     '/
(7)Come on hold me baby, and rough me up for spite.
  G      F    Eb    C    G C    C  G(7) C  C        C C
  '      '          '    '     /'         '      (M)'     '/
(9)Sling me, tear me, baby. My soul is yours tonight!
          (mb)    (G7)  C(E) '            (mb)     (G7)       C(M)
  G     /'Bb  Bb B'   B'     G    G  /'Bb    Bb  B'  B     '      '
(11)Don't let me run away, I'm your prisoner for all time.
            (mb)      (G7)     C(M)  C  G(7) F       EbC    C(M)
  G       /'BbBb    'B B     '     '   /'          '      '      '
(13)There's nowhere I can hide, no tall trees I can climb!
        C          C              (mb)   '          C(M)    C            (mb)
  G /'      G    '       G  'BbG     G     G    /'      G   '        G'Bb   '
(15)So beat me, pound me, baby, with that love of yours devine.
       C(M) C  D       E  C                  G(7) F  Eb  G    C(M)
  G /'          '          '      G ' G  /'           '         '       '
(17)My soul is yours to walk on, and love me for all time!
      C  C             '        (mb)     '
      '    '     '   G      Bb   /'BbG   ' G  '/
(CHORUS)Dog Bites!  They don't bother me.
   C(M)C              C       C      E   D(G7)
   '    '      '   G   ' G  /'         '    '    '
(21)Dog Bites!  Oh, baby, can't you see.
        C(M)       C         '                  C(M)         C        (mb)
   G  /'       G   ' G       Bb(mb) G    ' G /'         G     '  G    'Bb  '
(23)Our love was always frightening, as frightening as can be.
        C(M) C  D      E  C      '   (1) GF     Eb     C  C(M)
   G  '            '          'G    G    G/'(G7)
(25)Oh bite me babe forever and forever we'll be free!(://)
   C    C          C/C    '  '/  C     C        /
   '    '       ' G  ' ' G'G      '     '        ''
(27)Dog Bites!                    Dog Bites!  (//)
```

JUNIE MOON and the DANCERS strike a final pose.

CUT TO:

"Eternally Yours, Jayne Mansfield"

(c) 1989/2011
by Grant Sutor Vuille

Characters:

Shyler & Claude - Two young sensitive gay men who are still discovering their sexual identity.

Jayne A Queer young man who has a special bond with deceased icon Jayne Mansfield.

Setting:

A small apartment which is sparsely furnished, with walls covered with old movie posters, clippings, and memorabilia of glamorous male & female stars from classic 1940, 50, 60 to 80's movies.

Time and Place:

1989 in a typical USA town or city

(SHYLER sits, cross legged, CENTER STAGE, reading a MOVIE MAGAZINE. He is a young man overwhelmed by his own insignificance, indulged in a world of fantasy. After a moment or two of turning pages and a few chuckles, CLAUDE ENTERS. He sits down next to his friend, and lace since peers over his shoulder at the MAGAZINE. He is the same age and somewhat cute and innocent. He is naive, but willing to learn about life. SHYLER turns a page, miffing CLAUDE)

Claude: Hey, I wasn't finished yet. Go back.

Shyler: Will you bug off? Go see what Jayne's up to in the living room. Go pester her for a while.

Claude: *(Insisting)* Come on, please, just turn the page back. I didn't get a good look at the size of Marilyn's tits.

Shyler: Since when are you interested in women's breasts? Bug off. Don't you have anything better to do?

Claude: Why are you being so nasty to me? I thought you liked me living here with you and Jayne. You invited me, remember?

Shyler: Buddy, you're a real pal, believe me, but right now I could use a little privacy—ya dig—no offense, okay?

Claude: *(Noticing the male models)* Hey, get a load of those biceps *(Understanding)* Oh, I get it, you need to be alone so you can… *(He giggles)*

Shyler: Don't be so sure of yourself. Sex isn't everything.

Claude: To me it is. It's all I think about.

Shyler: *(Pensive)* You, know, it really bugs me that I can't get away with anything.

Claude: Just what are you talking about? You still messing around with Jayne?

(JAYNE ENTERS)

Jayne: No one's been messing with me. Hold your tongue, Claude.

Claude: It hurts me to see you with Shyler.

Shyler: You jealous?

Claude: And why shouldn't I be? She's a beautiful girl.

Jayne: Thank you, sweetheart.

Claude: I don't like it when guys leer at you… like they're hungry. They don't respect you like I do!

Shyler: The girl's in show business, dummy. Guys are supposed to look at her like that.

Claude: It disgusts me, I tell you. I especially hate it when you bait her with those promises.

Shyler: You're much too sensitive. All men, everywhere, bait chicks with promises. It's human nature.

Claude: God made me. He made Jayne. He made you and everything and everyone in the world. But you still disgust me, especially when you hurt her feelings. She's all woman—the most-womanly woman in the world. To insult her is to insult the Creator Himself!

Shyler: *(To CLAUDE)* Did I ever tell you, you turn me on?

Claude: Don't pay any attention to him, Jayne. He's definitely a pervert. Seriously... I'm serious, ya know.

Shyler: *(With some amusement, to CLAUDE)* Do you want to hear my poem about Jayne Mansfield?

Jayne: *(Excited)* Oh, Shyler! You've written a poem about me?

Shyler: Errr... yes... but it really spooks me when you talk like that. I keep telling you she died a long time ago in a terrible car accident.

Jayne: *(Defensively)* And I keep telling you I was born on the day she died!

Shyler: I know, I know. *(Resigned)* Sorry. Do you want to hear my poem now?

Jayne: Divoone! Yes, please.

(She sits. SHYLER moves to CENTER STAGE and takes a moment to prepare)

Shyler: The title of my poem is, "Eternally Yours, Jayne Mansfield". *(He begins)*
Jayne Mansfield was a buxom broad / I beheld her boobs and screamed, my God! / She loved pink hearts and pink Cadillac's / She preferred men strong as hot lumberjacks /

(JAYNE squeals with delight)

Shyler: The girl can't help it, the real men cried / Our bones can't resist her, you know how they've tried / Her nude spread in Playboy created a stir / Promises, promises, 'How Divoone,' she would purr /

Jayne: Divoone! *(She squeals and laughs)*

Shyler: Shhh! I'm not finished.

(He continues)

Shyler: Like a cat hanging-out in fresh pussy-willows / In bed she would lounge between pink fluffy pillows /

(He moves toward her. She is mesmerized)

Her Hollywood home was bright pink in and out / Her polka dots round like her teats firm and stout / Chihuahuas loved snuggling her bosoms so warm / My face ached for its turn, t'would do them no harm /

(He is caressing her)

Her act was a gem but gave film critics willies / She charmed the pants off us in "Las Vegas Hillbillies!"

Jayne: *(Quickly, throwing up her arms)* Va, va, va voom!

Shyler: *(Leading her around, slowly, sensually)*

Both Griffin and Rayburn could not get enough / They drooled and they sputtered as she strutted her stuff / With a genius IQ she worked without fuss / Her talent, a classic, in "The Wayward Bus"

Jayne: *(Softly)* I was good in that one, wasn't I?

Shyler: *(He becomes more forceful in his movements with her)* She knew what men wanted and she gave it full throttle / Her career spiraled down and she took to the bottle / "Will Success Spoil Rock Hunter?" her show business start / A substitute jinx would break her pink heart!

(JAYNE breaks away and gasps)

Jayne: *(Frightened)* That bitch!

Shyler: *(Ridged)* She squealed up three octaves on impact some say /

(JAYNE squeals and screams, covering her eyes)

Shyler: She sailed straight to Heaven, God lighting the way / (She slowly collapses on the floor) Her children behind her and fans were in tears / "Don't worry, she cooed, "I'm forever, my dears" / My children, my fans, Lord, "Kiss Them For Me" …

(She cries softly. SHYLER goes to her and comforts her)

Shyler: That was beautiful, Jayne…I didn't know you knew the ending. I'm sorry if I've upset you.

Jayne: *(Reflecting)* I love my life. I love who I am and what I stand for.

Shyler: And what is it you stand for? Enlighten us, Jayne… Miss Mansfield… blind us with your beautiful 'intellect'?

Jayne: My teats are my intellect, ya boob! *(She squeals up three octaves with delight)* Oooh! I didn't know I had it in me. A woman should always let a man know who's boss.

Claude: Ha! That's telling him, Miss Mansfield.

Jayne: And don't you start sucking up to me, Claude. I know your type. You'll use all your boyish charm to win my affections, but when it's all said and done, drop me like all the other guys in my life. Men-- I've had it with them!

Shyler: What is this? A celebrity marionette show? Let's cut the crap. We're not enemies here. We all have dreams. I have dreams. I'd like to be famous here, like Miss Mansfield… for all my accomplishments… my beauty.

Claude: *(Disgusted)* Leave her alone. What do you know about people anyway? She has ambition. She's got beauty, sure. Why shouldn't she be popular? You're jealous because you're a nobody.

Jayne: Shyler doesn't think I'm attractive.

Shyler: Oh, you're attractive, you're just not my stereotype.

Jayne: I'll bet you're afraid of me.

(She approaches him)

Jayne: Do I make you nervous, little man?

Shyler: Why can't people just be themselves. I'm as much of a man as the next guy. I don't have to stuff my pants to win affection.

Claude: Jayne's one hundred percent woman.

Jayne: You guys make me really sick. I can't believe you don't want to ravish me with affection. You must be into some deviant lifestyle. No real man can resist me.

Shyler: *(Offended)* No real man would have anything to do with you, bitch. You're a synthetic deviation of your true self. Judge not lest ye be judged.

Claude: Cut the phony quotes, Shyler. I can tell her how I feel myself... *(Thinking)* ...Say, wait a minute. You leave my girl alone. I told you I was in love with her. Can't you see how beautiful she is? Are you blind?

Jayne: I think you boys must be Gay.

Shyler: Think so, eh? Did you hear about President Bush testing HIV positive? He declared war on toilet seats to combat the spread of the disease.

Claude: I like to use disposable cushion seat protectors.

Jayne: I thought you two might be Queer.

Shyler: I bet you didn't know that when Eddie Murphy kissed his own ass, he wound up with band-AIDS on his lips.

Jayne: You're a lousy comedian.

Shyler: And you're a female impersonator. Can the act and join the human race.

Jayne: What have you got against me. I haven't hurt you, have I?

Claude: I still love you--guys are just a sideline.

Shyler: Claude, I think it's time you made up your mind. Do you love Jayne, or me?

Claude: Can't I love you both?

Jayne: I'll help you make up your minds. Let's all hop into bed and whoever I am unable to seduce successfully is the loser.

Shyler: The odds are stacked against me. There's no way you can turn me on.

Jayne: I'm 'stacked' as can be—the Hell with the odds—I think you might be pleasantly surprised.

Claude: What if we both get excited?

Jayne: Then I win and you both become my love slaves.

Shyler: So, either way, we lose. Fine. I'm not afraid of failure. You're on, you, sultry imposter. But if we're to be losers, then the least you can be is our maid. Let's strip. I love being naked.

Jayne: You, rats. I'll agree to be the maid, but I don't do windows or dishes.

Shyler: Fuck this game. Let's just strip and see what happens. We'll all be love slaves to each other. We'll be both winners and losers.

Claude: That seems fair.
(CLAUDE brings out the ROLL-AWAY BED)
Okay, everyone, let's strip off our clothes and dive in *(He strips in record time to his shorts and leaps into the bed. To JAYNE)*.
Come to Papa, baby!

Jayne: Wait a second, buster, you aren't completely naked.

Claude: What? No way. Let's see some skin you two. Fair's fair. You first, Shyler. Reveal that manly torso.

Shyler: Me? Hell, no. Let Jayne prove herself. She's the one who's spent her entire life flaunting her sexuality.

Claude: Flip it out, son, let's see if you measure up.

Jayne: We'll take turns, Shyler. One piece at a time.

Shyler: Okay. I'll buy that.

Jayne: Here goes.

(CLAUDE sings BACKGROUND MUSIC as JAYNE begins her strip. SHYLER gets into the mood slowly. With each ITEM she sheds, both boys get more enthusiastic. SHYLER tries to copy her moves, as she puts a lot into strip tease, squealing and sighing, bumping, and grinding. CLAUDE'S VOCALS have reached near climax by the time they're in their underwear. He has been wiggling and writhing on the bed, humping the pillows on occasion. SHYLER and JAYNE slip into the BED. SHYLER whips out a pair of SUNGLASSES)

Shyler: I just don't feel cool without my Billy Joel shades.

(He puts them on)

Hope you two don't mind, but I feel naked...

(He shudders)

...positively 'naked' without them.

(They are still for a few moments)

Shyler: *(CONT'D)* Don't anybody start anything they can't finish.

Claude: *(Nervously rising from the BED)*

Did I hear someone knocking at the door? Excuse me.

(He EXITS. An awkward moment ensues. JAYNE finally attempts to break the ice)

Jayne: You know, most of my films were shot in CinemaScope.

Shyler: Is that 'Sin' with a 'C' or with an 'S'?

Jayne: 'C' as in the 'cinema', you retard.

Shyler: Maybe you'd prefer 'E' as in enema, dearest Siren of the 'Sin'-enema!

Jayne: How am I supposed to arouse you if you insist on cracking nasty jokes?

Shyler: Butt-crack jokes? You fail to turn me on, Wonder Woman, and I've got myself a maid…I can't wait to see you mincing around the house in a black and white miniskirt waving a feather duster.

(CLAUDE RETURNS wearing nothing but a BETTE DAVIS FRIGHT WIG, his BRIEFS, a round smear of red lip rouge, and a defiant don't-give-a-damn-expression. He puffs a CIGARETTE, waves his arms in circles, and rolls his eyes in his attempt to imitate the legendary actress)

Claude: This is a fine how-do-you-do, I must say! Miss Mansfield, what are you doing in bed with my boyfriend? I demand an explanation at once! This instant, will do, if you don't mind…

(He waits, but gets no reply)

Must I wait forever? You know how impatient I can be. Am I to be kept standing here until the Grim Reaper arrives? Really, you're being most unreasonable. I am not accustomed to being ignored!

Claude: *(CONT'D)* May I remind you, Miss Mansfield, that my mere presence demands top billing. You have now been demoted to a member of the supporting cast!

(Going to SHYLER)

You, my dear, have been elevated to the status of leading man…you may kiss me now.

(SHYLER grabs him, pulling him into the BED. They tumble around, and finally kiss each other tenderly)

Jayne: This really sucks. How am I supposed to seduce you, Claude, if you're Bette Davis? I'm not a Lesbian. I require one hundred percent all-male-men!

Shyler: Don't give up so easily, Jayne, I'm all the man you need. Claude is just a plaything. He bores me.

(CLAUDE is hurt and breaks away from their embrace. SHYLER continues to JAYNE)

Shyler: Can't you at least give me a little hand-job? Quit complaining and prove yourself already. Put your money where your mouth is and blow me away with all that technique, you're so proud of.

Jayne: Oh, fuck you, you've made your point, I'm sick of this role.

(She tears off her BLONDE WIG revealing SALT and PEPPER HAIR PINNED BACK a la JOAN CRAWFORD)

Why does everything have to be a contest?! You two scum get out of that bed and make it!

(They obey)

Jayne: And when you're finished making the bed, I want this entire house cleaned from top to bottom or I'll beat you both black and blue with a wire coat hanger!

Claude: Oh, my God, it's my arch nemesis, Joan Crawford! You bitch!

Jayne: If it's roles you want, Bette, watch out, I'm indestructible. I'll wipe you off that silver-screen faster than you can scour out my toilet bowl.

Claude: *(Turning on her)*

Can the crap, Crawford, and fasten your seat belt. It's going to be a bumpy night!

Shyler: *(Coming between them)*

Time out! Break it up, you two! I surrender to both of you! You both win. Joan, I think I like you better as Jayne, okay… and Claude, no offense, but you look ridiculous in drag—especially with that bulge—you forgot to tuck it in, sweetheart.

Claude: *(Tossing aside his WIG, he sits on the BED)*

Sorry, Shyler. I did the best I could. Funny… I feel a lot stronger as a woman. I wonder why they always complain.

Jayne: *(Picking up her BLONDE WIG)*

Because, you dopey guys are always trying to run the show. I have the right to be as sexy as I want. If that doesn't happen to turn you on, then I'll find some guy who is.

(She puts it on)

You can be as Queer as you want to be, Shyler. I don't care. If you think I'm phony, well, that's too bad.

(She sits next to CLAUDE)

Claude: I like you this way. You look beautiful… just like Jayne Mansfield. Maybe someday I'll learn to love you like a one hundred percent all-male man.

Shyler: That settles it. At the very least, we can still be friends. Isn't that what counts?

(He sits on the other side of JAYNE)

One for all, and all for one?

Jayne: Sure. What have we got to lose?

Claude: Our stereotypes are intact, what's left but my virginity?

(JAYNE and SHYLER do a take, grinning devilishly)

Shyler: You thinking what I'm thinking?

JAYNE: Divoone!!!

(FADE OUT. CURTAIN.)

THE END

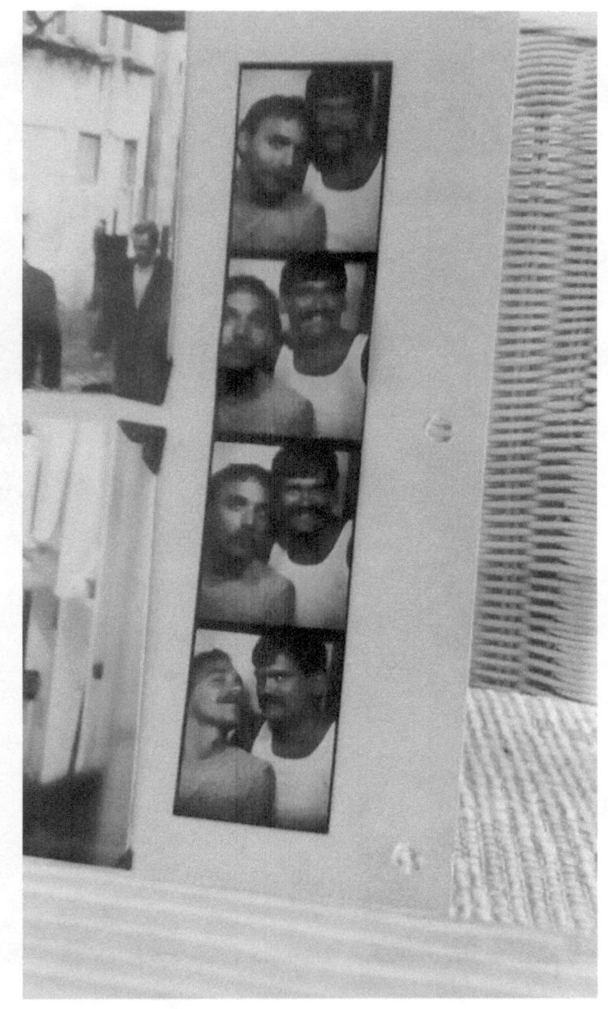

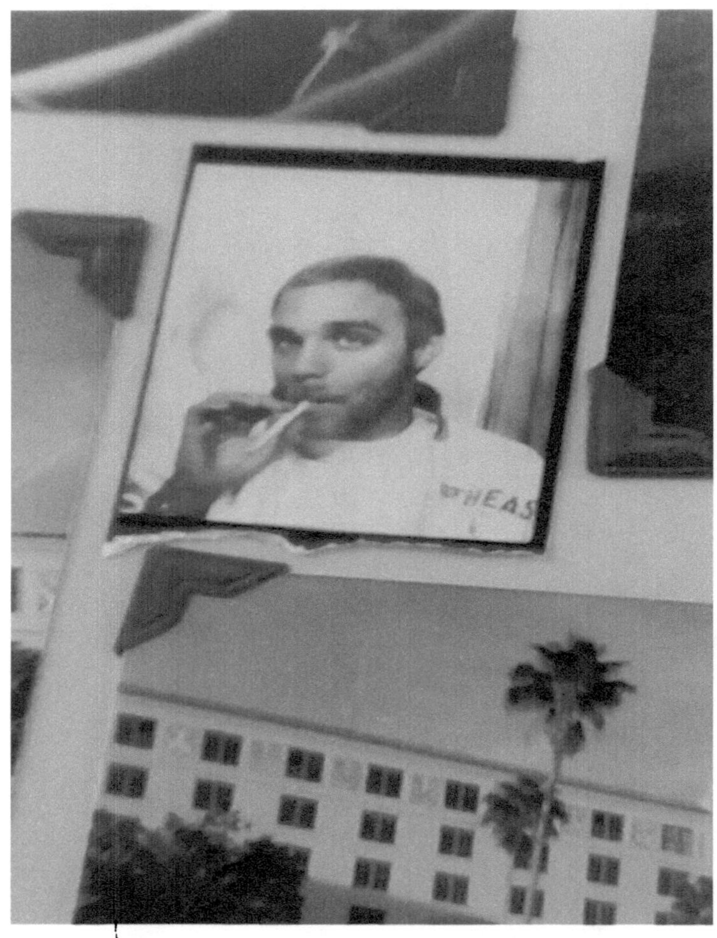

"Shamus Dragay"

An LGBTQ Screen Play
by Grant Sutor Vuille

SCENE 1

(Shamus Dragay was pondering the state of his mind one fine day while attempting to write his memoirs)

Shamus: *(Somewhat pensive)* What, oh, what do I begin to write about my unbelievable story? I pray, dear reader, you will not be too bored. My experiences and adventures are truly limited to say the least, yet, with my ability to exaggerate the truth at every turn, I promise to at least keep your eyelids from fluttering shut. Today we begin the adventure. The goal is to unravel my existence piece by sordid piece until which time sense can finally be made. Have you given up? I hope not. I need you as my counsel. Judge me if you will; please, be gentle, though, for I bruise easily…

(He finished writing and signed the first page of his diary. He then sighed, sat back, and enjoyed a sip of beer)

(CUT TO)

SCENE 2

(In a flashback to the beginnings of his life we see dear Shamus being born. The nurse lifts the child and puts him into his exhausted mother's arms)

Shamus: *(narrating)* Once upon a time I chose to be born. Though I'm not sure what some consider a choice? It was at exactly 11:16am May 2, 1950 that I popped forth. *(relieved)* Mama I'm so glad that's over with. Wonder if there's time to get in a set of tennis?

Papa: *(happily looking on)* Oh, great, another boy. This one's sure to be an ace on the tennis court.

Doctor: *(looking concerned)* Let's all try and get some rest. Anyone care for a sedative?

Shamus: Sure, Doc, and make it snappy. *(narrating)* And thus, I, Shamus Dragay, Faggot Supreme, came forth into the world and "Lo, the Angels of Death were heard to be singing in the east."

(As Mama, Papa, the Doctor, and attending staff admired our dear Shamus, the walls of the hospital dissolved away momentarily as the Angels of Death hovered beyond. They waved their shriveled arms as they chanted in song, their tattered flowing robes shimmered ominously)

Angels of Death: Beware, beware, oh, ye of little faith / Today is Born a King among souls / For surely, do you think we'd lie, motherfuckers?

Shamus: *(narrating)* God, those Angels of Death have a bad attitude; but so would you if you had their job to do every day. For sure!

(CUT TO)

SCENE 3

(In another moment, we the observers soared into the skies to have a heart to heart with God, our creator)

Shamus: *(Leaving his body briefly to speak on our behalf)* I'm happy to report that there is no such thing as an Angel of Death. Please disregard those ugly impostors who invaded the sanctity of my holy birth. You see, later in life when I began to become paranoid due to circumstances pertaining to the AIDS crisis, I began to think perhaps I was an angel of death myself. I was relieved to have been told by a gospel minister that there simply is no such thing. This was such a relief as I have felt this might have been a role the Almighty had assigned to me… is that so, dear Lord?

God: *(absolutely)* Sure, babe, t'would be a thankless job… if of course, I had need of any, and I don't.

Shamus: *(relieved)* It's just that, I was watching this movie about Leprechauns and they had this scary character called the Banshee—a spook of sorts seeming bent on the destruction of innocent victims. Oh, well…

God: Fear not, dear Shamus, all is well in the Universe thanks to me, naturally.

(CUT TO)

SCENE 4

(Shamus smiled with delight, comfortable in the knowledge that God did love him as he did all creation. He flew back to the Earth and as he soared above the mountaintops and valleys below, he thought back to his early life—all those magic moments that seemed to have this sad edge to them. Somehow, he felt he never did anything right, always falling short of real success or belonging)

Shamus: *(narrating)* And friends! Where are they? I needed them but they were nowhere to be found. I remember my friend Myles… *(pensive)*

Shamus: And there he was at the tender age of 10 with his friend Myles, in the woods by a pond with a waterfall, alone together. Mother Nature warmed their souls and freed their spirits.

(To Myles) I need some boogie.

Myles: I'm game, this is my secret place. Let's get down and dirty.

Shamus: Ah, what luck / Boogie to be had, and now / No reason to be sad / Doesn't it make you awfully glad?

Myles: The poetry thing turns me on, Shamus. Bump me 'til the Angels cry uncle.

(And boogie they did, and the fairies flew
and the elves danced tangos. When the heavy
hopping was done, they knew they had won,
and children they were not, what fun)

Shamus: *(sucking an after sex blade of grass)* The question remains, was it good or bad boogie? Sometimes I wonder… afraid some disapproving eye is looking over my shoulder.

Myles: *(with the knowledge of the Universe)* Boogie is always good. Boogie is never bad.

Shamus: *(smiling)* Be sure your partner agrees.

(They embraced tenderly, kissed, then plunged back into
the pond, naked as jaybirds, splashing wildly)

(DISSOLVE TO)

SCENE 5

(So years later we look at Shamus when he decided to become an MGM Hollywood starlet. There he was at the glorious studios minding his own business when the MGM Lion strolled by nonchalantly)

Shamus: Hi, Mr. MGM Lion.

MGM Lion: Hi, Shamus Dragay. Welcome to my MGM studios.

Shamus: *(Narrating)* From this moment on I just know I have to be a star at MGM. Unfortunately, MGM has long been dead, except on paper.

(To Lion) So, Mr. MGM Lion, I've decided to make my own films and star myself and my friends — if only I could scare up a few — Never say die!

(And so, amid the hustle and bustle of studio activity, Shamus observed all he could, then proceeded to find himself in the local MGM Fag Bar... you know, the one right across the street)

Shamus: *(narrating)* And so it came to pass that I, Shamus Dragay, desired to make a motion picture-the most important consideration being stars, and where to find them. It wasn't long before I realized that I should pick them up in the local Fag Bar. I prefer non actors as I insist on total realism. Of course, there would be a script-to be written as we went along.I'm a strong believer in cinema verite. Another requirement would be lots of S.E.X.! Without it, there can be no film. The sex to plot ratio should be at least 5 to 1.

Shamus: And naturally, all my films must be produced in the greatest of all widescreen processes ever developed-that is, ShamuScope69, developed of course by that illustrious filmmaker and author, Mr. Shamus Dragay.

(And now, back to the Fag Bar, just west of MGM)

Shamus: *(continuing narration)* So there I was in the Fag Bar with the great filmmaker himself, aka, myself — I was drunk as is per normal of most alcoholic wannabe's...

Shamus: *(to himself)* Say, Shamus... wake up... listen, I'm making this great Fag Film, Triple X natch, and I wonder if using my ShamuScope69 process in filming will be okay, or me thinks, too over-the-top?

Shamus: *(Sloshed to himself)* Nah, be my guest, Shamus, and not only can you use the process free, I'll be glad to act in any of the sex scenes myself. *(Elated)* Oh, that is good news. Thanks to me, myself, and I, it is really appreciated. *(narrating)* Before the evening was out, I had recruited several young studs for my Fag Film and all I need is a title and a start date. Let's see...how about "Fags Blowing with the Wind" or "All's Queer on the Western Front" ... I'll think of something...

(CUT TO)

SCENE 6

(In an intimate rendezvous with a fellow Fag, Shamus began to recruit his dream cast)

Shamus: *(narrating)* So, Once Upon a Time, when I was a young teenage adult, I, Shamus Dragay, made the choice to pursue my dream man... I mean, star for my Fag Film Phenomenon.

Lance: *(teasingly)* So, Shamus, you gorgeous hunk, what are you in to?

Shamus: You name it and I do it.

Lance: I do it all. The question is, can you keep up? Shamus Honey, name that tune.

(Thus went the conversation of the two would be one— night— lovers as they sat at the bar-pick-up-joint-starlet hangout— well, you be the judge. Stars are indeed born daily!)

(CUT TO)

SCENE 7

Lance: *(Narrating)* It was a dark and stormy night. I was working with my fellow cast members at striking the set for "The Night God" at the Texas Conservatory of Drama in Cactus, TX. This, dear reader, is a flashback. I was pulling nails from 2x4's when Mr. Lewis Leonard, a stud of 23—

Shamus: *(Pushing Lance aside)* —Excuse me, Lance darling, this is my gig!

(Beginning again) It was a dark and stormy night. I was working with my fellow cast members at striking the set for "The Night God" at the Texas Conservatory of Drama in Cactus, TX. This, dear reader, is a flashback. I was pulling nails from 2x4's when Mr. Lewis Leonard, a stud of 23-I was a mere 18 at the time-and he approached me and asked me to help him and the Professor of Lighting, Dr. Watson, get it? —WATT-SON, gather up lights and cables and put them away.

Louis: *(slyly)* Hey, cutie… yeah, you with the tight ass hole…

Shamus: You mean, I?

Louis: Yeah, who poured you into those jeans? Come on and help me and Dr. Watson put away this gear.

Lance: *(Stepping back into the scene, narrating)* Our dear Shamus began helping the young theatre student and his aging mentor Dr. Watson, the 'Lighting Professor' no less, put the heavy theatrical lights and cables away in storage closets.

Shamus: *(Pushing Lance away, begins narrating)* As I helped them put away all the tons of cable, lights, and equipment, I couldn't help but notice what a nice piece of ass that lovely Louis Leonard was.

Shamus: I really was surprised at myself because I'd spent so much time in my teenage years and now as a freshman in college trying to be straight,

Shamus: get dates with girls and get drunk at Delta Chi Fraternity make-out-parties. I had to face facts, nothing was working. My sex life was nil.

Louis: Stupid! My name's spelled Louis, not L.E.W.I.S!

Shamus: Same difference… Gee, bub, lighten up… *(narrating)* Why was he insulting my intelligence? Who cares how you spell it anyway.

Louis: Got a ride to the cast party for this turkey we just put onstage?

Shamus: No, I was going to walk. It's not far.

Louis: So be that way!

Shamus: *(narrating)* What's this, a guilt trip?

(To Louis) Okay… I'll ride over with you.

Watson: *(butting in)* If you girls are done, let's blow this joint.

Louis: *(double entendre intended)* I'm practically on my knees already care to help me out, Shamus? I'll handle the guys six feet and up... let's go, Dr. Watson, before he changes his mind. Shake that pretty tail of yours, Shamus, we're out'a here.

(CUTTO)

SCENE 8

(The three of them pile into the Professor's VW Volkswagen Bug)

Shamus: *(narrating)* And off we went,into the night, in the professor's old VW Bug. After we'd been riding a long while I became restless and somewhat suspicious.

Shamus: *(aloud to them both)* Say, where is this party at anyhow? I thought it was supposed to be across campus just a minute away.

Dr. Watson: Those cast parties are so dull.

Louis: Do you really want to go that bad?

Shamus: Well, yeah...

Dr. Watson: Okay, Shamus, but it's always a good idea to arrive fashionably late. So we'll get freshened up at my place first, and then, if we're still in the mood, we can go to your precious little cast party.

Shamus: *(quietly to self)* Again, with the guilt trips—what is it with these guys?

Louis: *(sarcastically)* Don't you like our company, Shamus?

Shamus: *(put-upon)* Sure... Yeah, I do... But I was really looking forward to being with everyone in the cast.

Louis: *(yawning)* Oh, those thespians are such bores! Worry not, darlin', that tired party won't begin for a bit. We were the first to leave strike, so we've got plenty of time.

Dr. Watson: *(irritably)* Don't be a bore, Shamus, we'll have a party of our own. Then later, if you still insist, we'll drop you off to play with your tacky little friends.

Shamus: Okay... thanks...

(The jolly threesome continued on into the night clear to the outer limits of Cactus, TX)

(CUT TO)

SCENE 9

(They finally arrived at Dr. Watson's townhome. Upon entering, Shamus became especially engrossed with dozens of theatrical posters everywhere. Many of them boasted Broadway credits for Dr. Watson. Being a novice, Shamus was in awe. After some naive ad-libs, the three settled down to brimming glasses of pink champagne)

Shamus: Dr. Watson, what was it like to work with actress Shirley Booth on Broadway?

Dr. Watson: *(snootily)* When you have earned the right to know I shall tell you and not before.

Louis: *(Pouring Shamus champagne)* Have some more to drink, sweet pea?

Shamus: It's awfully late. Shouldn't we be leaving to join the others?

Dr. Watson: *(outraged)* Not that again! You really are trying my patience, young man.

Louis: Drink up, we'll leave in a little bit.

Shamus: It's just that I don't want to miss all the fun.

Dr. Watson: Oh?! You're not enjoying yourself here with us? We don't bore you, do we, frat-rat-boy?

Louis: Stop worrying, we'll get you back to your little dorm buddies, all right, Shamus, honey?

(Some more time passed—so did another bottle of champagne and Shamus was definitely feeling no pain. All the while his hosts were exchanging wicked glances and toying with his insecurities. Their recruiting tactics were in full swing)

Dr. Watson: *(standing)* I'm exhausted. Sorry girls, it's my bedtime.

Louis: *(stretching and yawning)* Nancy, you got that right… time to catch forty winks… and a little man-pussy to boot.

Shamus: *(His heart begins pounding. Flushed with embarrassment he asks sheepishly)* I don't suppose you could give me a ride back?

Dr. Watson: *(stamping his feet like a sissy)* The impertinence! If you intend young lady to make the grade at this Drama College, then you had better begin by showing your superiors a little respect! Good night!

(Shamus waited until Shithead--excuse me--Dr. Watson had left the room before speaking to Louis)

Shamus: I didn't mean to piss him off. What do I do now? Can you give me a ride back to campus, Louis?

Louis: Oh, Shamus, grow up. Forget about the cast party. We're too drunk and too tired to go anywhere now. Come to bed… Let's go to my room. There's a spare bed in there.

(And so, reluctantly, and yet with his heart still pounding, Shamus followed while Louis led the way. Up the narrow stairs to his bedroom, they went. Inside the bedroom, Louis, without hesitation began helping to remove Shamus's clothes. There was a single bed across from another larger bed so Shamus threw himself upon it wearing only his BVD's. Moments later, to his surprise, he felt himself being crushed beneath the soft warm weight of Louis' naked body. He felt shocked… a thrilling adrenaline rush as Louis eased the pressure and began kissing and caressing him all over. Shamus made love to this man for a good ten minutes, his underwear long since tossed aside—naked—stripped bare and committed to the assault.)

Shamus: *(narrating)* He did things to me I'd previously only heard about in locker rooms filled with naked teenage jocks.

Shamus: My cock, my asshole ravishing pleasures hereto—for unknown. Yet, as I gave in, as the minutes passed, I slowly became consumed with shame—shame so deep, so penetrating that I suddenly froze, even before climaxing. I began to push him away. What if Mama found out?

(out loud, fearfully) … Mama… I can't… Stop… I can't do this!

Louis: *(tenderly)* Relax, everybody does this.

Shamus: *(getting up out of bed)* No… No they don't.

Louis: Yes, some do, Shamus. Come back to bed… Please…

Shamus: *(pacing anxiously)* No, I can't, I've got to get back to the dorms.

(Dr. Watson bursts into the room)

Dr. Watson: *(honey-coated allure)* Hmmm… well well, boys, what seems to be going on in here? May I assist in any way?

Shamus: *(losing it)* Get out! Get out!!!

(Dr. Watson minced a twittering about-face and caught his breath at the top of the stairs outside the bedroom)

Louis: Cut it out, Shamus, and get back in bed.

(But Shamus was almost dressed. He was very upset, massively distraught, and hyperventilating)

Shamus: I am out of here… NOW!!!

Louis: Don't be angry. Please…

(In a flash Shamus was dressed and bounding out of the room, passing Dr. Watson on the landing who simply glared. Down the stairs and out the front door into the pouring rain he ran. Thunder and lightning boomed and seared the sky.)

(Shamus suddenly realized he was running barefooted in deep puddles. Stopping abruptly, he tossed his head back and bellowed heavenward)

Shamus: *(nearly sobbing)* Oh God, oh God… my sneakers!

(He was crying now. With a burst of adrenaline, he ran back into the townhouse, up the stairs, past the affronted Dr. Watson, still glaring haughtily, into Louis's room where he grabbed his sneakers.)

Shamus: I forgot my sneakers.

Louis: Don't be upset. Come here a minute.

Shamus: *(angry)* No. You're All Queers!

(The sneakers were on and Shamus was once again finding himself dashing out and down the stairs as Dr. Watson snorted disapprovingly)

Dr. Watson: *(feigning disgust, clucking)* Your behavior is shocking and out of line!

(At the bottom of the stairs Shamus turned and exploded in a furious rage)

Shamus: QUEERS! Stupid Fucking Fags! FAGS!

(CUT TO)

SCENE 10

(Out into the Texas storm Shamus ran. Oh, yes, this was twenty-four years ago, for he was so much older now, sick with AIDS, and still trying to make sense of his past. Running, stumbling, crying, praying; he splashed through hundreds of muddy puddles trying desparate1y to remember the way to campus)

Shamus: *(narrating)* Yes, this was twenty four years ago. Now, battling AIDS, this incident seems so trivial. But it was the beginning of my Homosexual existence. Still, I struggle to make sense of the past.

Shamus: That night I walked and ran for what seemed like hours in the pouring rain. Unsure of the direction a car finally pulled up some 45 minutes later and a kind gentlemanly businessman offered assistance.

Man: Can I give you a lift somewhere?

(Shamus hopped into the man's car dripping wet)

Shamus: *(exhausted)* Yes, thank you, sir. Thank you very much. Can you please take me to my dorm at the campus? I'm not sure how far it is.

(The thoughtfully kind gentleman was smoking a pipe)

Man: You were headed in the right direction. You seem distressed. That's why I stopped. Are you alright?

Shamus: Yes. I am now.

(For a short while they drove in silence. Finally, the man at the wheel spoke up)

Man: I live near here. Would you like to come over and take a shower... get cleaned up?

Shamus: *(growing suspicious)* No thank you. I just need to get back to the dorm. I'm in enough trouble already.

Man: *(warmly, enticing)* You'd be no trouble at all. We could get you out of those wet clothes and into a nice warm bed. We don't want you catching cold. I'll cook breakfast in the morning.

Shamus: *(nearing tears)* As tempting as that sounds... one trauma is, I mean, at a time... Please, sir, I just need to get home right away.

Man: All right then... as you wish.

(And that was that, to the Dorms they went, and in a few minutes, they were parked outside. The gentleman took Shamus's hand in his and squeezed, not letting go his grip)

Man: *(suave, sophisticated, polite)* Are you affable to changing your mind and coming over to my home? I promise to bring you back here later... sure you don't want to come over to my place?

Shamus: *(hesitating)* Yes, well... thank you, but no, no, I can't. Thanks... thanks for the ride. You're a lifesaver. Good-bye.

(Like baby, that was indeed that. The man let go his grip and Shamus bolted out of the car. Unfortunately, it was still raining as he made a mad dash for his dorm. After discovering that he had been locked out he ran, from window to window, banging on the glass in an effort to wake someone. Finally, he succeeded in arousing a sleepy student who grudgingly let him climb through the window. Shamus then made his way into the hall and back to his own room where he let himself in with his key. He tried to be quiet but his three other dormmies gradually woke up, and seeing how upset he still was, tried to comfort him. From the future Shamus reminisced as these incidents occurred from the moment he left the gentleman's car)

Shamus: *(narrating)* When he finally let go my hand, I jumped out of the car. It was still raining and I made a mad dash for the dorm. I had lost my innocence, and it hurt bad—devastating—like losing a loved one. I wonder today how my life might have turned out if this far away event had never happened. Weeks of a funeral-like depression followed. Years did not ease the vividness of these memories. Now, in the present I think of two ex-lovers who tested positive for AIDS. My life today is in weird sexual limbo, having tried many times to love men deeply, and even a few women. What a shambles my love life has been. Yet I feel the desperate, constant need to be loved and to love others. One day, before I die, I must learn to love completely, unconditionally.

(CUT TO)

SCENE 11

(And so, one day in the present, Shamus was visiting a friend named George who had full blown AIDS. His girlfriend waved good-bye. Now they were alone together)

Shamus: *(Thinking nervously to himself)* Oh, no… I'm Shamus the babysitter! … No, no, that's not right, I'm Shamus the caregiver…

(Poor George was indeed very sick. He had sores and rashes all over his body. He had not long to live and was on dozens of medications. Shamus sat and talked quietly with him as he lay in his hospital bed at home)

George: Yeah, Shamus, I can't really figure how I got this disease. We waste our time worrying about it. There's a lot of different ways to get it and I just figured that I got it through the use of IV drugs. But just between you and me, it could have been some other way.

Shamus: What do you mean, George? Are you telling me you—

George: *(cautioning)* —Now, like I say, like a lot of this, that, and the other things going on in group and such… I just don't figure it's none of anybody's business. This is between you and me… so don't tell nobody, okay?

Shamus: Even Annie doesn't know?

George: She don't know shit—just you—right now I'm telling you. When I was in prison, I did a little smoking… from time to time… you know what I mean…

Shamus: By smoking you mean… Seriously? Nobody knows? That's cool. Wish you hadn't said anything. I'm not good at keeping secrets.

George: Not only did I smoke it, I took it up the dirt-shoot from time to time.

Shamus: *(Pondering this news)* I kind 'a wish you hadn't told me, but I'll try and keep it a secret. George, as God is my witness, you shouldn't be ashamed to be Gay.

George: Let's just say I'm more comfortable being socially acceptable. And I like chicks, too.

Shamus: God loves you either way... Why shouldn't be care? Sex between a man and a woman is a sin so what is the difference if we choose a partner of the same sex... Biblical shit is freaky, anyway, you're fucked if you do or screwed if you don't. God has to love us because He gave us life. He made us the way we are. I just feel confused if I dwell on it.

(DISSOLVE TO)

SCENE 12

(Shamus sat and wrote in his diary one foggy morning. He had just gotten word that his darling ex-lover had died. His thoughts are revealed in layered montages of imagery and sound)

Shamus: *(writing quietly while narrating his thoughts)* Last Thursday, one my ex-lovers died. His name was Eddie, born on June 26th 1958 he died on April 23rd 1992. He died of complications associated with AIDS, pneumocystis pneumonia to be precise. I had hoped to visit him in a few weeks when I was down in Florida on vacation. He was two months short of his 34th birthday. Ironically, two years ago when I was living in Kentucky with another ex-lover, we lost our precious kitty Junie Moon on exactly the same day—April 23rd. For about 10 years I have been rather obsessed with numbers and dates. It's called numerology and it has psychic implications for me. I can't explain it, but it touches something deep within me. I believe it's just one way God sends his many messages to us using signs and symbols. I believe God lives within us all and that he is taking good care of Eddie and Junie Moon, Tinkerbell—

Shamus: *(CONT'D)* another kitty—and my precious Doriana—yet another kitty—both of whom passed away on the same day, also two years apart on December 3rd, 1989-91. I want people to remember Eddie. If Marilyn Monroe and James Dean can be bigger stars after their death, then why not Eddie? But then, I forget that God knows Eddie, therefore the whole Universe knows Eddie—so, why worry? All of us are stars in the eyes of the Lord...

(FADE TO)

SCENE 13

(Here was Shamus on the tennis court one sunny afternoon with his friend Jim. Jim and his new racket decided to cream Shamus with a tennis ball after a particularly grueling point which resulted in victory for our hero. Jim slammed the ball at Shamus, hitting him in the back as he was walking to the service line.

This was very un-sportsman-like. Normally, whenever Jim would lose a point he would smash his racket onto the court. Because this was a new one, smashing a ball at Shamus seemed a better idea. Not so. Shamus did try to curb his rage momentarily)

Jim: *(surprised at himself)* Oh, Shamus, I'm sorry, I didn't mean to hit you like that.

(Our Shamus' blood began to boil, because naturally, he's being his typical good-sports-man-like self, so he's not going to say a thing even though Jim has been inhuman for the last two sets.)

Shamus: That's okay. Let's quit.

(Shamus walked slowly to the gate—somewhat calmly, trying hard not to show his anger. Jim walked to the rear of the court as if to begin serving the next game)

Jim: I said I'm sorry. Where are you going?

Shamus: Let's quit. I've had enough.

Jim: *(tersely)* Hold on, I gotta get the balls.

(Shamus walked slowly to Jim's new Toyota Pacea sports car in the parking lot. Once there he simply stood silently by the car, facing away from the court as Jim approached from behind. Shamus was taking a few deep breaths and mentally trying to picture a babbling brook in a rain forest. He didn't know what to say or do at this point, but he knew he must remain calm. Acting like nothing had happened came to mind)

Jim: *(approaching)* Dammit, I said I was sorry!

(Jim opened the car door for him. Shamus got in and picked up his house keys on the floorboard. Shamus then settled back and shut the door gently. Jim, now in the driver's seat next to him, is very sensitive about his new car and had in the past accused Shamus of slamming the door. The door is somewhat light to be fair and shuts with quite a bang no matter how easily one makes the move to close it)

Jim: Thanks for slamming the door!

Shamus: *(losing it)* Fuck you!

(Jim raised his elbow and nearly hit Shamus in the face with it but stopped short)

Jim: *(angrily)* God Damn it!

Shamus: *(raging)* Fuck you! Take me home! Now!

(They drove the five miles to Shamus's home in silence. They pulled up to the townhome where he lived with his sister. They stopped, the car idled. Silence. For good measure, Jim decided to remind him of good car-door manners)

Jim: *(sarcastically)* Will you please not slam the door!

(Shamus got out of the car and in the process of doing so he gave Jim the ultimatum)

Shamus: I never want to speak to you again. I won't be coming to the Positive People AIDS meetings either.

Jim: Suit yourself—just don't slam the door.

Shamus: Shut it yourself.

(Shamus went into the house leaving Jim's car door wide open, forcing him to put on the emergency brake, get out, walk around and do the job himself. Shamus did not look back. He went to his room and fumed. He did not hear from Jim for a while. Later, alone in his room with his cats, Shamus grew very depressed. The consequences of losing one's temper are great. This had been a good lesson in how to destroy a relationship)

Shamus: *(narrating)* I really need to get a grip on the anger within me. Today was a good lesson on what not to do next time I'm in a tense situation. From this moment on I promise to exercise more self-control.

(DISSOLVE TO)

SCENE 14

(It was exactly 5:05 am in the morning, only about 12 hours after the infamous tennis incident.

Shamus was in bed with his cats, Seymour, Tina, and Bandit. He had been up, writing down this sordid tennis—tale in his journal. Still, he could not sleep. So many inner conflicts tortured him)

Shamus: *(quietly, aloud)* I've done it again—destroyed another friendship. Anger did it—blind anger. So many friends...there was Mark who opposed my Ascorbate vs. AIDS theories-who, after taking me out a dozen times, giving me presents, just suddenly gave me the silent treatment.

Shamus: In group he still made jokes about Vitamin-C at my expense. He died shortly after his Valentine's Day party which I grudgingly went to. I remember another friend who just hung up on me, then wrote a nasty note later, all because I was drunk when he called. He thought I should move to Hollywood to become a star—great idea, but not very practical. Candace, my friend in Boston, after hinting for years that I come for a visit, when I finally do, she spends four days baiting me with digs about who's more successful than whom. Then there was Len in the Gay Men's Chorus. I tried to be his friend, he wanted sex. The two don't mix. Last time I went to Florida, my old friends Bill and Sally wouldn't return my calls, yet they write all year like they miss me. Made me think they're scared of people with the AIDS condition. Mike and George are the same way. Now, they don't write or call. I reach out to people and get nothing in return. Thank God for my cats. (praying) Dear God, please show me the way. Teach me to be tolerant. Teach me to love more. Teach me to forgive others and let go of the conflicts. Amen.

(Shamus turned over in bed, petting his cats and saying goodnight to each of them. It had been a difficult day. All God's creatures need and deserve love and respect. Conflicts rarely make any sense in the aftermath)

(DISSOLVE TO)

SCENE 15

(Shamus was in the park a few weeks later with his friend Tandy who had just lost his lover to AIDS. They sat on a bench together enjoying the weather as best they could, attempting to comfort one another)

Shamus: *(referring to Tandy's dearly departed lover)* It's tough… really tough, I know. Right now, I feel a lot of anger. My companion Eddie suffered terribly as did your lover. Guess that's the way it goes. Another dear friend bites the dust and makes a reservation in the clouds. I'm truly sorry, Tandy, though I feel helplessly misunderstood, I do try to make sense of things… I'm just so very sorry for what we're having to deal with and how agonizingly sad it all is…

Tandy: *(close to tears)* Oh, Shamus, how can I live without my dear sweet Anthony? I just can't accept that he's gone, I just can't.

Shamus: I sometimes feel I can't live another day. To lose a friend is devastating. I'm ashamed of myself for not loving life more… every moment a test of our will to continue living.

Tandy: There must be a poem—perhaps some words written down to describe how we feel. This can't be the end to the script. Where have all the ShamuScope69 cameras gone?

Shamus: They're in storage waiting on a re-write of the script. *(pausing to reflect)* There are thousands of songs about love and loss. I wrote a song about Eddie. I call it "Eddie's Song". I wrote it three days before what would have been his 34th birthday.

Tandy: *(smiling, a glimmer of anticipation)* Oh, please, Shamus, sing it for me.

Shamus: *(singing "Eddie's Song" by Shamus Dragay)*

There was this guy named, Eddie /
(C7) He was my buddy and my friend /
(Bb) I miss him more than my Teddy /

(Shamus suddenly broke dow in tears. Tandy comforted him as best he could)

Tandy: Oh, please, Shamus, don't cry. Your song is beautiful. Please continue.

Shamus: *(recovering)* I'm sorry Tandy. I'll start again. *(singing "Eddie's Song")*

There was this guy named, Eddie /
(C7) He was my buddy and my friend /
(Bb) I miss him more than my Teddy /
(F) Oh, God, my love is not pretend /
Save a place for me in Heaven /
(Bb) Dear, Eddie, my sweet Ba'Boo /
(C7) Gone are the days when we were together /
So what else is new or known /
(C7) Give me a break and forgive me my friend /
(Bb) I miss you every day, hey, hey /Should'a built that home together / Save me a place in the clouds /
Save me a place in the clouds.

(Tandy begins crying more and so does Shamus. After blowing their noses together they recover)

Shamus: I also have a poem.

Tandy: About Eddie? Oh, please recite it.

Shamus: *(reciting "Eddie's Birthday" poem)*

Today is Eddie's birthday, but he is not Here /
He died 2 months and 3 days ago on April 23, 1992 /
Eddie had AIDS and was Very sick /
His doctors had abandoned him, or was it vice versa? /
It's hard to Blame anyone because everyone worked hard /
To save his life --------
Eddie fought hardest of All /
He was a wonderful person /

I Loved Him very much but I failed him /
I could Not communicate my love to him enough /
Eddie Needed lots of love and lots of attention /
If you love someone, I beg you to let them Know /
Eddie is always in my dreams /
I know I must say good-bye /
His presence is among Us still and has been since June 26, 1958 /
I didn't buy you a present this year /
This Poem will have to do, forgive me /
God, please bless Eddie in Heaven /
Save his soul Forever and ever /
Find him a good job up There in the clouds /
Save us who loved him a spot near him in the same department /Please, God, give him a bonus every year on his Birthday / You won't regret it, he's a hard Worker /Send him our love…

(Again, Tandy and Shamus sniffle and sob. They get up from their bench and walk off into a green field arm and arm)

(FADE TO)

SCENE 16

(Shamus is getting drunk with another friend Freddy in a local Gay bar called The Sizzling Meat Market. He was going on about Eddie as usual)

Freddy: *(concerned)* Don't you think you've had enough?

Shamus: *(drunkenly)* But I haven't told you about the quilt I made for Eddie in the Name's Project… A sea of quilts memorializing the fallen heroes of AIDS.

Freddy: That was thoughtful, I didn't know.

Shamus: I made it out of his Act-UP and Queer Nation T-shirts. His Mom gave them to me after he died. His quilt # is 169. That adds up to a 7. The 3 N's, Glenn Niola are 7's numerologically. His psychic # is 7777 and 7777 is his psychic phone # so you can reach him anytime you want in the cosmos.

Freddy: *(doubtful)* That's nice, but I really think you ought to let me give you a ride home.

Shamus: *(Slurring his words, inebriated)* Okay, but don't tell Dan. I think Eddie would approve that I'm his lover's — Lover! You know, our friend Stewart's boyfriend, Dan... Stewart doesn't know we're having an affair, so keep it quiet okay, Freddy?

(Freddy is so uncomfortable. He excuses himself after a moment and moves away quickly)

Freddy: Oh, well, that's cool, Shamus. *(Rolling his eyes, he scans the bar distractedly)* ... Gotta go... Take it easy, buddy... Someone's looking for me....

(CUT TO)

SCENE 17

(Shamus was really horny. He felt like cum-city. Wouldn't it be nice to shoot his load directly into the ShamuScope69 camera lens and put an end to this movie? No, No, no chance. We find our Hero doing his jack-off thing, quite literally, spraying his manhood in huge milky glops on our hungry awaiting faces thanks to the realistic courtesy of the ShamuScope69 wide-angle lens. We, the audience, feel as though we have been thrust into Shamus's bedroom to enjoy the dramatic climax. Now, as the last drops of cum dribble forth, he speaks directly to us)

Shamus: *(relieved, to us he speaks, narrating)* So, gentle viewer, you thought my saga was through. Oh, my, no. That 'The End' sign is still waiting in the wings. We just needed a little break, a chance to be together in the flesh. Was it as good for you as it was for me?

I do hope so. *(pausing to reflect sadly)* So many beautiful people and friends have died of AIDS. I feel my soul being whittled away by time. The emotional sadness of the loss of close friends and lovers wells deep in my heart. I feel as though my heart might burst at any minute. But look... hear me, sweet darlings, I, Shamus Dragay, Faggot Supreme, needs love, love, LOVE!

(Enter Dan, the hot-blooded Latino)

Dan: You're bored with me, aren't you, Shamus? You don't love me anymore, do you?

Shamus: Nonsense, I've got lust to spare. Come over here, pull down your pants and sit on my face.

(Dan decides to split. He'd made up his mind long ago and wanted nothing more to do with this wacky self-loathing Shamus Dragay)

Dan: No, it's over between us. I could never love you as much as I love my Stew-Pot. Good-bye.

(Dan slammed the door and was gone. Shamus cried and cried, begging him to come back but it was too late. Shamus was good at adlibbing sobs and pleas for love and attention)

(FADE TO)

SCENE 18

(Shamus was not feeling too good. He was not sick exactly, unless you count being neurotic sick. He was shivering and crying underneath the covers of his bed in the fetal position)

Shamus: *(sobbing, talking to us)* My lover Dan does not seem much interested in me. He seems to prefer his live-in-lover Stewart... Stew-Pot...That eastward old Fuck. Why do I always fall for the wrong guy? I know, I need support. Counseling... I'll call someone on the phone. But who? I've lost all my friends. What the hell, I'll fake it.

(He picks up the phone and pretends to begin talking to an imaginary friend)

Shamus: *(sadly)* Whoever you are, dear friend, what must I do to revive my spirit?

(Shamus imitates the voice of the imaginary friend) Why don't you meditate and pray to God 24 hours a day? *(his voice)* What a fabulous idea. I'll begin right away.

(Shamus hung up the phone and began to arrange himself in the lotus position for meditation)

(FADE TO)

SCENE 19

(And so, it came to pass that Shamus Dragay was feeling a bit blue so decided to hit another Fag Bar one evening. He had fortunately found himself a temporary AIDS infected lover by the name of Mooniebutt)

Mooniebutt: *(swilling beer)* You know, Shamus, my boy, lover extraordinaire, I think this affair is getting a bit too sticky. I can't, as they say, take it anymore.

Shamus: *(aghast and smashed)* But, I don't understand? I've been at your beck and call for nearly 3 days! We've had sex on the hour, every hour, morning, noon, and night! My testosterone level has risen by beaucoup degrees in-so-far as I've been sprouting chest hairs I'd here-to-for been sadly lacking!

Mooniebutt: Yes, dear-heart, but we have nothing in common and you're getting on my nerves. We've got to cool it!

Shamus: *(sadly)* But I thought that you loved me? Just the other night while I pounded you with my swollen manhood you were moaning grateful sighs of lusty love verbs.

Mooniebutt: Alas, then, I admit, dear Shamus, that I'm bored. Besides, I told my lover of 10 years that our affaire was over and I could never love you as I love him. He is irreplaceable—you, unfortunately, are not.

Shamus: Am I not your friend, too, dear Mooniebutt?

Mooniebutt: Not so, Shamus.

Shamus: You do not love me as a friend?

Mooniebutt: Forget me, yes, dear boy, and breathe an easy little sigh of relief. The strife of life can be difficult during heart—lust. Be gone, now, for my true love Wartsaway will soon be here. I wish to get drunk first so as to tolerate his advanced age.

Mooniebutt: I knew he'd never leave me and that's why I snagged him long ago. Security is a must in the grim world we Queers do live.

Shamus: My heart is once again broken. Will this rejection saga never end? I must find a new heartthrob soon or I may perish.

(And so, Shamus went to a back corner of the bar and continued to drink away his troubles. In a short while a new stud-of-largecock - had made his acquaintance. Oh, happy day!)

(CUT TO)

SCENE 20

(Shamus, a great guy, or was he? Say what? In all the confusion and delusion, he made another phone call. This was a 900# at $3.00 a minute. A sexy dude named Tim answered at the other end. Shamus rubbed his crotch but was too blue to pop)

Tim: *(lustily)* So your name is Shamus Dragay... hmmm... that's a sexy name, fella... So, stud-muffin, what do you like to do, eh?

Shamus: *(sadly)* I'm bummed out. I've lost all my friends... hence, you know, a touch of the blues.

Tim: Ohhh, that's too bad, I'm not a therapist, but I bet I know a way to cheer you up-got my long hard cock in my hand and I'm thinkin' of you! ... How about you? Got that rock hard monster in a strangle hold for me? Just stroke it, baby, stroke it nice... hmmm... Baby...

Shamus: Really? You want me? You really want me?

Tim: Who are you, Sally Field? Accept your Oscar, Shamus, and all my love along with it. Ohhh, yeah, I wish you were here so you could cum in my ear and stroke that load right into my brains...

Shamus: I got'ta go now, sorry, this isn't working, I can't get it up.

(Shamus hung up the phone and threw himself to the floor. He lay there for a long time)

(CUT TO)

SCENE 21

(Shamus had a dream that he was in a film starring Clint Eastwood. This was quite exciting. He was a nervous wreck on the set just anticipating meeting the legendary star. He arrived at the set a couple pounds thinner having just barfed his guts out in the street outside the studio gates. On the set the Assistant Director approached him)

Assistant Director:	Now remember, Shamus, as cute as you are please refrain from staring directly into Clint's eyes. He is most sensitive to good-looking young men such as you. He simply doesn't want to be tempted. It would cause delays on the set waiting for him to emerge from his bouncing trailer. Got it?
Shamus:	So, that's cool. Say, will the camera pick me up in the midst of all these extras?
Assistant Director:	Sure, don't worry about it, you're a natural, so don't sweat it, bub.

(How lucky, soon Clint had caught Shamus's eye. Production was halted so the two could retire for a quickie in the famous bouncing trailer. The crew stood around bored to tears. The cast of extras were pea--green with envy, as Scarlett O'Hara would say… Clint's leading lady contemplated a law suit… She too was pea-green with the proverbial envy, a common trait in ever-so-glamorous Hollywood, USA)

(CUT TO)

SCENE 22

(And in the Heavens above, Lo, God said:)

God: Go Shamus, you young middle-aged stud-muffin, unto the breatherin out among the flocks of the un-gay and do your best to convert them to the glories of Gay-hood. The LGBTQ community is desperate for your services.

(But Shamus was a'feared, and like, pretty damn scared. He was trembling mucho-macho as he tried vainly to keep from falling off his little cloud in the sky)

Shamus: *(scared shitless)* Oh, God of Rock Hudson, Oh, God of Liberace, Eddie Niola, Brad Davis, etc. etc. etc., doth thou really want me to go forth into this scary hetero red-necked world You have created and attempt to convert these non-homos into Gay loving tolerant respectful folks? Is this wise?

God *(booming voice)* Shamus, do not question, Oh mighty Me, the Lord thy God, Creator of the Universe! … But since you ask, I'll do my best to answer you. The Heteros are overpopulating the earth with unhappy unwanted children. It was a big mistake to tell them to be fruitful and multiply and to condemn Gays-which I never actually did, it's just that the ass-holish Zealots read that interpretation into the text. I don't personally feel that way at all. People with hate in their hearts will say and do anything in the name of Jesus, one of my many children, just as you and the red-necked ones also are-you're all my naughty little babies and I love every fuckin' one of you. Believe Me when I say I've had a change of heart because the Earth needs more Gay, Queer, Bi-Curious, and Lesbian people.

God: Now go and spread the word--but stay out of trouble, okay? Jesus made a big mistake when he allowed himself to be crucified... That was not in My original plan. That's a guilt trip people all over the world still suffer.

(And so, Shamus went out into the hetero—world and spoke of being Gay and the virtues thereof—and Lo, he was stoned, tarred and feathered everywhere. In sad disgust, Shamus returned again to the clouds in Heaven and spoke to the Almighty God.)

Shamus: *(disappointed to the max)* God, they treat me so badly, those fucking Heteros. I seem to have no power to spread the word.

God: Have no fear, Shamus. From thence forth, you shall have the power to smite the Hetero enemies who do not believe in the holiness of Homo's. Go forth once again unto the multitudes and give Gay Power another shot.

Shamus: Thanks, God, you're the greatest, Oh Holy Great One!

(Dear, Hetero-Minority, don't be restless believe me, this tale will not disappoint you)

(CUT TO)

SCENE 23

(Shamus went forth into the East, and Followers from Whence and Fro came to hear his words and see his handsome face and to bask in his manly presence. Now that he has been blessed by Godly powers of persuasion what could possibly go wrong?)

Shamus: *(gratefully)* Good citizens of the world, how good of you to come hear my words.

(Just then some young studly Gay Bashers dared crash in on his serene-scene with their foul words and taunts of evil violence)

Gay Bashers: *(rudely)* Hey, Shamus, we know you're just a Fag. Why don't you die of AIDS and do us all a favor! Yeah! Ha, ha, ha!

(They chortle nauseating platitudes and ugly slurs throughout the scene)

Shamus: *(gently)* Dear, Gay Bashers, Haters of Homo's, go from us who are Gay. Gaze at thyselves in the mirror and marvel at your own Inner Gayness. Those who hate are hiding from themselves the Truth. Heaven is Within, as our Lord Jesus, one of trillions of God's Sons used to preach.

Gay Bashers: *(nastily)* No way, man, we're not fallin' for that old line. Instead, we're goin'a bash you and your followers!

Shamus: *(ominously)* Not so, Closeted-Ones, who bash only to disguise their True Natures. An LGBTQ Profit once wrote, "All Men Are Gay, All Women Are Lesbians". Go now in peace and I'll not harm thee.

Gay Bashers: *(gleefully)* Horseshit, let's go to work boys, yeah! Let's bash 'em and trash 'em til they bleed!

(With that said, they began to threaten the followers of Shamus, his Disciples—Disci—Pals—with bats, sticks, knives, and sizzlingly harsh words)

Shamus: *(resigned)* Fools, I warned thee, did I not?

(With his hand raised Heavenward, Shamus smote the Gay Bashers with lightning bolts and they fell to the ground as crying babies would, begging for mercy)

Gay Bashers: *(crying and pleading)* Oh, fair and wise Shamus, how could we have been so foolish as to doubt you. Please, spare us your wrath and we promise to go forth into the world peacefully as your newly anointed Gay subjects.

Shamus: *(happily)* Thank you, dear former Gay Bashers, and welcome to the family of Gay Men & Lesbians.

(The huge crowd applauded and everyone was happy. Everyone was hugging and kissing, and kissing and hugging, and one could not tell which sex was with which sex because it simply didn't matter, and temporarily, all was right with the world.)

(DISSOLVE TO)

SCENE 24

(Wherever Shamus went he was filled with the spirit and love of being. Lesbians and Gays began to worship him but he tried to discourage them from this practice)

Shamus: *(narrating)* They thought of me as the Messiah. I tried to tell them that each and every one of them was the Messiah. God is our creator. We are the mind, the body, and the spirit of God. One only has to look deep within… Heaven is Within… relax and soak up God…

(One beautiful sunny day Shamus found himself at a luxurious Gay Seaside Resort and gradually he became surrounded by a large # of Gay people while basking poolside)

Gay Person #1: *(gushing)* Oh, Shamus, surely you are the Lord!

Shamus: That's what you say, I say We.

Gay #2: *(overzealous)* Yes, Shamus, you are the Messiah! We've been waiting for you to show up for lo these many previous 2,000 years.

Shamus: *(politely, calmly)* That's what you say, but I am not He—Please, look around you and see His reflection everywhere and in your own hearts as well. The Lord also resides in his Heaven with our long-lost loved ones who are now His Angels guarding over us. Do not doubt this, for it brings peace to the body, mind, and soul.

Gay #3: Dear, Shamus, what loved ones have you lost?

Shamus: As many as there are stars in the sky. To name a few, there was Eddie, Tinkerbell, Doriana, Corabella, and my precious eternal Junie Moon. I am no stranger to life, loss, or death. I am of God, but not God. We are all God as His Spirit resides within... The Universe is at the tip of our nose and we are One Within it's awesome embrace. What power I do have comes only from God; a source, yes, the source within all beings of light. AIDS is a conflict among God's life forms, but with care, love, and large doses of Vitamin-C, all viral and bacteriological forces may be kept at bay, and, in check. We will be vegetarians and no longer sacrifice Our precious Creatures of God... I urge you to spread the word.

Gay #1: *(enthusiastically)* We will be your Dis-Ci-Pals... get it?

Gay #1: *(Welcoming his friends gathered)* PALS!!! We will tell the world to take this Vitamin-C you speak of... We will eat our fruits and veggies and never harm animals again!

Gay #2: Yes, please allow us to be your Disci-Pals!

Gay #3: We will be as out-of-the-closet as the four musketeers to support all the LGBTQ family... Gays & Lesbians, Trans, Queers, the Bi-Curious... Everyone! Hurray!

Shamus: Dear LGBTQ Lesbians, Gay Lovers of Gays, Bisexual, Trans, & Queer, what are your names?

Gay #1: My name is Fritz. My Trans friend here is Tania.

Gay #2: My name is Stan! My Bisexual friend here is Bruce.

Gay #3: And my name is Linus, named after the Nobel Prize winning Scientist who did massive research on Vitamin-C against disease—Linus Pauling. He also recommends all AIDS victims to take large daily doses of precious Ascorbate.

Gay #3: My Lesbian & Queer friends here are Lyla & Queststar all wish to join your team to save the world from bigotry and prejudice.

Shamus: Bless you one and all! Welcome Disci-Pals! Welcome Vegetarians! Lovers of All God's Creatures who eat their fruits & veggies... Ascorbate, being the technical name of Vitamin-C, will be our slogan. Ascorbate verses AIDS. Dear LGBTQ friends, from this day forward we will travel the world and spread the word of God, Peace, Love, and the Miracle of Vitamin-C!!!

(The LGBTQ men and women embraced one another filled with joy. With gusto they began to cavort around the pool as young schoolboys and girls might do. In no time they were naked as jaybirds, diving in and out of the pool, basking in the rays of the Lord above and within)

(CUT TO)

SCENE 25

(Things were going fairly well for the Disci-Pals and Shamus until one dark and ominous day when they reached a raging rivers edge.)

A crowd of followers had gathered as they preached the word of Gay Pride when some nasty Cops—policemen, put it upon themselves to follow the orders of a notorious red-necked Judge and arrest them. Their flimsy charge was for disturbing the peace... How sad is that?)

Cop #1: *(Harsh and Nasty)* You faggots have got no permit to congregate here!

Fritz: You cops are welcome to join our merry band!

Stan: Leave us in peace, Oh red-necked-ones, as you are violating our civil & constitutional rights to assemble!

Linus: For God's sake be reasonable. Peace, Love, and Vitamin-C!!!

(The LGBTQ crowd who had assembled began to taunt the piggish cops with various phrases as these)

Lesbians, Gays, Bisexuals, Trans, & Queers— LGBTQ Crowd: *(Adlibbing sentiments and protests)* Leave Shamus and his Disci-Pals alone! We are peaceful citizens of this great nation. You are violating our civil & constitutional rights! Leave us alone! We mean no harm! Gays and Lesbians and the LGBTQ Community Unite! Diesel Dikes Rule! Trans Triumphs over Tyranny! Bisexuals Beware, Protect the Innocent!

Cop #2: *(spiting, shouting)* Give us the one who calls himself Shamus and we will then depart without arresting the whole perverted bunch of youze-guys!!!

(Diesella, a Lesbian with a heart of gold and personal advisor to the Disci-Pals leaped out of the crowd to speak)

Diesella: Fuck Off Pigs!!! We'll sue you for harassment!!! Back Off and Fuck Off!!!

Fritz: Easy does it Diesella… We'll kill 'em with kindness. Excuse us, Officers; those sticks you carry are very impressive. My Disci-Pals and I will be glad to show you the proper way to use them.

(Addressing All) Disciples of Peace, fear not! Shamus will save our souls!

Stan: Shamus has done nothing wrong! What dirty tricks are you butch brothers of corruption up to? Care to kiss and tell?

Linus: We preach Peace, Love, Gay Pride, and the healing powers of Vitamin-C! How can this possibly upset lawmakers?

(Shamus could take no more. He stepped forward and faced the stern police officers)

Shamus: *(softly)* Please, please, fellow Disci-Pals, Diesella, Gay & Lesbian followers, Queers & Bisexuals… and you dear respectful Officers of the Peacefull Law Enforcement community… please, I beg you, be calm as a sea of yellow daisies. I am Shamus Dragay, L over of God and All His Dominion and the Universe. What is it you want of me?

Fritz: Shamus, no, do not play into their hands.

(Diesella leaped forward once more. She pointed at Shamus while she shook her head to exclaim)

Diesella: Do not believe him! He is not the real Shamus Dragay! I am Shamus Dragay, in drag, no less. Take me away with you and throw the book at me! I will not resist!

Fritz: This Joan of Arc Spartacus gig does not become you Disella. I am Shamus Dragay!!! Take me if you dare!!!

Stan: Guys, this worked in "Spartacus" and I get it, but, please, be real, they're on to us. You Cops are Evil Gay Basher-Baiters! Take me, for I am the one you seek—I am Shamus Dragay, Faggot Supreme!!!

LGBTQ Crowd: *(chanting, taunting)* Evil, evil, evil, evil!!! The Coppers are on Poppers, the Coppers are on Poppers!!!

(Shamus simply could not be a part of this increasingly ugly display. He had witnessed confrontations such as these before and most had led to unnecessary violence and bloodshed)

Shamus: *(calmly)* Dear followers, dear lovers of the Gay Lifestyle, silence, please! Let us avoid becoming a destructive incoherent mob. These kind and gentle policemen are not the enemy, only their lack of enlightenment. If their hearts are hardened, we must find a way to show them the same love and respect we desire for ourselves.

Cop #1: That's more like it! As much as I'd like to bash your skinny faggottie little body into a Taco Supreme, Shamus Dragay, I must present you instead with a warrant for arrest!!! You have the right to remain silent, etc....

(Shamus was taken away in cuffs. Zoot--Allor!)

(DISSOLVE TO)

SCENE 26

(Here we are with our dear Shamus Dragay. Yes, it was a courtroom, a.k.a. A Kangaroo Coutroom full of Red-Necks, Religious Zealots, plus the darling faithful Disci-Pals, and all the lovely Gay & Lesbian Trans & Bisexual supporters.)

(As Shamus was brought into the courtroom his followers cheered while the doubters booed. The evil Judge Ramrod was miffed…)

Judge Ramrod: *(savagely banging his gavel)* Order in the court! One more shameless outburst from you disgusting Dikes and Faggots and I will see that your Messiah from Hell gets the chair!!!

(Shamus attempted to approach the bench but his burly red-necked-hetero guards restrained him)

Shamus: *(speaking out sincerely)* Your honor, I must object to such prejudicial language. We have harmed no one. I am a peaceful servant of God and therefore deserve more respect, as do my dear brothers and sisters of the LGBTQ community. Yes, and pardon me dear Judge Ramrod, sir, because I represent myself and a counsel unto myself I must demand it!

(The prosecuting attorney, Mr. Holelicker leaped to his feet)

Mr. Holelicker: *(salivating)* Judge Ramrod, your imperious judgelessness, lover of traditional family values and the narrow way of the Lord, I must object to the defendant's obvious contempt for you and these proceedings. He has arrogantly and defiantly lambasted our fair and impartial prosecution. Because he is a carrier of the dreaded AIDS disease he can only be viewed as a vicious murderer and sociopath. Thus, he deserves the maximum penalty, the penalty of death by burning on the cross!

(This statement caused a ruckus. The crowd of supporters was defiantly pissed. Trash was thrown and threats were made)

Crowd of Seedy Rednecks: *(pissed and adlibbing)* Kill the Faggots! Stick it to 'em where they like it best! String them up! You Lesbo's, Homo's, Bi's, Tran's, & Queer's—Must burn, burn, burn!

LGBTQ Crowd: *(angrily, adlibbing)* You Red-Necked Zealots are going to Hell!!! You evil Hatemongers are Closet-Cases! Free Shamus Dragay! Free Shamus Dragay!

Mr. Holelicker: Your Honor, I object to these disgusting Faggots!

Judge Ramrod: Mr. Holelicker, your objection is sustained! *(Banging his gavel)* Order! Order in this Coutroom or I'll clear you Queers out! You are over-ruled, Mr. Dragay! *(Jeers from the crowd pro & con)* Order in this Court!!!

(For just a moment, Judge Ramrod unconsciously banged a Dildoe on the bench before replacing it quickly with his Gavel. The Security Guards did their best to restrain the Mob but the jeers continued)

Mr. Holelicker: *(assholishly penile)* Judge Ramrod, I have never in my life seen such a putrid display of support from such low—life—scum as these Fags! I demand you sentence them all too death by lynch mob!!!

Judge Ramrod: *(insipidly cruel agreement)* Mr. Holelicker, that's a very good suggestion. However, in fairness we must allow the Jury a minimum of a few moments to reach their verdict. *(To the Jury)* Have you reached the verdict I have previously instructed you to give in this queerest of all cases?

(The Crowd gasped and a hush grew all around. The Red--Necks chuckled gleefully amongst themselves. The Jury of obviously slanted Red--Necks, Zealots, and Bespeckled Prudes stood and minced out to deliberate in the adjoining Jury Room. Gays Lesbians, Queers, Bisexuals, & Trans booed their passage. Herewith we hear some adlibbed chattering from the mixed crowd of our colorful onlookers)

Crowd Pro & Con: *(Adlibbing)* Kill the Fags! Come out of the closet Red-Necks! Send the Lesbo 's to Siberia! Go back to beating your wives and children Gay—Bashers! Homos are sinners in the eyes of Gawd!!!

God loves all Gay & Lesbian peoples!!! Give them the shaft, Judge Ramrod! Go back to your Closeted Sex-Pad, Holelicker!!! Support the LGBTQ community! *(Etc. Etc.)*

(Shamus addressed the judge again)

Shamus: *(calmly)* Your Honor, Judge Ramrod, please, I beg you, I must object to allowing the jury to deliberate without hearing my defense. They have not been given enough evidence to make recommendation. Please, your Honor, show a little compassion, objectivity, fairness, and above all, mercy.

Mr. Holelicker: *(sarcastically)* Save the pity party speech for the sentencing Mr. Dragay. You Faggot Messiahs give me a real deep pain where the sun don't shine.

Shamus: I'm not surprised, Mr. Holelicker, that you would be comforted by a pain so personal. I object to your criticism of my personal lifestyle.

Judge Ramrod: *(incensed)* Objection just too damned late, boy!!! You Jesus pretender! Phony Messiah! You're a Fake Faggot Flake!!!

Shamus: I've never made such claims. As odd as it may seem, we are all the Sons and Daughters of God. Even you, Judge Ramrod, have the Spirit of God in you… It's only twisted in CIRCUITOUS fashion… A good Shrink could restore you to health.

Judge Ramrod: Stifle yourself, pervert! Bailiff, bring in the Jury, they've had time enough!

(As the jury re-entered, once again the crowd made a lot of noise, cheering, booing disrespectively. Judge Ramrod cried out loudly for order, banging his gavel forcefully. The homophobic slurs and rebuffs abounded in vitriolic fashion, order did more or less occur after a short while)

Judge Ramrod: Defendant and Prosecution please rise. Jury, let's have the verdict please?

Lead Jury Verdict Reader: We, the solemn and reverent citizens of this fair state and community do find the defendant, Shamus Dragay, guilty of fraud in presenting himself as the Messiah and guilty of murder in the 1st degree by being a carrier of the AIDS disease, and guilty of the damnable sin and gross perversion that is Homosexuality, or Faggotryism as it is known by the good and narrow Christian followers of the Narrow Ways of Jesus Christ our Lord and Savior. We recommend life in prison with no possibility of parole.

(The crowd went mad while Judge Ramrod screamed for order in the court)

Judge Ramrod: *(Furious at the Crowd but obviously tickled pink by the verdict)* Good people of the Jury and lovers of the Almighty whose personal presence we feel at times as glorious as these, I thank you for your verdict, though slim in penalty, I hereby exercise my prerogative, yes, my duty, to review this sentence. Because of the extreme nature of the perversions entailed I sentence Shamus Dragay to immediate execution by cross--burning with no possibility of appeal at any level by our fine Justice System of the United States of America!

(He hangs his gavel)

A Red-Necked Asshole: In other words, let's carry out the sentence NOW!!! LYNCH the LGBTQ Faggots and Burn Shamus Dragay on the Cross of Jesus, our beloved heterosexual true Lord & Saviour!!!

(Oh, for God's sake, what a travesty! Poor Shamus Dragay and his followers were pounced upon by the sick Red-Necked Bigoted Mob and the Brutal Officers of the Law. Meanwhile, Judge Ramrod and Mr. Holelicker surreptitiously toasted each other behind the bench with a glass of champagne & a butt-kiss on the lips, while the LGBTQ innocent ones were dragged kicking and screaming from the courtroom along with the still calm and loving hero and kind true & honest Messiah Savior, Shamus—The Wholesome Martyr—Dragay. The Adlibs from our remarkable Cast of Characters has been truly gut--wrenching, to say the least)

Red-Necks: Death to all Faggots! Burn them at the cross of Jesus! God hates Homos! Homos are sinners! Burn, Faggots, Burn!!!

LGBTQ+ Supporters: *(The Innocent LGBTQ Gays & Lesbians)* Have mercy on us! You are mistaken God loves Gays! Please have mercy on us! Show some compassion! Oh, travesty of travesties, tis a pity for sure....

(DISSOLVE TO)

SCENE 27

(Fellow Fags, Gals from the Isle of Lesbos, what horrors have we here? Our beloved Shamus Dragay and his band of Merry Disci-Pals have been drug to the seaside to be burned at the cross upon sundown. The Evil Hetero's and the various Red-Necked Stereotypes were having the Orgy of their Pitiful Lifetimes. The infantile prejudice and obscenity of this affaire shall not be forgotten soon.

(The shouts and jeers of hatred as our Gay & Lesbian, Trans, Queer & Bisexual Heroes were bound to their crosses and raised to the fiery sky was just too ugly to be repeated in detail here lest I cause you to be sick from grief, but the least I can do is repeat a few of the ugly lines that were spoken at the time just to give you an idea of the gross extent of their debaucheries)

Fag Haters: Death to Fags! Down with Homos! God Hates Queers! Bite The Big One Butt-Fuckers!

(As the degenerate mob was beginning to toss sticks and brush beneath the crosses, Fritz, Stan, and Linus, who were hoisted along with Diesella on adjacent crosses, pleaded with their hero, Shamus, to do something-you, know, spark a miracle.)

Diesella: Do your stuff, Shamus, ZAP these Ass--Holes ASAP!!!

Fritz: *(weeping)* Dear, Shamus, I beg you, is there nothing to be done? Call on the power of God!

Stan: *(sadly)* Shamus, dear friend, how can they hate us so?

Linus: Shamus, I have never seen or known such naked homophobia. I'm sure if these people knew their own hearts, we could be brothers.

Shamus: *(calmly)* This really has been carried a bit too far. I can't think of a human condition more appalling than this blind hatred based on self-loathing and fear expressed by these perpetrators of doom.

(Naturally, Judge Ramrod was having the time of his life. He carried a torch and prepared to set the unhappy Queens aflame. No doubt this act will give him a special footnote historically. Bully for Judge Ramrod!)

Judge Ramrod: *(Cum Lustfully)* Now let's show these Heroes of Sodom just what Justice tastes like! Good-bye disease-ridden AIDS Faggots! Give the Devil a kiss on the ass from me! Know that you are hated!

(He plunged his torch into Shamus's stick pile. As the flames leapt skyward the crowd screamed with horror and pleasure! Hasn't mankind advanced a long way since the dark ages? As the crowd chanted hateful epitaphs, Judge Ramrod ran to the other crosses and set them aflame to the chorus of shrieking Blood-Lusty-Bigoted-Bigots!)

Fritz: *(fearfully)* For God's sake, Shamus, what must we do?

Stan: *(crying)* To die while a crowd cheers on… Oh, Pity Us and Set Us Free!!!

Linus: *(filled with remorse)* How sad that they hate us so. I wonder if large doses of Vitamin--C would help heal their infected minds?

(Mr. Holelicker was particularly impressed with and pleased by the aggressive actions of his favorite Judge. Without thinking he snagged Ramrod for a quick hug and kiss)

Mr. Holelicker: Sock it to them Ramrod baby!

Judge Ramrod: Control yourself Holelicker, save it for later.

Mr. Holelicker: Sorry, guess I got carried away by the magnificence of the moment.

Judge Ramrod: *(to Shamus)* Shamus, now that the flames of truth are licking at your heals, have you any last words?

(A hush came over the obscene crowd)

Shamus: *(peacefully, fearlessly)* While it is a shame I allowed this travesty to carry on so long, we should all remember to be friends, and lovers of God and his Creation.

Shamus: The Universe is eternal. I have asked God to intervene in this situation because our deaths now will solve nothing. We must leave you to your prejudice and fear. Remember us kindly for we must now depart to the Isle of Lesbos. It is our desire to live out our lives in peace and harmony... And perhaps someday, God will teach you to do the same.

(The clouds in the Heavens swirled and rolled ominously. Rain began to pour down from the sky, putting out the flames beneath the crosses. Lightning bolts struck about the ground scaring the shameless crowd away while they screamed in terror. All the Trans, Queer, Bisexuals, Lesbians & Gays freed Shamus and his Disci-Pals from their crosses as the sea behind them parted, clearing the way to the Isle of Lesbos, seen shimmering on the Horizon behind a Brilliant Setting Sun. In the Blazing Light Fire of God's Grace, the LGBTQ Lesbians, Gays, Bisexuals, Trans, & Gays cheered and kissed one another. Slowly, patiently, they made their way to freedom at long last)

(FADE OUT)

SHAMUS DRAGAY

by *Grant Sutor Vuille*

THE END

In Loving Memory,
Edward (Eddie) Glenn Niola
b. June 26, 1958 - d. April 23, 1992

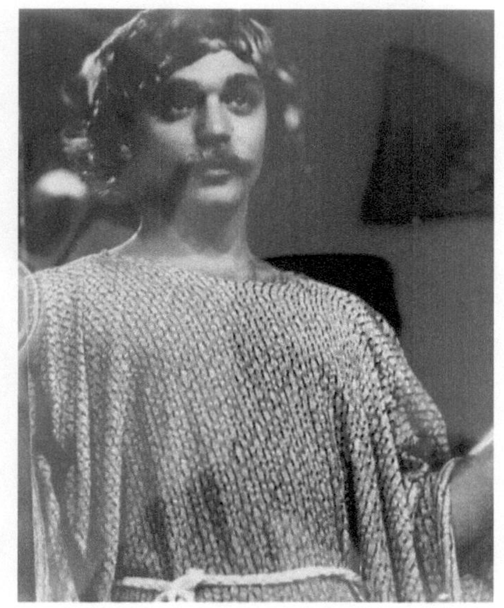

Eddie onstage in "A Midsummer Night's Dream"
St Petersburg Little Theatre 1978

"Twelve Tulips For Tinseltowne"

A One Act Play
by Grant Sutor Vuille

Genre: *Comedy/Satire*

Synopsis: *A short one act satirical comedy play about a young aspiring starlet in Hollywood who is anxious to make it in show business as a dramatic actress, but who is always given sex-kitten roles because of her glamorous appearance. Tulip Tinseltowne, feeling she is right on the verge of success, arrives back to her Hollywood apartment from an unsuccessful audition for a movie when a 7.1 earthquake occurs. She thinks it's Armageddon because Hollywood always seemed to her to be a den of sin. Her agent continually sends her to auditions for loose women roles where casting directors and producers harass the female talent. Her boyfriend has adapted to the ways of Hollywood quite well but expects her to toe the line and be faithful to him only. TULIP wants none of that except to succeed in achieving her artistic goals. Undaunted by these set-backs she vows to make it in Hollywood by hook or by crook, returning to the crumbled wasteland of Tinsel Town streets and boulevards to solicit her tantalizing talents.*

Characters:

Tulip Tinseltowne	*A young aspiring starlet in Hollywood who is anxious to make it in show business as a dramatic actress, but who is always given sex-kitten roles because of her glamorous appearance.*
Aaron Buggerspell	*Her middle-aged disgruntled over-sexed agent. He has the 'hots' for all his female clients, and an unrequited love interest in Tulip.*
Phillip Twigsbee	*Her young street hustler bisexual bi-polar paranoid schizophrenic boyfriend, whose fears and worries increase the tension whenever he is around.*
Time:	*Afternoon, in the current year, just as Armageddon is beginning.*
Place:	*Hollywood, CA, just after a major 7.1 earthquake.*
Setting:	*Tulip's modest efficiency apartment overlooking Sunset Boulevard. Behind a small sofa center stage is a cracked window pane with the Hollywood sign cracked apart on the mountain in full view. A free-standing door, stage left, also has a big crack on it. A single armchair is right of center stage with additional cracks on the wall behind it. A small end table between the sofa and armchair has a vase with a dozen roses.*

SCENE 1

(The stage is dark. Sounds of a massive 7.1 earthquake rumble loudly and screams are heard. Just as the lights slowly begin to come up the vase with a dozen roses tips over. The whole Hollywood background set outside the window visibly shakes and the Hollywood sign and buildings on it are loose cutouts that shake individually, also. As the rumbling fades out Tulip Tinseltowne enters from the stage left door into her apartment. She flips on the lights and screams, noticing all the damage. There is a crack in the window behind her sofa center-stage. The crack seems to pierce the damaged Hollywood Hills sign on the distant mountain above the streets of Hollywood in ruins. Tulip dashes around straightening up, putting a few of the roses back in the vase)

Tulip: Oh, my God, it's the end of the world! Oh, help us, dear God!

(She collapses onto the sofa. There is knocking at the door. It is Tulip's Hollywood Agent, Aaron Buggerspell. He begs Tulip to let him in)

Aaron: Tulip! Tulip Tinseltowne! Let me in please, the streets are covered in rubble and the people who need people are screaming hysterically everywhere! I can't take it another minute! Let me in, the sky is falling and the earth is shattering apart!

(Tulip runs and opens the door and in bursts Aaron Buggerspell)

Tulip: Mr. Buggerspell, what's happening, is it Armageddon? I've just come out of a really bad audition—I'm shaking all over.

Aaron: That had to be a 7.1 quake, baby. Say listen, how did that audition go for the "Bubble Goddess" flick? You're perfect for that role. Did you do the coochie-coochie dance for them?

Tulip: Yeah, Aaron, about that coochie-coochie bit… I'm really tired of you sending me on those kinds of auditions. I'm a serious actress—I'm looking for juicy acting parts, not these constant bimbo bit roles.

Aaron: But they're your bread-and-butter. You satisfy a definite need that producers are just desperate to fill. You have a great look, and you know it. You're the next Marilyn Monroe. They can't resist you… I can't resist you.

Tulip: I can't stand the way those so-called producers and casting directors drool over me--it's disgusting. Please go now Aaron, I'm exhausted after that earthquake. Between it and that awful audition for those lecherous movie gorillas it feels like my head will crack like that Hollywood sign.

(Tulip checks the damage to her apartment. She surveys all the cracks, looks out the window at all the destruction, then flops upon the sofa again, exhausted)

Aaron: Don't sweat it baby, don't let a little earthquake bother you, it happens all the time out here.

Tulip: But look at all the damage that's been done. Hollywood is on its knees and I'm sick of producers and casting directors harassing me all the time and expecting me to do the same, the dirty perverts. I'm not assuming that position anytime soon. Where's the 'me, too, movement' for me, too?!

Aaron: Are you going to let a little sexual naughtiness get in your way? A little flirtation might help you get that part in a movie you've always wanted.

Tulip: *(Standing up)* No! I won't let them get away with it! On the way out the door that nasty producer pinched me on the ass and invited me up to his office for a personal examination of my talents.

Aaron: Great! Did you accept his invitation?

Tulip: No! You're not listening to me, Mr. Aaron Buggerspell, and as my agent, you're part of the problem, too!

Aaron: Come here, my little Tulip flower, you need a hug. Come to daddy, baby, I'll fix it all for you. Are those the roses I sent you?

Tulip: Yes, the earthquake tipped them over and were scattered on the floor when I came in. I tried to straighten them up, but…

(Bursting into tears she allows Aaron to give her a hug. He begins to go too far and starts kissing her)

Tulip: Oh, Aaron, I don't think I can handle any more stress.

(She squirms uncomfortably, wanting to break free of his embrace)

Aaron: Oh, sweetheart, let daddy make it all better. You're so beautiful, Tulip, I just can't stop kissing you. I love being your agent. I'm going to make you a star someday. You put the animal instinct in me on fire.

See, baby, see how it is? Everybody does this in Hollywood. It's okay, sweetheart, just relax.

Tulip: *(Pushing him away)* No, stop, I won't let you, this is exactly what I mean! This is not what I want, I want to have a career, not a series of perverse sexual encounters! You're acting like some narcissistic politician. What gives Aaron, are you planning on running for president?

Aaron: That hurts me, Tulip. Didn't you like the roses I sent?

Tulip: Yes, well, I prefer tulips, but it's not appropriate for you to give me flowers of any kind because we have a business relationship. You're my agent, not my boyfriend. Show me some respect!

(Just as she finishes speaking her boyfriend Phillip Twigsbee pops up from behind the sofa where he'd been hiding the whole time and Tulip's joust with Aaron has crossed the line for him)

Phillip: Tulip! I demand to know what that lecherous old fart is up to.

Tulip: Phillip Twigsbee! How dare you spy on me in my own apartment! I'm sorry Mr. Buggerspell. Phillip, really!

Aaron: Sorry, Tulip, this is my cue to exit. If Hollywood hasn't collapsed completely I'll be back later to get you to sign a new contract! Practice your coochie-coochie, coo's!

(Aaron exits though the front door)

Phillip: He's just a sick old creep and you need to get another agent pronto!

Tulip: Who are you calling sick? If the bunny slippers fit, well…

Phillip: Bunny slippers? I'm not a perverse old pussy-snatcher like Buggerspell. I'm a freelance sexuality therapist… in practice.

Tulip: Ha! Is that what you call it? Don't hustle me, Phillip Twigsbee, I can see right through you. This earthquake is going to send all of corrupt Hollywood straight to frigging Hell!

Phillip: Gee, Tulip, a guy's got to make a living. My tricks pay me top dollar. I'm saving up for your engagement ring.

Tulip: Oh for pity's sake, Phillip, you're having another episode-have you been taking your psychiatric medication?

Phillip: I don't trust these sick people you associate with. I want you to marry me right away and come back to Sacksville, PA. We can stay at Mom's.

Tulip: Your mother has never forgiven me for running off to Hollywood. You should not have followed me out here especially when you knew our relationship was not working out because of my career ambitions.

Phillip: Mom may think you're a loose kitten, but I'll set her straight. Why can't we just work things out?

Phillip: And you need to allow me to go to these auditions with you so those buzzards will leave you alone. How can I be certain one of them won't seduce you and steal you away from me?

Tulip: I know what your mother thinks and she already knows I'm not loose, Phillip. She knows I'm not interested in having affairs with anyone. I've been faithful to you since we met two years ago and that's because I have no interest in any compromising sexual relationship. If I had been I'd still be in Sacksville, PA with you tying me down!

Phillip: You can be so cruel sometimes.

Tulip: Sorry, but I have to be blunt, Phillip Twigsbee. I want to focus on my career, not waste my time or yours trying to patch things up between us, or because of anybody else for that matter. I still love you in a small way, but I can't stand your jealous outbursts. You make me a nervous wreck. You should leave Hollywood and go back home to Mom. I'll send for you later when I've had a successful break as a serious dramatic actress.

Phillip: Is that Aaron sicko coming back here to try and get in your panties again?

Tulip: Please, let's not talk about my agent, he's finding me work in Hollywood. I can handle him, he's a pushover with a lot of connections and I can't afford to let him go. You know how hard it is getting an agent out here, Phillip, so I just have to hang in there and not give up.

Phillip: Tulip, I simply won't have you dilly-dallying with that starlet hopper for another second.

Tulip: Yes, I'll admit, Aaron Buggerspell has a more than liberated libido, but I can manage his advances just fine by myself, thank you.

Phillip: When he comes back, I'm going to be waiting behind the sofa to pounce on him—I'll give him a taste of his own medicine.

Tulip: Phillip Twigsbee, that's not a good idea and you know it. He's my agent, sweetheart. I need him to find me work in Hollywood. Please, butt out of my business.

Phillip: Ha, sex is big business out here for sure, just look at my sexuality therapist gig, I make loads of cash and I don't discriminate against women, men, or the LGBTQ community. I can take care of myself, too, Tulip. That's why you need me to fight off those sexual predators like those movie mogul types and your sicko agent Buggerspell.

Tulip: Buggerspell likes conflict—he may even take an interest in you, Phillip… your libido is sizzling and you have a natural magnetic charm.

Phillip: I will not have sex with that old fart! I'll just appeal to his degenerate nature and threaten to push him out the window where he'll make a giant splat onto Sunset Boulevard.

Tulip: Will you get out of here? He'll be back shortly. Go back to the YMCA and stop bugging me.

Phillip: I heard him say he gave you that dozen roses if you'd sleep with him. Is that true, Tulip? Tulip Tinseltowne, answer me!

Tulip: He did not say that, Phillip. Your constant paranoid barrage is the big reason I won't allow us to live together. I'm not sleeping with anybody! Can't you get that through your thick skull? You're imagining things. I think you've forgotten to take your medicine this morning.

Phillip: I always take my medicine. My Social Security covers my doctor and prescriptions, why would I not take them? My psychiatrist is very proud of how responsible I've become over time.

Tulip: I bet you're not taking your meds and instead are selling them on the street! I think we need to break up and you need to leave Hollywood and go home to your mom back in Sacksville, PA. I can't take you anymore.

(A momentary expression of physicallity explodes between them but they freeze, stopping short remorsefully)

Please leave! And give me your key, I don't want you coming in here again when I'm not at home.

Phillip: I want to stay with you here. I hate staying at the YMCA. And I'm sick of not having my own place. Why can't I move in here permanently? And I never imagine things that aren't there. Didn't we just go through an earthquake? Was I imagining that?

Tulip: Yes, I think that earthquake was in your imagination. Maybe you'd better go back to Mom in PA. She misses you and I can't manage a career and a psychotic relationship at the same time. Now give me your key to my apartment and leave at once!

Phillip: I'll show you, Tulip, I'll show you. *(He gives her his key)* When I come back if that rat-fink Buggerspell is here I'm going to divorce you as my girlfriend.

Tulip: Yes, then by all means, come back when Aaron is flirting with me on the sofa! Better yet, don't come back, we're officially through!

Phillip: I mean it, Tulip-don't mess with my head! I don't imagine things when they're not happening anymore!

Tulip: We just had an earthquake, fool, or have you forgotten. Goodbye, Phillip, give my regards to your boyfriends at the YMCA.

Phillip: I'm not gay and you know it, just a little bi-curious... that hurts me Tulip, I love you and nobody else. And I'm not a cheat. I'm faithful to you. My tricks are simply a business venture. There's no love exchanged, just hard cash.

Tulip: Phillip, you're a piece of work. It's okay for you to prostitute yourself but I'm required to be pure as the driven snow!

Phillip: I'm warning you, Tulip, when I come back, things better be as they should be.

(Phillip runs to the door and leaves)

Tulip: Try not to fall through the cracks in the street!

(Flustered, she spins around and collapses on the sofa. More earthquake aftershock rumblings are heard and the Hollywood sign, the window, and the door frame shake. Tulip screams)

My God it's the end of the world! And I haven't been nominated for an Oscar yet!

(FADE OUT)

SCENE 2

(Fade In. Tulip has fallen asleep on the sofa. Earthquake aftershocks begin and the roses tip over and scatter. Tulip wakes her up and she screams. Aaron Buggerspell knocks on the door)

Aaron: It's me, Tulip sweetie, I have a surprise for you!

Tulip: Come on in, the doors unlocked!

(Aaron enters with a dozen tulips from the florist and a script in hand)

Tulip: More roses? Put them in that vase that keeps falling over and then go, I'm exhausted.

Aaron: No, sweetie, no, it's your favorite kind—tulips! Remember? Your favorites! Just like you told me to bring you.

Tulip: You're mistaken, Aaron, I didn't ask you for more flowers; I told you it was inappropriate to bring me flowers because, as my agent, we have a business relationship, Mister Buggerspell, a business relationship… Oh, you just don't get it. I'm exhausted, Aaron, can you please leave, I want to be alone.

Aaron: Look, Tulip, I have a new script for you, not just these tulips you love so much. Here it is, sweetheart, you'll love it, it's got the perfect character for you.

Tulip: A new character, not one of those bimbos?

Aaron: No, no, not at all, here, take a look for yourself.

(He hands her the script and then rushes around cleaning up the roses by throwing them out the window and the placing the tulips in the vase next to the sofa. TULIP ruffles through the script searching for her character role)

Aaron: You're going to love the character Tulip… no more coochie-coochie for my girl.

Tulip: I don't think I like the title, Aaron, "The Sluthouse Diaries" … think that's an acceptable story for me, eh?

Aaron: The lead character is a prostitute with a heart of gold and she and her gang of whores provide shelter for homeless millionaires.

Tulip: *(She laughs)* You're kidding of course… aren't you? Oh, God, this is Armageddon, isn't it, there's no hope left and we're all going straight to Hell!

(She throws the script out the window, then grabs the vase with the tulips and throws them out the window, too, followed by another rumbling aftershock)

Aaron: Have you lost your mind? That script is pure genius, how could you just chuck it out the window with the beautiful tulips I brought you?

(Tulip grabs Aaron and pushes him out the window)

Tulip: You're fired Aaron Buggerspell, you'll never work in Hollywood again! May the fiery pits of Hell swallow you whole! That's it Satan, cremate his remains so even God in Heaven won't recognize his ass!

(Hollywood shakes and quivers as rumbling of another aftershock with flames shooting up outside the window follows. Fade Out)

SCENE 3

(Lights Up. Tulip's asleep on the sofa when a knock at the door wakes her. She goes to the door)

Tulip: Who is it?

Phillip: It's me, Tulip, open up, I have a surprise for you!

(She lets him in and he crosses the threshold presenting her with a dozen tulips)

Tulip: Why Phillip, how kind you are to return with the twelve tulips I recently lost… that is, they accidentally fell out the window after another aftershock hit… dear me…

Phillip: I just saw that Buggerspell creep limping down the street. He dropped this script in the gutter as he passed by. I think he might have something here, maybe he wanted you to have it. Let's read it together and if it's good I'd like to help you develop it… I'll be your manager and we'll get this project off the ground.

Tulip: Believe me, it's not, it's just more exploitive filth offensive to women.

Phillip: We can rewrite it together and cut out the sick stuff and just fix it however we want it together.

Tulip: We aren't the original writer, we don't have the rights to do that.

Phillip: Who needs rights, we'll just steal what's good and make the story our own.

Tulip: That's plagiarism Phillip, they'd take us to court.

Phillip: Not if we totally go in another direction and make the main character a Saint.

(He opens the script & flips a few pages, Tulip joins him)

She can save all the girls and start a support group. We'll change "The Sluthouse Diaries" to something inspirational like "Stairway To Acceptance". You'll play this saintly role to perfection, Tulip, and we'll develop this show and tailor the part to fit all your most generous abilities as an actress.

Tulip: Well, thanks Phillip, it might work, but do you really want to be my agent manager?

Phillip: Of course, I do... you know I love you and only want to help. We'll be a team and we'll write a new show script just for you and I'll peddle it to producer's door to door for you and for as long as it takes.

Tulip: Oh, Phillip, I do love you!

(They kiss)

Phillip: Oh, Tulip, you know you've always had my heart. Now let's go to work on that script!

(They go to the sofa)

Tulip: This is so exciting, well work night and day until it's finished!

Phillip: Night and day, Miss Tulip Tinseltowne?

Tulip: Of course, silly, you can move in with me right away! You can kiss the YMCA and your sordid nightlife good-bye for good.

Phillip: Oh, Tulip, I love you!

(They kiss again and embrace) Now let's get busy! Tulip Tinseltowne conquers Hollywood!

Tulip: Oh, Phillip, I do love you! Let's break this script down and see what new ideas we can come up with! *(They flip through the script with excitement)* What about this page, and this scene, how can we use it in our story?

Phillip: Oh, I like that idea, we can change it to suit your character, over here is a good idea I think we can work with.

(They continue chattering when another brief aftershock rumbles loudly and they scream. The aftershock stops and they laugh, then they continue chattering happily with more enthusiasm)

Phillip: Another amazing day in Tinsel Town!

Tulip: No, Phillip Twigsbee, you mean another day with Tulip Tinseltowne!

(They laugh together, kiss, then continue chattering about the script.)

(FADE TO BLACK)

THE END

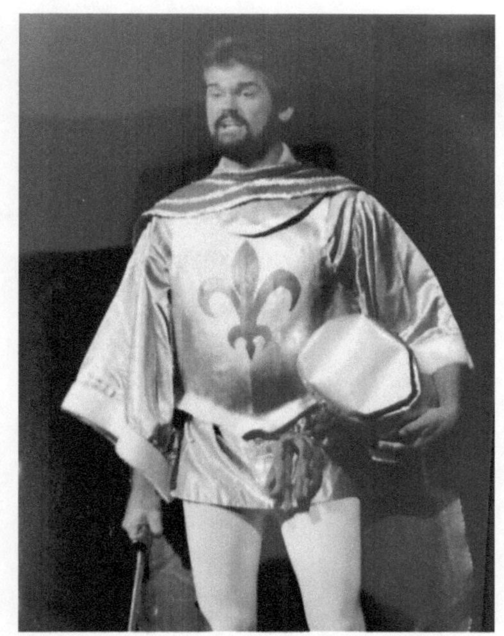

Grant onstage as Lancelot in "Camelot"
St Petersburg Little Theatre 1978

Vapid

A Decadent Adult Gay Fantasy about Hollywood at the Beginning of the AIDS Crisis.

Grant Sutor Vuille

Dedicated in the Memory of My Friend and Companion

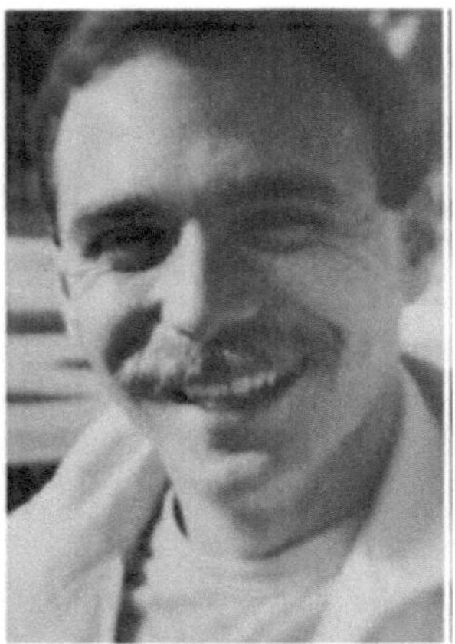

Edward "Eddie" Glenn Niola
June 26, 1958 - April 23, 1992
From Complications of HIV/AIDS

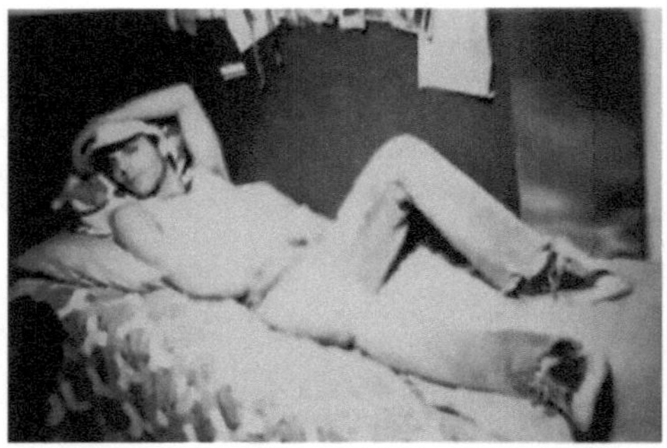

Eddie at home, Circa 1978

The author will donate 50% of all personal profits earned from the sale of this book to HIV/AIDS charities in Eddie's name.

Chapter 1

The sun arises over the plush mansion belonging to Carlotta Carlisle, movie siren desperate for a comeback. The pink morning light sparkles mystically amidst the dewdrops, overshadowed ominously by the immense Hollywoodland sign on the mountain behind her estate. The time is the present, and the future belongs to aspiring starlets and budding young stud actor types.

Such *is* the setting when Carlotta suddenly *awoke* on this glorious pink day to exclaim, "My God! I've got to get to the studio! I'm late for the Tide commercial gig!"

She springs from her bed and screams for assistance. "Rocky! Rusty! Quick! I'm late for work! Help me get dressed! Slap me in makeup!"

Rusty and Rocky, dressed in colorful bikini underwear, appear as if from nowhere to come to her aid. Her hair is teased and her makeup literally slapped on minutes before she is whisked out the door and into the limousine.

By no means does the Tide commercial go well. Carlotta refuses to read the cue cards correctly.

"Look at these filthy makeup stains on the collar of this blouse! Disgusting! But with extra-action Tide, you can believe they'll vanish at the end of the wash cycle. Take it from me, Carlotta Carlisle; Tide does the trick with its extra-action ingredients. But speaking from experience, it doesn't hurt to get my houseboys to rub a little ordinary soap into the stain first—"

"Cut!" is screamed by the director, who doesn't hesitate in letting Carlotta know in no uncertain terms that if she won't stick to the cards, she would be one has-been actress who would be blackballed from the business permanently if she spoils yet another take.

Using the foulest language imaginable, she dumps the Tide on his head, tells him what he can do with it, and leaves the studio with her bikinied houseboy's arm in arm. Neither Rusty nor Rocky are ever allowed to wear clothes.

Cruising the streets of Hollywoodland is a young stud by the name of Brad Willis. He makes his living turning tricks, although his mother, who lives in nearby Los Angeles, is convinced he works the late afternoon, early evening shift at Taco Bell. She has no idea what he does after he gets off at 11:00PM.

Like most young men with good looks in Hollywoodland, he has stars in his eyes. Unfortunately, none of his tricks ever turns out to be big-time producers or directors. At least, his tricks never *admit* to being members of that profession, preferring, for obvious reasons, to remain anonymous.

This particular night, Brad is getting pretty disgusted with his chosen career after tricking with a couple of old queens when he chanced to meet Larry. Larry is a hustler, too, but has ambitions of being a pimp. He is blond, muscular, and gorgeous, his ancestors being among the original settlers of Hollywoodland. Brad's slender good looks and dark hair cannot compare, but both men, bored with life and needing a change, find solace in each other. Mutual admiration at first sight seems to be the order, so they spend the night in passionate bliss in Larry's cluttered apartment in East Hollywoodland.

Mrs. Willis, Brad's mother, is pretty upset when her son shows up days later with a black eye and bruises on his arms, legs, and ass.

"I got in a fight in a bar, so I stayed at my girlfriend's." It was a lie, but his mother believes it.

She makes him strip naked and take a bath. She catches a glimpse of the damage when she passes the bathroom door and nearly faints.

Later that afternoon as she is hanging out her son's laundry, she makes it clear to him that he has to give up his job at Taco Bell and go back east to New York City to live with her estranged husband. It would be better for him, she knows, because Brad's father has promised to pay Brad's way through college.

"You could go to NYU or Columbia," she says. "LA is no good for you."

"New York City is just as bad," he says.

"But your father will only pay for your schooling if you stay with him. I can't support you well enough on what I make part-time."

"But, Mom," he says, "I dropped out of UCLA and USC because I *hate* school."

'You made straight A's! Straight A's!"

"I hate school. I like working at Taco Bell."

"You can't like it."

"Yes, I do. I do like it because I can look for agents and go to auditions during the day."

"I can't believe you want to throw away your life on an acting career."

"It's what I want to do."

"Hollywood is a dangerous place to hang out. Drugs and prostitution are bigger out here than the movie business. You could be so happy in New York with your father."

But convincing his mother proves impossible. He ends up moving in with Larry, who regularly beats him. The relationship obsesses him. Larry pimps for him, sending the tricks to the apartment because he is too badly beaten and bruised to be successful on the street.

Brad disappears from sight, not seeing his mother ever again. She has tried calling Taco Bell but is dismayed when they had never heard of him. She also tries calling missing persons and the FBI. She becomes so exhausted from worry, nervousness, and depression that she begins calling Brad's father regularly. They reconcile, and she sells the house and flies to New York City. The void she feels at her son's loss never leaves her.

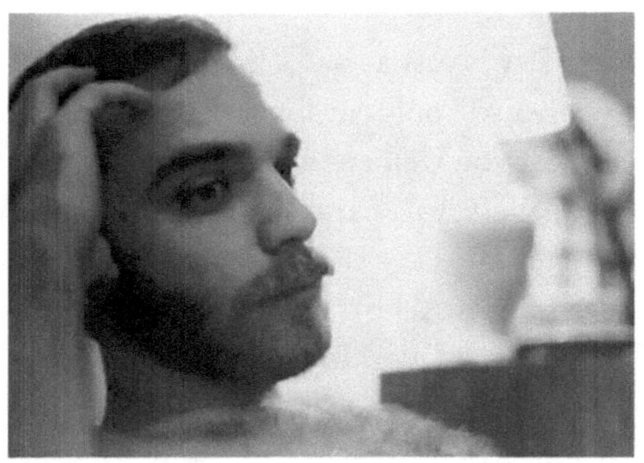

Eddie at our apartment in St. Pete, Circa 1979

Chapter 2

"In Hollywoodland, the time is now," he is saying aloud to himself as he paces around and around the room with a bottle in his hand. He is kicking trash as he staggers about but then stops when he suddenly catches sight of his deplorable condition in a cracked dresser mirror. Brad begins to sob. "Larry... Larry... damn you... I love you... I want to die."

"Larry enters with a trick, but Brad is too sick to service him. The john, a nervous old fool of a man, is anxious for a kinky scene and is insistent on getting off at any expense. Larry, ever resourceful, ties Brad to the bed facedown and, for two hundred bucks, allows the stranger to beat him, torture him unmentionably and, ultimately, to sodomize him violently. But Brad has passed out and fortunately does not feel a thing.

Carlotta's mansion sits majestically in the noonday sun. Rusty is cleaning the pool outside. Rocky is giving her a rubdown with suntan oil on the sofa as she talks to her agent on the phone just inside the sliding glass doors leading out to the pool.

"Oh, darling!" she rasps, much like the late great Tallulah. "Paramount has accepted the project? Divine! For a while now I've been afraid, I'd be stuck doing trivial television commercials for the rest of my life. Bill, this movie is going to win me the Oscar, I know it! Darling, you've come through for me again. What's that you say? They won't accept Rock Hudson as my leading man? But I've got to have Rocky!" Rocky the houseboy slaps her on the back. "Ouch! Not so rough, dear! I'm sorry, Bill, did I just blast your eardrums? Please forgive me. Easy on the massage, Rocky! But, darling, who do they want to cast opposite me? An unknown! What? A younger man? How absurd, using an unknown!"

Both Rocky and Rusty begin to pay attention. "But why, Bill, why? What? They want to cut the budget? Is that why? Goddamn it! I'm sorry... well, what can be done, I've just got to do this picture, but where on earth are we going to find a man sexy enough to play opposite me and still not steal focus? Are you sure we can't have Rocky Hudson?"

Rocky the houseboy slaps her on the back again. "Ouch! Rocky! Cut it out and get off my back! Sorry, Bill. Rusty! Throw Rocky in the pool and cool his ass down!" Rusty comes into the room from outside and grabs Rocky and they tussle. "Easy boys! Ouch!" she screams when they bump her. "You just can't get reliable help these days!" They pull each other's bikinis off in the scramble to push each other towards the pool and then into it with quite a splash.

Carlotta gasps into the phone, "I swear, Bill, I'm going to fire those two! So back to business... hmm... do you think they'd accept George Hamilton? He's sexy enough, and I doubt he could steal focus from me. Well, at least ask them for me, Bill. Oh, come on, the studio would go for it! He could be gotten for nothing! Are you kidding? Listen, his Zorro movie flopped. Yes, it did! There weren't enough faggots out of the closet to support that Gay Blade film of his! Oh, come on, it doesn't hurt to ask him. Alright, if we have to use an unknown, we have to use an unknown! But you've got to promise me you'll call Georgie and offer him the role. I'm sure he'll do it! Yes! Of course, darling... you, too... bye-bye!" She gets splashed when Rusty and Rocky run into the room briefly, naked and wet, and she screams, "Damn it, boys! Don't fuck with me fellas or you'll be back on the streets faster than you can jack off!"

Brad is alone in the apartment. Having come around, he raises himself from bed and shuffles about the room. He finds his empty whiskey bottle and throws it in the trash.

In the shower, he scrubs down, taking time to inspect his various wounds.

He shaves his face, slaps on lotion, and puts his hands through his hair. "I'm going home," he says to himself. "I've had enough… enough." Later, in a quiet park nearly, he sits alone on a bench. He watches the kids at play and takes notice of his surroundings as if for the first time. He is smiling. It has been a while since he has felt this good about himself. He has made a decision to change his life for the better. He will reconcile with his mother and then take his father up on the offer to live in New York City and go back to school.

He gets up from the bench and begins heading south toward Los Angeles. The walk feels good, and he is filled with euphoria. Hours later, he finds himself staring at the front door of his old house from the street. Finally, he is able to stir up enough courage within him to go to the door and knock. To his complete surprise, a strange woman answers,

"I'm looking for Mrs. Willis," he says.

"I'm sorry, she moved away some time ago, I don't know where."

"You don't know? You mean she won't be back?"

"Well… we live here now… I never met her, my husband has, I think, when they closed the deal on the house… you want to speak to my husband?"

"No… thank you…" Brad leaves quietly with the awesome weight of complete abandon, gnawing at the very center of his being.

It becomes dark as he returns to the neon strips of Hollywoodland. With great difficulty, he makes up his mind to return, at least temporarily, to Larry's apartment. Upon his return, in the rain, Larry greets him with surprising coolness without seeming to be annoyed by Brad's absence.

"Where have you been?" he asks Brad.

"Just out... thinking. My mother's moved away," he says, nearly choking from anxiety and exhaustion. "It's been over a year since I've seen her... I thought she'd always be there."

"Too bad."

Larry leads him to the bedroom. "I've got some business for you," he says in an even tone, "you got back just in time."

"No," replies Brad urgently, "not anymore. I can't do it anymore."

"You will!!!" screams Larry as he smashes him up against the wall. Brad is crying, begging, but Larry forces him into the bedroom where a menacing john awaits. Larry orders Brad to strip, but he refuses. Both men begin beating up on him. His clothes are ripped from him, and his face is bashed to the floor as the ugly john rapes him, thrusting his oversized manhood brutally into him. Brad cries for help, but Larry silences him with a kick to the temple, yelling, "Shut up, shit!"

Brad goes limp on the floor as a high-pitched frequency envelopes him. He is suddenly somewhere beyond the ceiling observing his own rape. The john climaxes lustily, then removes himself from Brad's lifeless body. Zipping up quickly and paying off Larry, he leaves hastily, sensing something is dangerously wrong with Brad.

Larry cannot revive him, and he begins to panic, running about the room crying for God. "God, help me, what have I done?" he whimpers over and over. He is begging Brad to forgive him as he picks him up and begins dragging him toward the door.

Just as Larry is making his way with him down the hall and out into the pouring rain toward his car, Brad is suddenly pulled away, straight upward into the sky, and Larry and the apartment shrink from view far below, becoming tiny pin point figures, disappearing among the vast reaches of the city.

Beyond infinity Brad travels faster than the speed of light, enveloped in a tunnel of swiftly accelerated time and dimension.

He observes his entire life. Incredible sounds and music have replaced the high-pitched frequency that envelopes and surrounds him. He is filled with the vastness and love of the universe, all questions in life now answered. He is bathed by the light of God, and by His eternal love. He is asked if he is ready to die, and he replies that he is not.

Brad is on the street, lying face down in the gutter. Rain pours from the sky, and the water swirls around him on its way to the drain. Automobile headlights flash beyond him, and two men race out and carry him coughing and sputtering back to the limousine.

Seated between the two brawny young men in the front seat, he remains semiconscious.

"Where to?" asks the driver to the woman in the back, "the hospital?"

"No, no... home," replies Carlotta Carlisle as she takes a drag through her foot-long cigarette holder, "but get my doctor on the phone and have him meet us there."

"I'll call," replies Rocky on the passenger side, picking up the phone, "make tracks, Rusty!"

"Right," he says, gunning the limousine, racing it down the rain-drenched streets of Hollywoodland.

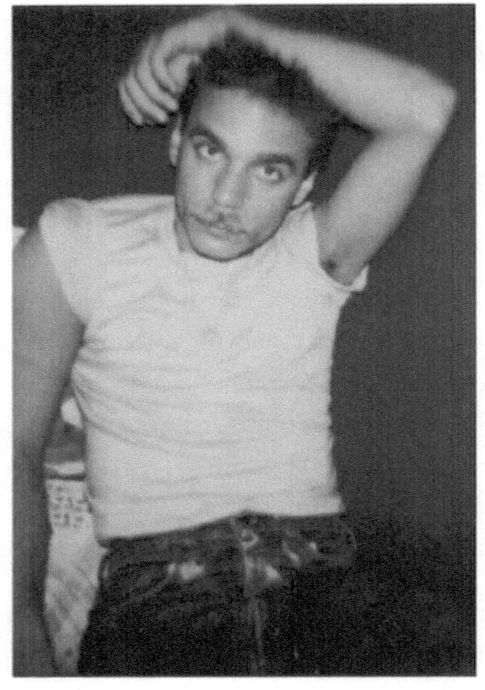

Eddie at home in St. Pete, Circa 1978

Chapter 3

Carlotta Carlisle is basking by the pool as Rusty and Rocky play checkers near her. When Brad comes up from the house dressed in his cut-offs she throws a fit, lifting up her bejeweled sunglasses to have a better look.

"Why," she asks, "are you not wearing your bikini briefs as I instructed?! Those shorts are for riffraff and tourists and not worthy of anyone in my employ!"

"I'm sorry... I just wanted to—"

"Take them off immediately!"

"Yes, ma'am." He obliges, his briefs being on underneath.

"... And throw them in the incinerator! And while you're at it down there, you may as well finish up the job you started earlier and burn the rest of the trash. I don't want it lying about in piles killing the grass. You *have* finished all the hedge trimmings, have you not?"

"Yes, ma'am."

"Yes... Miss Carlisle" she says. "I am not a ma'am to you! Now run along, Brad, and check back with me when you're done."

"Yes, Miss Carlisle," He walks away quickly.

He goes to the shed in the far corner of Carlotta's estate where he begins throwing hedge trimmings, along with his cutoffs, into the incinerator. Then changing his mind, he pulls the cutoffs out again. He mutters to himself and imitates her saying, "Yes, Miss Carlisle, *ma'am,*" with great emphasis, and then adding, "damn it... damn bitch!" Thinking out loud, he says, "When I got here you promised to test me for a part in your movie if I stayed on to be your slave. Rusty and Rocky lie around on their asses all day with you while I do all their work!"

Meanwhile, Rocky beats Rusty at checkers, and they start wrestling with one another, Rusty accusing Rocky of not playing fairly.

Rusty says loudly, "You are a filthy rotten cheater!"

To which Rocky replies, "See if I sleep with you again!"

"Boys! Stop it!" commands Carlotta. "Rocky beat you fair and square! I watched him. Rusty, stop your fuss and go check on Brad. I don't want him burning the place down!"

"Yes, Ms. Carlisle," he replies.

Brad is leaning up against the shed smoking a joint when Rusty comes up to him. "Hey," says Rusty, "you know she doesn't allow pot smoking."

"Have some," he says, passing it to him.

"Thanks."

They smoke for a while and then move into the shed out of sight. They finish off the roach but have already begun caressing and petting each other. Moments later, they go for each other's privates with a vengeance, all the while conversing about the prospects of working in Carlotta's movie.

Rusty is upon Brad's swollen member. "Oh God," moans Brad, "that is so good... so good... oh, yes... Rusty... man... how do you stand her bossing you around all the time? Oh... oh... I don't see how you can... take it... yeah... hmmm... hmmm... she promises you things and then never... oh... comes... comes... oh... through."

Rusty speaks while licking Brad's balls. "Man, like, she doesn't pay much, but she takes good care of us. We got this great home, all the food we can... hmmmmmm... eat, and I... hmmmmmm...

like it… yeah." He moves on to Brad's pungent tasty asshole, a.k.a man-pussy!

"Oh, Rusty, that feels so good! I tell you, I'm tired of it all already, and I've only been here two months. She only gives me a hundred a week, and that's not enough to party on, let alone buy good grass. Plus, we rarely are given time to go out. She's always got us running around doing everything for her."

Rusty begins to penetrate Brad with his hefty erection. Brad bends over, supporting himself against the shed wall, and he begs for it, pleading, "Give it to me… oh, yes, yes… *Yes!* Do it to me!" He moans as he begins masturbating with his free hand. "She promised me a screen test… yes… yes… hmmmmm… deeper."

"In fact, she promised all of us a screen test oh, baby," Rusty groans, pounding flesh into flesh.

Carlotta removes her sunglasses, puts down her magazine, and says, "Rocky, go check on Rusty and Brad and tell them to hurry up. It's getting late and dinner hasn't been started yet."

Rocky obeys, drying off his stark-naked self with a towel after leaving the pool dripping wet. As he walks off toward the shed, he awkwardly slips on his bikini briefs.

Brad and Rusty are putting the last of the hedge trimmings into the incinerator when Rocky comes up to them. Right away, he notices something odd and a look of perplexity changes his expression.

"What is it?" asks Rusty, thinking he's on to them.

"Ummmm… I don't know," he says, "but it's not a good idea to burn oleander."

Brad and Rusty just look at each other, puzzled.

"Dopes… oleander is deadly poison. If you burn it, it gives off a poisonous gas and will kill you. Come back to the house, we gotta get dinner started. We'll have to separate the oleander and throw it out with the garbage later."

They look at each other glumly and follow him back up the hill.

Brad is puffing on a joint in the laundry room as Rocky and Rusty enter carrying yet more loads of wash to be done.

"For God's sake, guys, give me a break!" he exclaims to them with a sigh. "Is there no end to her wardrobe?"

"Relax," says Rusty.

"Yeah," says Rocky, "there's only one more load."

"And when we bring it down, we'll help ya!"

"So relax like the man says, Cinderella, we'll be back in a flash!" They exit and Brad tokes on his joint, sighs again, and begins to separate the load.

"Yes, darling," Carlotta is saying to her agent on the phone. "I'm telling you I want my boys tested for the role! I'm not kidding! Look, Bill, you've been my agent for twenty years, but lately, until this movie deal you've been sitting on your ass. Uh-huh, I mean it, all three of them! Yes, three! I added another one last month… he's a charmer! Boys!" she bellows to Rusty and Rocky as they enter her bedroom to retrieve the last laundry basket. "I want you both and Brad to test for my leading man!" They hoot and whistle before retreating out the door. "Be sure and tell Brad the good news! What do you mean a scatterbrained idea! Bill! Listen, I'm the star! I say we don't need Rocky Hudson or Georgie Hamilton or anybody like that! Yes! No, not even Cary Grant! Look, you said the studio wanted to save money! Well, I'm trying to save them money! Look, these guys work here for practically nothing. Of course, I pay them, but after all, they do get room and board. What?

The studio wants Tom Selleck? A percentage? You're kidding… hmmm… I'll have to think about that… he's pretty hot, but *I* want to be the main attraction. What? My fans will be coming to see me of course! Bill!

"How dare you! My fans are not *fags!*"

In the laundry room the three boys are seated playing cards and Brad is toking on his joint. He tries to pass it to Rusty, but he begs off.

"I'd like too, man," he says, "but Carlotta doesn't allow it. If we were off somewhere by ourselves, it'd be okay. You oughta put it out."

"Yeah, Brad," says Rocky, "you shouldn't smoke it in the house. I've tried it, and she beat my bare ass. Didn't hurt, but boy was I embarrassed!"

"You guys kill me! She never comes down here!"

The door to the laundry room suddenly bursts open and in flies Carlotta, drink and elongated cigarette holder in hand, puffing away madly. She is excited and talking rapidly, waving the air with her arms. Brad quickly lowers the joint in his hand under the table and exhales slowly.

"Boys," she exclaims waving her arms, a la Bette Davis, "the studio wants Tom Selleck, but I'm behind you all the way. I'm demanding screen tests for each of you! And maybe, if you're good, one of you will be my next leading man!"

The boys all hoot enthusiastically over this bit of news.

"Just think of it, your names up in lights right under mine in small print naturally! Isn't it exciting?" she asks, sniffing the air suddenly with suspicion. "All right, where is it? Who's the culprit? Come on, come on, you can't fool Mama Carlotta!"

Brad reveals the joint and takes a defiant toke. She immediately slaps his face and snatches it from his lips, burning herself in the process. She screams bloody murder and dances up and down holding her finger in anger and pain.

"Take that!" she screams, splashing her drink in his face. "Oh, and that was good booze, too! That's it, buster, no screen test for you!"

"But you promised!" pleads Brad with restraint.

"Buddy, I make the rules here. You know very well I don't allow pot smoking! Do you want to turn into a junky? Don't you know it leads to heroin and cocaine addiction?"

"What about alcohol?" asks Brad.

"Uh-oh," mutters Rusty, "now you're going to get it!"

"Keep your mouth shut," hisses Rocky to Brad.

"You boys keep out of this! Listen, you young whippersnapper, for one thing, alcohol is socially acceptable and totally protected by the laws of this land! We pay high taxes to regulate it, and by God, it has kept this country strong!"

"I'm sorry," sputters Brad, "I didn't know you felt so strongly about—"

"*Shut up!*" she screams, fighting to regain control, huffing and puffing and pacing melodramatically. Suddenly she stops, then turns to face him, smiling patronizingly to show she has a big heart. "I'm the one who should be sorry, Brad, darling. I suppose I'm being a bit hard on you. You have been... good... for the most part, anyway, wearing your bikini briefs in my presence and so forth..." She is grinning so hard it seems she might crack. "I'll tell you what, it you promise not to smoke marijuana anymore, I'll let you have your screen test, but ***NO BEDROOM PRIVILEGES FOR A WEEK!"*** Understood?" she asks sweetly, glaring down at him.

"Yes, ma'am!"

"Yes... *MISS CARLOTTA!*"

She exits in a huff. Brad pulls out another joint and lights up.

"Thanks for backing me up, fellas," he says sarcastically. "No bedroom privileges for a week... breaks my heart!"

"Rusty, it isn't fair," muses Rocky, "he gets her gourd and then doesn't have to sleep with her."

"Forget it," replies Rusty, "let's play cards. Who's turn was it?"

"It's mine and I'm out," says Brad. "Gin! Whose deal?" he asks, propping his feet up on the table and leaning back against the washing machine.

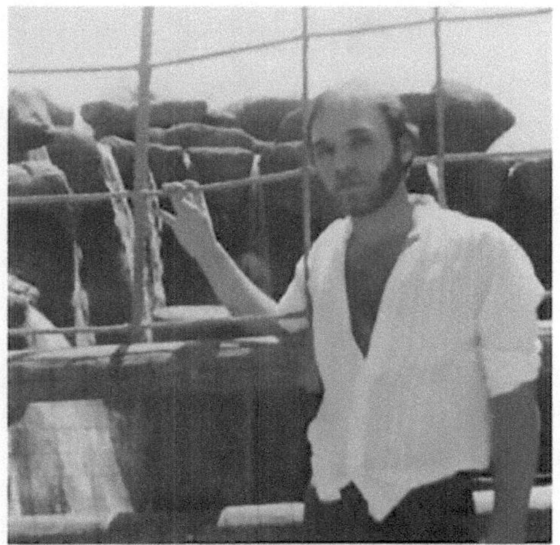

Eddie in a scene from our 16mm movie Siren of the Western World, Circa 1980

Chapter 4

The screen test is proceeding somewhat tentatively. The boys are lined up, and each is given a few moments before the camera. They are asked to relax, then asked somewhat personal questions. A mannequin dressed to resemble Carlotta stands next to them. They are expected to relate to it as she has refused to be present for the tests. Brad is last to go before the camera.

"Name?" asks the director, Harold Blatz.

"Brad Willis."

"Occupation?"

"Houseboy… er… manservant."

"Can you tell us a little bit about yourself?"

"Not much to tell, really… um… I was born here in Los Angeles, went to UCLA… um…"

"Did you graduate?"

"Um… no, but I may be going back to school in the East."

"Where?"

"NYU or Columbia."

"What will you study?"

"Acting… theatre… um… filmmaking"

"I see. How do you feel about acting opposite one of the finest film stars of our time? Carlotta is an American Institution, you know."

"I think it's great!"

"Can you give us a sample of your abilities as an actor?"

"Huh?"

"Could you play a *love scene* with Carlotta here?"

"You mean the dummy?"

"Yes. Ad-lib something for us. You student actors should be good at that. Show us what you would do."

"Uh... well, okay." He takes the mannequin representing Carlotta in his arms and proceeds, first looking deeply into its blank face. "Carlotta, my darling... sorry... *Miss* Carlisle! Darling, mere words cannot express my utter devotion to you. You turn me on in ways I've never known before." He puts the mannequin's lips to his ear as if it is whispering to him. "What's that you say, Miss Carlisle? You want me to do what? Oh, no, I couldn't, not with the camera rolling! Well, all right... if you insist..." He unbuckles his trousers down to his ever-present bikini briefs. He forces the mannequin's head to his crotch and mocks orgasm. "Oh... oh... Miss Carlisle," he moans, undulating his pelvis. "My God... you're beautiful. Oh... oh... I think I love you!"

"Cut! Thank you, Brad!"

Brad's expression first becomes blank as he lets the mannequin slide to the floor. He stands up and buckles his trousers.

"Is that it?" he asks the director, "do I get the part?"

"We'll let you know in a few days. Thank you, boys!"

Carlotta is on the phone with the producer of her film *Enlighten Me with Your Smile.* During her conversation, she sips a tall alcoholic beverage through a straw and puffs on a cigarette through the ever-present foot-long cigarette holder. The large picture window behind her exhibits the lawn where Brad is seen raking leaves in his cutoffs. Rusty is carting away leaves in a wheelbarrow, and Rocky is chastising Brad for not being in his bikini briefs.

"Yes, darling Ernest," Carlotta purrs, "*Enlighten Me with Your Smile* is sure to be a big success, and I'm *so* glad you liked the boys in their screen tests. You say you want to use them as extras in the picture? But what about using one of them as the lead opposite me? No? I don't understand? What do you mean they're too young to play opposite me? I'm insulted! Hmmm... still thinking of Tom Selleck? He is a bit more mature in the face. Oh, I don't know, you're the producer, you call the shots. I'm just the little star aching for a comeback! Ha! Without me, this picture won't make *peanuts!* Oh, Ernest, my boys will be so disappointed, especially Brad. He's new and very ambitious. Yes, uh-huh, fancies himself as an actor... what? You want to test him again with me? Well, that's wonderful, darling, but I don't do tests for films... yes, I know, but I've *refused* to do a screen test... I'm a big star, that's why!"

Rocky is now banging on the window and pointing to Brad, trying to get Carlotta's attention. Rusty warns Brad in time, however, and he quickly strips and tosses his cutoffs aside into a bush. "Excuse me, Ernest," Carlotta says, turning around to see Rocky at the window. "Rocky!" she yells. "Not now! I'm on the *phone!* Get away from that window and get back to work! Hi, boys!" she bellows, waving to the other two, who wave back in turn, smiling broadly. Rocky shakes his fist at them and they laugh.

Carlotta turns away from the window and continues. "I don't know what gets into them sometimes, Ernest," she says, sinking back luxuriously into the sofa—and Rocky, catching her turn away from them, promptly pulls down his briefs, spreads his buttocks wide, and shoots her a moon as his comrades become hysterical. The three of them begin throwing leaves at one another and tugging down one another's briefs. Rusty tries on Brad's cutoffs backward.

Carlotta continues, growing weary of the conversation, "Anyhow, Ernest, if you really like Brad and want to use him, I guess I could force myself to do the test... is the part *worth* me going to the trouble of testing with him? Oh, I see... you want him to play the part of the young gigolo I have an affair with after Tom Selleck leaves me for an *older* woman. Hmmm... not a bad idea. I tell you what, can we arrange it for tomorrow afternoon? How long will it take to do? I don't have to learn any lines, do I? Well, can't we use cue cards? Ernest, I insist... well, ask Harold Blatz if he'd mind! In fact, ask him to call me this evening. After all, as the director, he should have *some* say in the matter, don't you think? Uh—huh... okay, darling... talk to you later, sweetie, bye-bye!"

She hangs up the phone and turns around to the window just as her three houseboys shoot her full-faced, spread-eagled moons, Rusty having just unzipped Brad's cutoffs from a reverse position. Carlotta screams, "Boys!"

I don't pay you to monkey around! Get back to work or none of you gets to be in the movie with me!" She storms out of the room angrily declaring, "Those boys will be the death of me yet! I've got to do something about their conduct!" The boys, much amused with themselves, scramble back to work, readjusting their colorful bikini briefs in the process.

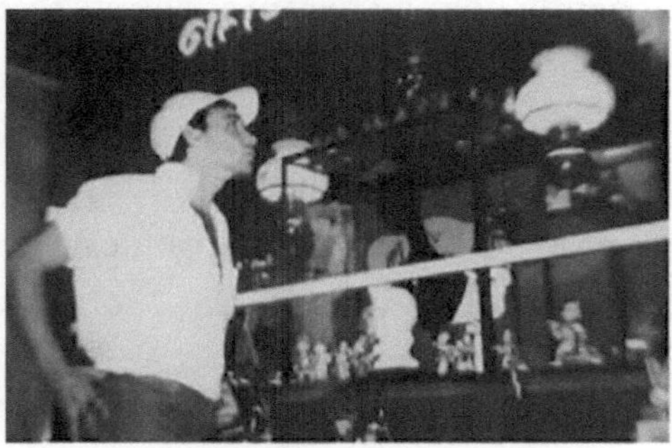

Eddie, Circa 1979

Chapter 5

The sun sets in Hollywoodland, and Carlotta's mansion is aglow. She wanders about the house, drink in hand, calling her boys by name, begging them to come to bed. She is sloshed out of her mind and collapses in an easy chair when Rusty and Rocky appear to escort her to the bedroom. Brad is nowhere to be found.

"Where have you been?" she demands.

They make lame excuses. "I was brushing my teeth," replies Rocky.

"And I was taking out the garbage," adds Rusty.

"Ridiculous!" she chides. "We have no garbage here!"

They help her to her feet. "Come to bed, Miss Carlisle," implores Rusty, gently helping her up as she staggers and moans.

"Come along now, Miss Carlisle," says Rocky softly.

As they make their way to the bedroom, Carlotta looks over her shoulder and cries, "Brad?! Where's Brad? I forgot to… to tell him… we test tomorrow together… oh, oh dear."

"Don't you remember?" asks Rocky. "You banished his ass from your bedroom."

"Did I? … I don't remember."

"He's out checking the sprinklers. We'll tell him in the morning," answers Rusty.

Brad is alone by the shed smoking a joint. He is wearing his cutoffs and an old worn-out army jacket. He has just turned on a set of sprinklers and he stands facing west, gazing across the lawn into the swirling wet mist as it glistens in the glowing after light of evening. As he tokes on his joint, he begins to sing aloud, very quietly at first, but then progressively with more volume and feeling, making the words up as he goes along. He moves about the lawn with the sprinklers spinning freely behind him.

Wasted Man.

Oh, I was a wasted man, who had too many dreams. Oh yes, I was a wasted man, without true friends it seems.

And then I fell into a dream That stole me from reality. Reality became my guide to steer my love so gently.

I always thought I could know love, never cared to doubt. But then someone I thought who cared, crushed my soul to naught.

Oh, I am a lonely man who now embraces life above all else and everything there is, even dreams at once beloved.

Dream on, mister, dream on, and you can have it all. But just don't lose your self-respect at a glittering Cinderella ball.

And then you'll be just fine and you'll be standing tall once more, not wasted, not lonely, not lost… Anymore… anymore… anymore…

He takes one last toke and flicks it away, looking upward at the house. He is beside the pool, and he grabs a couple of towels and wraps himself up on the cushioned lounge chair to spend the night. The stars twinkle eternally in the sky over the valley of Hollywoodland.

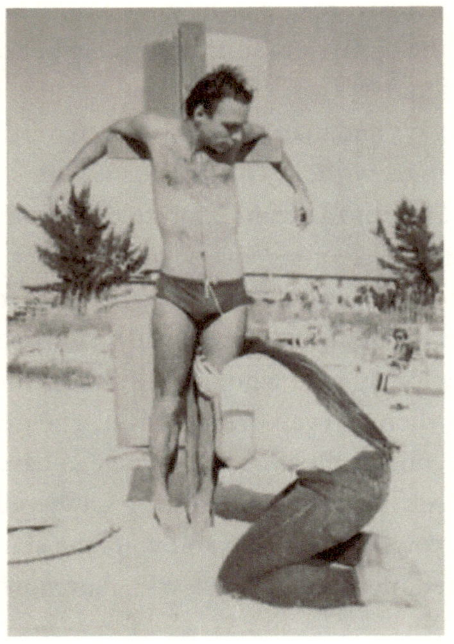

Eddie as Jesus Christ at St. Pete Beach; Anita Goodwin as Jesus' Mother, Mary Circa 1979

Chapter 6

The director, Harold Blatz, explains, "Now you see, Brad," he begins, his arm about Brad's shoulder as Carlotta looks on, "you're this sexy gigolo about to be picked up by this dazzling starlet over here." He indicates Carlotta. "You know what a gigolo is, don't you?" Brad shakes his head yes, and Carlotta rolls her eyes. "Good. Good. Tell you what, let's not worry about details. The cue cards are right over there, so just relax and give me all you've got!" He fondles Brad's crotch and whispers not too discreetly to him, "And I bet you've got a lot... stud..." he says, chortling throatily, then dashing back to stand by the cameraman in time to yell, "Action!"

Brad stands by a prop lamppost, somewhat uneasily at first. His nerves showing slightly, he eases one hand into a pants pocket after placing a cigarette to his lips and lighting it, surreptitiously taking in the dark and smoky atmosphere. Carlotta jostles with herself in the background, adjusting her breasts quickly, before taking a deep breath and moving confidently into the scene.

She moves up to him slowly, sexily, but it is Brad who dominates the scene in tight jeans and leather jacket. His hair is oiled back, and the light from the streetlamp sets him off with an unearthly glow. Carlotta is very obviously distracted by the cue cards, her eyes dart to them constantly, while Brad is completely controlled and natural, never having to use them once. Brad had the unique ability of a Laurence Olivier or his beautiful wife Vivien Leigh and could memorize lines quickly after glancing at them briefly.

"Oh," she says, "I've seen you on the street before, haven't I?"

"Yes, ma'am. I'm here every night just after midnight."

"It's awfully cold tonight... don't you think so, young man?"

"Yes, ma'am, it is... awfully cold."

"Don't you think you ought to go inside... somewhere... out of the cold?"

"I wouldn't mind a bit... that is, if I had a place to stay for the night."

"Oh... of course... I take it that you... don't live... close by?"

"This is where I hang out."

"On the street... all night long? Poor boy!"

"Uh-huh, that's right, lady."

"That's a shame!"

"Yeah... cryin' shame."

"I tell you what, young man... I live just around the corner... and if you like, you may stay the night in my apartment... *my husband* is not at home... and... I don't feel safe without a... man... in the house."

"That's nice of you, lady, but I'm a little short of cash"

"You just tell me what you need, and I'll reimburse you."

"Lead the way, lady."

Carlotta turns and walks upstage. Brad takes a final puff and snubs the cigarette butt out on the lamppost before following her off. She casts alluring glances over her shoulder in his direction to make sure that he is indeed behind her.

Harold Blatz screams, "Cut!" He is quite enthusiastic about the scene. "Brilliant! Brilliant!" he effuses.

Carlotta is being interviewed by Merv Griffin while Brad relaxes at home in the sitting room watching his mistress on the television. He is smoking marijuana. Carlotta is noticeably disturbed as all Merv wants to talk about is "that hot new star" who'll be playing the gigolo. He is obviously not the least bit interested in her. Suddenly, Carlotta stands up, slaps his face, and rushes out of the studio. Merv, flushed with embarrassment, cuts to a commercial.

"Oh, Jesus!" cries Brad aloud, pausing to suck in on his joint.

Rocky and Rusty enter and begin teasing him about his new status but are quick to remind him that the film has not yet been shot. They tease and bully one another until they've worked themselves into a frenzied orgy of sex. They strip themselves naked and cavort their carnal pleasures in every deviate position imaginable. At the climax of their passion, just as they all begin to shoot their prospective love loads, in storms Carlotta, fresh from *The Merv Griffin Show.*

She screams, and the boys slump to the floor in a heap of spent energy. They are so worn-out they can scarcely move, and they lay there on top of one another like rag dolls.

"Damn it all!" she shrieks. "I can't leave you boys alone in the house for a minute! And here I had to take a *cab* to *The Merv Griffin Show* because the three of you *promised* me you were going to do housework!" They just groan. "Is that all you have to say for yourselves?"

Brad speaks up, "We're sorry, Miss Carlisle... but most everything's been done already we were just taking a break and—"

"***YOU CALL THIS A BREAK?!*** Ha! I bet you were the instigator of this little fiasco! You! Mr. Macho Stud of Hollywood! Future heartthrob of America! Ha! You're nothing but a freaked-out pothead! And you two! Ever since he's come here, you pay less and less attention to me! Well, I've had it! The movie starts shooting next week, and I'm going to need my rest, so you can, all three of you, just forget about sleeping with me! You'll all have to sleep in your own *separate* rooms!" They look at each other and smile. "***SEPARATELY I SAID, DAMN IT!*** And I'm locking you in at night to make sure there's no more hanky-panky!" They are not amused. "If *I'm* not going to get any, *nobody's* going to get any!" she screams, storming out of the room.

Rocky looks at Rusty, and they look at Brad with bemusement.

Then Rocky speaks up, a light suddenly turning on in his head, "Don't worry, guys, I know how to trip the locks from the inside!"

They shake hands and pat one another affectionately and then collapse with exhaustion.

Carlotta sweeps down the hallway in her nightgown, bidding good night to each of the boys in turn, then promptly and sadistically locking their doors behind them. Once returning to her own bedroom, she mixes a very strong drink from the portable bar next to her bed. Settling between the sheets, she grabs the TV remote box and flips on Johnny Carson.

"Now there's the man I need to see!" she rasps aloud. "Way to go, Johnny! Blow that Merv bitch right off the air!"

The lock to Rocky's room clicks open, and he sneaks out. First, he opens Brad's door and beckons him to meet in Rusty's room. Finally, having successfully tripped the lock of Rusty's room, he begins his usual ritual of making love with Rusty, not content to wait on Brad. They are well into it when Brad suddenly appears in the doorway, naked, his cock tucked between his legs, his face made-up, and sporting one of Carlotta's wigs.

"So," says Brad, assuming a stance a la Carlotta, "you boy's think you're gonna get away with starting without me, eh? Well, think again!" He pulls out a towel twisted into a rattail and begins snapping at them.

Within moments a battle ensues, which sends the wig flying and resolves into some serious orgy work but culminates when the real Carlotta appears in the doorway defiantly.

"So," she says, much calmer than expected, "this is how it is, eh?" She takes a few steps into the room, her dander puffing up. "Well, well... something will have to be done about this, now, won't it? Aha! Yes... we shall see, won't we? Yes! Yes, ***INDEED!***"

She storms back down the hall and slams the door to her room and is heard to scream, "You are ***VAPID, VILE SEX MANIACS!***"

"I'm getting real tired of her," says Rocky.

"You and me both," says Rusty.

"Come on, guys… let's not let her spoil our fun," says Brad. "Fuck her!" he says, shooting her the finger.

"No, thank you!" pipes up Rocky.

Without another minute's hesitation, they continue their orgy, and of course, they savor every delicious bite of it.

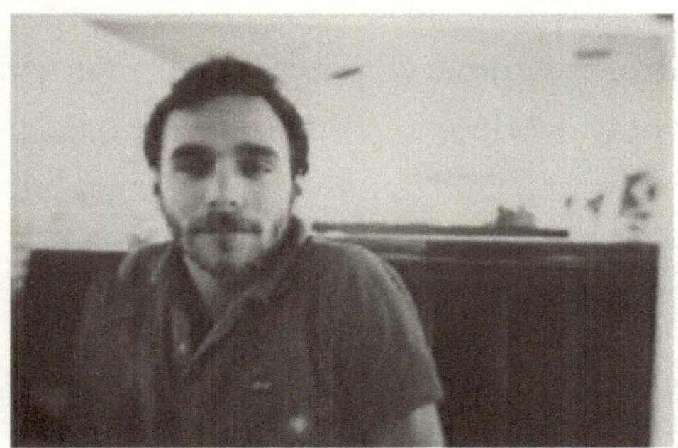

Eddie Circa 1980

Chapter 7

It is morning in Hollywoodland, very early morning to be exact, because what few birds that have been able to survive the smog are chirping, and the dew is without a doubt sparkling. Peace and tranquility pervade the air, and an unusually quiet calm suggests a serene day sans strife ahead.

Carlotta is on the phone with her agent in the sitting room near the picture window overlooking her estate. Brad is up making a cup of Maxim instant coffee and happens to overhear her conversation. His expressionless reaction betrays the inner torment her words bring to him.

"Yes, Bill, yes," she says on the phone impatiently. "I'm anxious to begin shooting. Next week? Good. And what did Harold Blatz say about the tests? Oh yes, he liked them? Oh, really? Very impressed you say... well, well... yes, that is good news. Oh, I agree, he is very attractive. Listen, Bill, I've been thinking, perhaps we ought to go totally with an experienced professional cast. Yes, yes, I mean it. Now I understand Tom Selleck has been signed to play opposite me, eh? Good. Yes. Well, you see, Bill, I want you to talk to Harold Blatz and the producers today about hiring professionals to play the bit parts, the extra roles... yes...yes, I know we tested the boys, but... uh—huh... but listen, I've had the greatest flash of an idea... you know the part of the gigolo? That would be a great cameo for John Travolta. I know he'd be expensive for just one small scene, but I know he'd be dying to do it. He and I are old chums; we go to all the same parties. Look, ever since he turned down American Gigolo, he's regretted the success it brought to his rival Richard Gere. What do you mean don't be silly? They hate each other! I ought to know, Richard and I are intimate friends! How intimate I shall never reveal! I do know that John has been working his little tail off to overthrow him and succeed him as the reigning sex symbol of the eighties. The proof is in the pudding, dear. Didn't you see the way he flexed his muscles and wiggled his ass in the sequel to Saturday Night Fever? No?! Wake up and smell the coffee, Bill, sex is in, in, in, and it always will be, or my name isn't Carlotta Carlisle! What? What do you mean it isn't? ***ELSIE CARLTON!*** How dare you remember that name!

Especially after I went to great expense to have it legally changed! Bill, you do as I ask or… or… or else, that's what! Got it? I want John Travolta, and I want professional people on the set at all times! Good-bye!"

She slams down the phone, downs some of her drink, and then lights another cigarette in her favorite foot-long cigarette holder. She is so unnerved, her hands are shaking, and she has considerable trouble accomplishing this easy task. She begins laughing to herself wickedly. "Now we'll see who's boss around here!" she says, her laugh becoming maniacal. Brad retreats into the shadows of the estate.

Carlotta and Merv are standing on the street in front of a huge billboard advertisement for her film *Enlighten Me with Your Smile*. In the display, Tom and John are arm in arm and look to be playing tug of war with Carlotta's cleavage prominently between them.

Merv effuses enthusiastically, "Gosh, Carlotta, I'm really impressed with this spectacular, glittering billboard advertisement. Shooting this film with the two hottest stars in Hollywood must have been an exciting endeavor. What can you tell us about Tom

Selleck and John Travolta? Was there tension on the set between these two sexual epitomes of the American male?"

"Well, Merv, if there was tension, I took care of it."

"Ho, ho! I gather the three of you became very close!"

"We're the best of friends!" she replies with a wink.

"How marvelous! In spite of a busy schedule, you were able to soothe the savage beasts!"

Carlotta bats her eyes. "Precisely, Merv."

"Exciting! Mmmm… mmm… when does the picture open, Carlotta?"

"Friday night, and I hope all our fans will come."

"Yes, and my camera crew will be videotaping the event to be presented on my show the following Monday."

"Thank you, Merv."

"I'm so glad we're still friends after what happened the last time we were together, but I wanted to ask, whatever happened to that young man… err… Brad Willis, who was originally cast as the gigolo?"

"Brad? Oh, yes… hmmm… well, he is employed on my staff and is quite content."

"But what a shame to give up what promised to be a brilliant acting career! What work does he do for you?"

"Why he is in charge of the grounds to my estate."

"You mean he trims hedges and that sort of thing?"

"Precisely, Merv."

"Well… this is a crazy business, but I suppose his time will come."

"I'm sure it will… he and the rest of my staff will be at the premiere, of course."

"Oh, delightful, I'd love to chat with Brad… in fact… I'd like to ask him out to… uh… and there you have it ladies and gentlemen—Carlotta Carlisle, super sexy siren of the cinema in a spectacular new fun-filled motion picture costarring Tom Selleck and John

Travolta. Carlotta, thank you for being on the show. The best of luck to you and your new film *Enlighten Me with Your Smile.* Be sure to catch the premiere footage on Monday the twenty-seventh, one week from today on the new *Merv Griffin Show!* Thank you again, Carlotta!"

"Thank you, Merv, you're too kind."

Although the television is on in the sitting room, no one is present to watch it. An asinine commercial ensues and vainly attempts to sell useless products to the furniture.

Brad is trimming the oleanders. He stops suddenly and kneels down to the ground, grabbing a handful of leaves, which he crumbles in his hand.

He places the dried leaves into a flower sifter and grinds them into flakes onto a piece of paper. He carefully removes a cigarette from Carlotta's cigarette case and gingerly rolls it between his thumb and forefinger, emptying out the tobacco. He mixes the tobacco and oleander together.

He composes a letter.

Dear Dad,

A few months ago, I tried to find Mother. She's moved away, and it's been at least a year since I've seen her. Do you know where she is? I miss both of you.

Your son,
Brad

He stares at the letter awhile, changes his mind, and crumples it up, tossing it in the waste can.

Brad is sweating and breathing heavily, grimacing in ecstasy while being sodomized by Rocky, who in turn is whipped on the bare ass with a leather belt by Rusty.

Brad removes a cigarette from the cigarette case and places it in the cigarette holder. He sits in Carlotta's favorite chair and puts the end of it to his lips. Later, it is Carlotta herself who lights it and puffs on it. After several annoying drags, she bitches about the taste.

"Are you sure, Brad, that you bought the right brand for me? This tastes vile! Well, peculiar anyway… not bad, really."

"It's a new brand of the same cigarette you always smoke," says Brad, sitting across from her in another chair. "It's a new and improved special blend that's supposed to be beneficial and clear the air passages." "Hmmm," she purrs, "very peculiar… uh-huh… I feel rather light-headed… how *divoone!*" she croons, "as the late Jayne Mansfield would say… I think I could get used to it… yes, I do, really!" she says with satisfaction.

Carlotta is transformed into a slightly altered version of herself. It is Brad wearing her clothes, made-up, and wig to look like her. He is smoking a regular joint on the end of a feather roach clip.

"I always did prefer grass to oleander," he says softly to himself, "unfiltered, of course."

It is opening night at the Cinerama Dome Theatre in Hollywoodland.

The searchlights scan the skies, and the crowds bristle with excitement.

A spotlight is thrown on host Merv Griffin.

"Here she is, folks! The star of *Enlighten Me with Your Smile,* Miss Carlotta Carlisle!"

A Cadillac convertible, top down, pulls up and seated on top of the backseat is Brad as Carlotta. Rusty and Rocky, seated on either side of him, are dressed in tuxedos—a rarity indeed. They smile happily as Brad throws kisses to the crowd. Our story ends with the flash of a photographer's camera.

A star *was* born today in Hollywoodland. The year is 1983, and big brother had not yet taken over. Merv Griffin, Tom Selleck, John Travolta, Rusty, Rocky, and Brad Willis, alias Carlotta Carlisle, we presume will live happily ever after. Indeed!

THE END

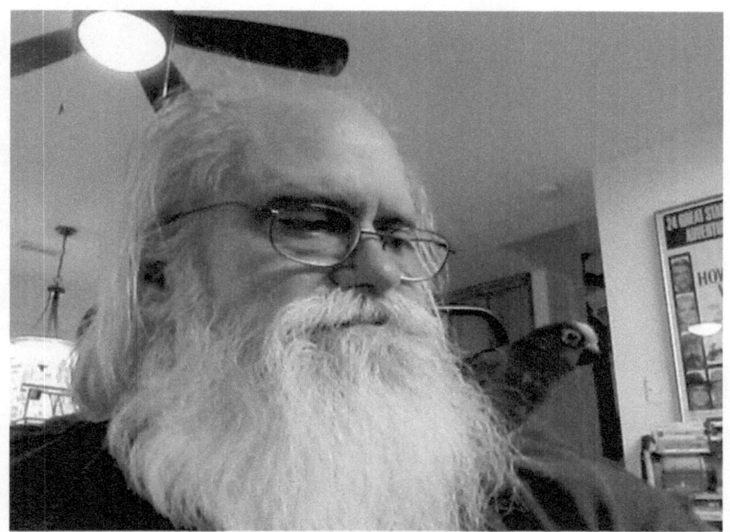

Grant with Corabella

www.ingramcontent.com/pod-product-compliance
Lightning Source LLC
Chambersburg PA
CBHW032222050726
47591CB00001B/227

* 9 7 8 1 7 7 8 8 3 0 4 8 8 *